Library of
Davidson College

# Societal Reconstruction in Two African States

**Victor A. Olorunsola**
Iowa State University

University Press of America

Copyright © 1977 by

**University Press of America**™

division of
R.F. Publishing, Inc.
4710 Auth Place, S.E., Washington, D.C. 20023

All rights reserved

Printed in the United States of America

ISBN: 0-8191-0207-5

For Carol Ann Bradley Olorunsola

Political Reconstruction in Two African States:
A Study of Military Regimes' Performance
in Ghana and Nigeria

by

Victor A. Olorunsola

## Table of Contents

### Part I.

Introduction: States the objective, scope and method of the research

Chapter I: Reviews the literature briefly, develops the theory and postulates relevant to the studies.

Chapter II: Outlines the background material necessary for the understanding of the problems of the countries and the performance of the military regimes.
  a. Political tradition.
  b. Problems of the countries.
  c. Civil-military relations.

### Part II. Economic Performance

Chapter III: Discusses the economic development performance of the Nigerian military regime.
  a. What are the economic goals set?
  b. How much of these have been accomplished from the point of view of the military regime?
  c. How much has been achieved from the objective viewpoint?
  d. How much can be achieved?
  Relate all of these to the economic performance propositions clearly set up in Chapter I.

Chapter IV: The economic performance of the National Redemption Council of Ghana. Repeat the same outline of approach as in Chapter III.

### Part III

Chapter V: Discusses "Legitimacy Engineering" under:
  a. The Ironsi Military Regime.
  b. The Gowon Military Regime.

Chapter VI: Discusses "Legitimacy Engineering" under:
  a. The National Liberation Council of Ghana.
  b. The National Redemption Council of Ghana.

### Part IV
Deals with the military regimes' relationships with crucial segments of the political communities.

Chapter VII: Focuses upon the Nigerian academicians and students in their relationships with the military regime.

Chapter VIII: Examines the relationships between the students, academicians and the National Redemption Council.

Chapter IX: A. Discusses the Nigerian press and the Gowon regime.

B. Seeks to understand the Ghanaian press and the National Redemption Council.

Chapter X: A. Discusses the Nigerian labor and the Gowon regime.

B. Discusses the Ghanaian labor and the military regimes of Ghana.

Chapter XI: Examines how the citizens perceived the performance of these military regimes. (General and brief discussion of highlights of questionnaire administered.)

Chapter XII: Political style.

Part V.

Chapter XIII: Conclusion

## ACKNOWLEDGEMENTS

In this short space, it is not possible for me to acknowledge everyone who has contributed, in one way or another, to the writing of this book. Nevertheless, let me single out a few.

Professors Mazrui, Rothchild, Crawford Young, Lovell, Talbot, Hadwiger, Dorfman, Leighton, and Esedebe read parts of this manuscript and offered very valuable criticisms. In addition, Professors Dejo Ikediji and Olu Okediji, Frimpong, Mr. Samuels and Ms. Olorunsola offered encouragement. Suzy Peters, Judy Rooks, and Brian D'Silva worked for me, at various times, as research students. Without the assistance of the late Dr. Florence Okediji, the Nigerian study might not have materialized. My interviewers worked through thick and thin. I found their enthusiasm infectious.

I am grateful to the Departments of Sociology, and Political Science, University of Ibadan; the Institute of African Studies, and the Department of Political Science, University of Ghana, Legon, for providing me with many academic courtesies. To the many citizens and government officials who allowed me to study their countries and intrude upon their valuable time, I shall always remain thankful.

The funds which made this study possible, were provided by the Ford Foundation (Ford Faculty Research Fellowship in Political Science), the Social Science Research Council, and the International Development and Research Center, Indiana University. Moreover, the Vice President for Research, Iowa State University, supplied the money for typing the manuscript. Ms. Shuping, Smith, Bognar and Cook typed the manuscript at various stages.

There are three families to whom I am bankrupt in gratitude: the Anders, Okedijis and Olorunsolas. They probably do not know how selflessly they have given, but I hope they know how much they mean to me.

Needless to say that none of the people, organizations and institutions mentioned should be responsible for the views expressed in this book. Finally, I should take full responsibility for the possible weaknesses which might have stemmed from my failure to accept all of the advice proferred.

Victor A. Olorunsola
January 1974

PART I

INTRODUCTION

OBJECTIVE

The involvement of the military in the politics of many developing nations is not an entirely new phenomenon. What is comparatively recent is its involvement in the politics of Sub-Saharan Africa. It is, therefore, understandable that the subject has only just begun to demand the attention of some Africanists. In this short span, however, the literature has steadily mounted. Claude Welch's effort in Soldier and State in Africa and Henry Bienen's The Military Intervenes[1] are cases in point. Welch, in particular, argued that the African military is different from the Turkish and Israeli armed forces and that the African military cannot be viewed as the institution which will bring about political development. But, he added,

> "Scholarly analysis of intervention and its effects, particularly by Africans, has been scanty. Many of the African states in which the take overs have occurred could not be analysed in time to meet the deadline for this book - particularly Mali and Nigeria."[2]
> (p. viii)

I am not interested in the intervention per se, but in the performance of the military government. I assume that coups and counter coups attest to gross political instability. Thus, their seemingly bright prospect in Sub-Saharan Africa are disturbing. The motivation behind this effort is that, ultimately, the data gathered (from the research) will enlighten us further on how the military governments can institutionalize, within the civilian framework, the political and economic gains which might have been made under the military order. Obviously, this goal cannot be achieved without a sound understanding of (a) the goals of the politico-military leaders, (b) the methods used in pursuit of their goals, (c) their administration, (d) the citizens' reaction to their administration and (e) their achievements.

## SCOPE

Political Science should be interested in examining how the new leaders of Africa attempt to cope with the problems of their various countries. It appears that these men have set for themselves two rather broadly defined but crucial goals which fall under the rubric which political scientists call "development." They proclaim an interest in the creation and forging of a nation out of the independent state. Moreover, they express a keen desire for gaining and maintaining the central government's capacity to institute and manage modernization and cope with its "socio-economic concomitants." For the most part, their predecessors have failed in both dimensions. Presumably, these men took over because of this failure. The crucial question, then, is whether or not the new leaders will succees where the former politicians failed.

Most germane to a study such as this are the three stages of governance by the new leaders. These stages are: (1) message proclamation, (2) plan fulfillment, and (3) status maintenance. Briefly, let me explicate upon these stages.

Usually, in the African experience, these new leaders had no legitimacy prior to the seizure of power. The problem of engineering legitimacy is, therefore, paramount. The chief concern in stage one is to examine how the new leaders seek or sought followers; a study of their messages and the political skill and style used in their proclamations should be most instructive.

The second stage represents the interest in how the new leaders fulfill their "state of the union" promises. Under this rubric, one must ask a number of questions. How much have the new leaders promised? How much have they delivered? How much do the nationals think the new leaders have delivered? It must be borne in mind that the perception of "reality" by citizens may be quite different from objective reality. The former is by no means less important than the latter because attitudes and behavior patterns are very dependent upon the perception of reality. More importantly, do the citizens believe that the new leaders are succeeding where the old politicians have failed? Moreover, I am interested in finding out whether the leaders' approach to development could be classified as "Mobilization" or "Reconciliatory."[3]

The third stage is a study of the attempt to institutionalize the political gains so that a condition of political stability and development may continue to exist even after the exit of the present leaders. To put it more succinctly, have the new leaders really succeeded in curing the ills of the state and are they creating the proper propensities for the establishment of nationhood? The answers to these questions rest largely upon how much the particular military regime has succeeded in the institutionalization of whatever gain has been achieved under it. If this third stage is successfully attained, the dim prospect of a vicious cycle of coups and counter coups would have been short circuited.

METHOD

The universe of interest consists of Nigeria and Ghana. Ghana is particularly interesting for two reasons. First, the military government in Ghana (NLC) has handed power over to the civilian rule. Therefore, one is in a better position to undertake a complete assessment of its performance and to investigate what kind of relationship prevailed between it and the civilian politicians who succeeded it. Second, it should be easier to obtain more valid data from the citizens regarding the military leaders' efforts since the latter is no longer in power. Ghana (NRC) and Nigeria are ideal for the study of the dynamics of the military government as it seeks to achieve national integration and political development.

Two research techniques were emphasized. First is a content analysis of national and local newspapers in the country. Here I was interested in the examinations of speeches, writings and pronouncements of the leaders; the citizen's reaction to the leaders, i.e. editorials, articles, letters to the editors; the leader's access to radio and television. Second is the interview technique. The first goal in this respect was to reach the populace who may not be inclined to write letters. Moreover, I also interviewed "political brokers." Finally, I addressed myself to the civil servants. In some of these instances the sample was randomly selected. Where this was impossible, quota sampling was employed. The interview schedule consisted of closed and open-ended questions. Of course, in the final analysis, there can be no substitute for a first hand observation of these leaders at work, wherever this is possible.

## FOOTNOTES

1. Claude Welch, Jr., (ed) Soldier and State in Africa. A comparative analysis of military intervention and political change. (Evanston: Northwestern University Press, 1970).

   Henry Bienen (ed) The Military Intervenes: Case Studies in Political Development. (New York: Russell Sage Foundation, 1968).

   J. M. Lee, African Armies and Civil Order (New York: Frederick A. Praeger Publisher, 1969).

2. Claude Welch, Jr., op cit., p. viii.

3. David Apter, The Politics of Modernization (Chicago: The University of Chicago Press, 1967).

CHAPTER I

INTRODUCTION

As I indicated earlier, my interest is not in military intervention per se, but in the performance of the military regime. Therefore, in this chapter, first, I will examine the three major theories which seem relevant to the performance of military regimes. Second, I will try to point out the critical shortcoming of each.

I contend that the examination of military performance must be viewed from different vantage points if we are to get a maximum understanding of it. First, we must attempt to see the performance as the ruling politico-military leaders see it. Second, it is necessary to look at their performance objectively from a detached examination of their real performance, i.e. how much of their promises are being or have been redeemed? Third, we must find out how the significant politically conscious and vocal segments of their society view the performance of the military. Fourth, we need to know how the majority of their people--usually non-literate--see the military's performance. No correct diagnosis of the military's political performance could be produced unless one takes cognizance of these multivarious vantage points.

For the purpose of this research we also need to recognize different types of performances: economic performance, strategy of modernization performance, and political performance. It will be evident in the course of this chapter that these are not mutually exclusive categories.

The problem of the legitimacy of African military regimes interests me because I feel that it is very central to the ways different sectors of the society perceive the military regime's performance. More than that, it is important for the objective assessment of the military performance as well as the prospect for the institutionalization of its achievements, ultimately, within the civilian framework. In short, legitimacy is a necessary support mechanism which can affect the input and output of political systems. Furthermore the nature and extent of military regime's legitimacy vis a vis the various sectors of their society is an important index of the life expectancy of the reforms and changes introduced during the period of military governance. This chapter concludes then with the stipulations of some general legitimacy propositions and descriptive generalizations about two typologies of legitimacy engineering.

THEORY

The formal organizational model is one of the main models used for the study of the military and political development. It contends that military organizations are characterized by centralization, discipline, hierarchy, communication, espirit de corps[1] and it ascribes to military regimes in the developing world certain qualities and characteristics of military organizations. Consequently, the armed forces in developing countries are presented as organizations possessing ideological and structural cohesion, internal discipline, a commonly shared belief system of secular rationality, puritanic asceticism, patriotic nationalism and commitment to modernization and public service. Ipso facto, therefore, military regimes in developing states are positive agents of modernization.

The problem is that the formal organizational model fails to consider the effect which the transplantation of institutions or organizations, from a Western milieu to a transitional one, would have on the nature of such transplanted organizations. Institutions so transferred are seldom complete carbon copies of the metropolitan model. Certain fundamental or significant transformations occur in the process of transplantation. Because of this significant oversight, propositions emanating from this theory can be misleading and inadequate. Finer's portrayal of nationalism as a distinctive military ideology or Janowitz proposition of puritanic outlook and strong sense of nationalism with pervasive overtones of xenophobia are cases in point. Both of these propositions have been called into question by R. Price's "emulation paradox"[2] which, he claims, produces in the military elite of the new states 'non-nationalistic' and non-puritanic' policies and postures. In addition, Claude Welch queries some of the contentions of the formal organizational model. He wonders whether centralization without acceptance mean much in terms of political performance and he expressed some serious doubts regarding the military's ability to develop societal authority. Is the weakening of traditional authority necessarily due to centralization? In any case, he sees qualitative differences between the military organizations of the African countries and those of the more developed ones.[3]

Instead of the seemingly organizational determinism of the formal organization model, Huntington proposed a model which, for want of better terminology, I will call "mass political participation determinism." He views organizational factors as largely irrelevant. To him, the role of the military in modernization is not dependent on its organizational characteristics, but broadly on the social and political conditions of the society. More specifically, it depends on the degree of mass participation in the system. In effect, he postulates that the role of military in development varies with the nature of the society. Thus, "In the world of the oligarchy, the soldier is a radical, in the middle class world, he is a participant and arbiter; as the mass society looms on the horizon, he becomes the conservative guardian of the existing order."[4] All in all, therefore, Huntington implies that a certain degree of conservative dogmatism is deeply embedded in the attitude which military regimes have towards the creation and maintenance of mass societies. The military elite's orientation towards mass political participation thus becomes a most crucial factor and, in a sense, monolithic. He writes, "The extent to which a politicized officer corps plays a conservative or reform role in politics is a function of the expansion of political participation in the society."[5] Does this then mean that we cannot consider the military as viable agents of political development unless we change one of the major aspects which recur in most definitions of political development, i.e. that of increased participation? In any case I tend to feel that it is one thing to wonder whether increased popular participation can be decreed and it is another to talk about a monolithic negative response of military elites to popular participation.

The third theory I would like to consider is the "reference group theory."[6] I will discuss this theory at some length because of its relevance to this study. Reference group theory contends that identification with a social group involves internalization of the group's core values and norms. A distinction is made between social interaction and psychological identification. One may interact with a group socially without viewing members of the group as his "significant others." Similarly, he may psychologically identify with a group with which he has no social interaction. In all cases, the group with which one psychologically identifies constitutes one's reference group. In most, but not in all, cases, an individual's membership group constitutes his significant others.

To some extent, then, the formal organizational theorists and the reference group theorists are on common ground. They both ascribe great efficacy to the socialization process. The formal organizational theorists, as we have pointed out, believe in the efficacy of military socialization up to a fault. Perhaps it is this that has made them gloss over or even ignore the effect of transformation and transplantation on the military organizations and personnel of new states. Price, the advocate of the reference group approach, writes:

> "The military training officers undergo can be viewed as a socialization process within which the recruits' identification with his previous civilian reference group are broken down and replaced by the new ego-involved associations that are centered in the military organization.
>
> In the case of military officers from newly independent states, one likely consequence of this training process is the development of positive reference group identifications with the officer corps of the colonial power, for, as we noted earlier, the top officers in such states receive their training at European military schools. . . . At Sandhurst, at St. Cyr, at Mons, Camberley, Saymur, and the like, the ideology, values and traditions that are carefully impressed upon the student are those of European military. And the impact of the military academy on such matters can be expected to be great, for the socialization process in these institutions is structured in ways that experimental social psychology has shown to be extremely effective in shaping attitudes and behavior.[7]

Military socialization is effective, therefore, because it

(1) isolates its new recruits from previous membership groups;

(2) baptizes them by immersion into a "network of new membership group" with high cohesiveness and by reinforcing ideological homogeneity;

(3) rewards conformity and severely punishes deviation.

Price quoted generously from two of the participants of the Ghana coup to show that foreign military socialization is powerful. He went on,

> "These men (officers) were being promoted into what was an exclusively European officer corps, and their eligibility for promotion was determined solely by European officers. Consequently, promotions were given to those who manifested the attitudes and behavior considered appropriate from the standpoint of the European military profession . . . the NCO or Warrant Officer who rose through the ranks to General had to undergo what Robert Merton has termed 'anticipatory socialization: identification with and concomitant adoption of the values of a group to which the group aspires but does not belong.'"[8]

Four points central to Price's theory are (1) that the socialization of officer corps of many of the new states produce reference-group identification with officer corps of the ex-colonial power and "concomitant commitments to its set of tradition, symbols, and values"; (2) that these identifications and commitments affect the officers in their relationship with civilian political authority; (3) that they also affect the behavior of these officers as governmental leaders should they accede to political power--a situation which he correctly noted the organization model neither explains or predicts; (4) that military socialization is more effective than civilian socialization.

But some additional explanation is necessary in view of the supposed efficacy of foreign military socialization. One of the cardinals of indoctrinations of the British and American military is the notion of civilian supremacy and the non-interference of the military in politics. Yet, the participation, indeed the leadership of coups in Nigeria, Sierra Leone and Ghana involved officers whose military training tabooed such exercise. Price has argued almost convincingly, quoting from Lt. Generals Afrifa's[9] and Ocran's books, that these generals were most affected by their British military training. How then does one explain the National Redemption Council (NRC) policies and specifically these assertions of the engineer of the second successful Ghanaian coup? The interview granted to Peter Myers, a British journalist, by Col. I. K. Acheampong, the leader of the coup detat against Dr. Busia's government, is very enlightening on this score.

Peter Myers:

> "It is often said that Commonwealth officers training in Britain go through a military process that is so British in character that in the end the Ghanaian, Indian, Nigerian or Canadian graduate returns to home base more English than English. As one who went through the mill what do you say?"

Col. Acheampong:

> "This depends entirely on the individual, I was not English anymore than I was before entering Britain."

It should be noted that Col. Acheampong was not only trained in England but was in fact seconded to the British army for a while![10]

How could the officers of the NRC and the National Liberation Council (NLC) who were exposed to the same military socialization pursue such different policies and exhibit different ideological predispositions? One claimed to have intervened solely to bring tyranny to an end. The other intervened to shorten the life of a "duly elected democratic government" because "the principle of one man one vote is meaningless without the principle of one man one bread." If it is true that the NLC subscribed to the "emulation paradox" the NRC up till now, seems to be singularly unaffected by it. I will strongly suggest that NLC situation is not as clear cut as it appears. This point will be discussed later. Quite apart from the Ghanaian case, there are evidences to point to the failure of the foreign military academies to influence the behavior of key military officers.

> "No convincing evidence exist of a correlation between the American military aid and military involvement in politics. And, it must be pointed out, the opposite hypothesis also is not true: the hopes of many people that the propensity of foreign military to intervene would be reduced by a course at Leavenworth, indoctrination in Anglo-American doctrines of civilian supremacy, and association with professionalised American military officials

> have also turned to naught. Armies which have received American, Soviet, British and French military assistance and no military assistance have all intervened in politics. So also, armies which have received American, Soviet, British, French and no military assistance have refrained from political intervention. Military aid and military training are by themselves politically sterile. They neither encourage nor reduce the tendencies of military officers to play a political role."[11]

Huntington's argument casts doubt upon the potency which Price, Finer and others have ascribed to foreign military training and socialization.

What is needed is not the abandonment of reference group approach but its constant modification and refinement. There is the suggestion that the recruit's identification with his previous civilian reference groups are broken down and replaced by new ones through isolation from past reference and membership groups ". . . thus, isolating him from the sources of social and psychological support for his previous beliefs."[12] Is it impossible to resocialize officers especially foreign trained ones? What happens to these officers once they are re-emersed, at least partially, into their old membership and reference groups? The utility of reference group theory as it is presented by Price can be enhanced by the probing of these questions. To my mind what is more important is not the 'emulation paradox' *per se*, but the concept which it implies--that of cross pressures arising from membership or even identification in two organizations with sometimes conflicting demands and expectations.[13]

It can be argued that in some cases, military regimes subscribe more to non-military reference groups while in others the reverse may be true. What factors will guide us in predicting? Is it more in depth analysis of the social, professional background, and psychological data? Or is it the case study of decisions and, or, analysis of influential segments of societies in military regimes? If we opt for the latter, in terms of significant civil-military relations, we would need to know the relationship of the:

  (a) military regime to old politicians
  (b) military regime to key politicians

(c) military regime to civilian intellectuals

(d) military regime to labour

(e) military regime to farmers

(f) military regime to traders

(g) military regime to traditional rulers

(h) military regime to religious groups

(i) military regime to foreign constituencies

(j) military regime to the rest of the armed forces.

All these call for a combination of Huntington and Price.

Price has started us in the right direction by suggesting that the performance of military officers in military roles varies according to reference group identification. But can it be hypothesized that the reference group identification varies primarily only according to differences with the professional socialization process of the nation's officer corps? Does this not, in fact, suggest a great efficacy of military socialization over civilian membership groups. In Africa, at least, this is a debatable proposition. Does not the Ghanaian case of NLC or NRC dispute this contention of the great efficacy of military socialization over civilian ones? I should note that in general, conformity to formal organizational norms in Africa--be it in the bureaucracy, intellectual establishments or others--tends to be low. This suggests that in fact it may well be that primordial membership groups are very salient.

I have dealt at some length with the reference group theory because I would like to test some propositions suggested by Price's reference group model[14] particularly as they relate to Ghana's NRC and NLC and the Gowon Regime of Nigeria. These propositions can be divided up into economic performances proposition, strategy of modernization performances proposition, and political performance proposition.

I. Strategy of Modernization Performances Propositions

1. In states with a recent colonial past a strategy characterized by heavy foreign participation of a financial and technical nature and limited mobilization of indigenous resources both human and material will be followed.

2. There would be a "low profile" approach to nation-building and political integration: government makes only minimal effort to penetrate society. Political integration occurs with trickle down effect because of the application of political _laissez faire_ strategy.

II. Economic Performance Propositions

1. Military governments of an ex-colonial army would behave in non-nationalistic fashion and would often give high priority to their identification with reference groups connected to another political community. Thus there would be an absence of economic nationalism.

2. Military rulers will not necessarily introduce rationality and pragmatism into economic policy making; military officers trained in the 'West' will behave in just as irrational and unpragmatic ways towards the "Eastern bloc's" economic interest as many left-leaning nationalist leaders are alleged to behave towards Western economic interest.

3. When military officers have governmental control they will be unconcerned with the realization of economic change and reform. Moreover where there are civilian organizations or groups pressing for such economic changes these military officers will oppose them.

III. Political Performance Propositions

1. The political leadership potential of military officers is decisively undermined by the fact that military elite is unlikely to relate to the political symbols that have meaning in their own society. To the extent that the process of modernization involves mobiliation of popular sentiment around collective values and goals as a means of increasing input of human and material resources to the development

efforts and/or as a means of building solidarity in a fragile political community, the military elite may be unsuited.

2. As a result of foreign reference group commitment, the military tends to be cut off from the "expressive symbols of resonance" for the society. They will tend to rely instead on martial rituals and symbols of a foreign cultural milieu and this tendency will reduce their political capacity.

3. Armies are not democracies. Therefore where military organizations become the state, order is maintained, but training in "democratic civility is the less probable outcome."

Claude Welch cautioned against the attractive temptation to see the armed forces as a "paragon of modernized political system."[15]

> ". . . unless one realises that centralization is effective only if the right of the central entity to rule is widely accepted."[16]

This caution is at the heart of the matter regarding the connection between political development and military rule. The issue of the societal perception of the seizure of power is central. Is it seen as usurpation or deliverance? To whom is it deliverance? To whom is it usurpation? By themselves the answer to these questions do not completely resolve the issue. After all, people are capable of changing their opinions. Alliances can be made and unmade. Consequently, we need to know how the seizure of power is transformed into legitimacy and ultimately to authority. Can the military in fact do this? As Welch put it, "Can the military develop the communities of opinions, values and beliefs as well as interests and needs that constitute authority?"[17] The acceptance of the legitimacy of a government tantamounts to authority.

To Welch the prospect for success depends upon developing political institutions with a capacity for effective change. He argues that the "creating of traditional sources of authority does not necessarily result from centralization of government functions.

> "To replace traditional, religious, familial, and ethnic political authorities by a single, secular, national political authority

obviously requires time, favourable conditions, communications based upon similar values, and a growth in mutual confidence."[18]

In the absence of favorable conditions, attempts at centralization may lead to disintegration. The stress of military intervention may in fact lead to the disintegration of 'modern' organizational characteristics of the armed forces. He concludes:

> "The loss of authority can as readily afflict commanding officers as presidents. The semblance of centralization accordingly must not be mistaken for an effective central, military authority that reserves unquestioning obedience."[19]

On the whole, Professor Welch's theoretical arguments are sound and his more cautious appraisal of the military's political capability most welcomed in view of the currency given to the suggestion that "frequent coups are a sign of change and progress."[20]

However, I feel it is imperative to take serious cognizance of the subjective perceptions of the general populace, and influential sectors of the populace with regards to their view on the performance of the military in the field of development both economically and politically. It is quite probable that what constitutes economic and political stagnation by objective measurements may be at variance with the perception of the members of the polity. This observation has two important implications: First, a favorable rating by a significant sector and/or majority of the populace of the system even when it may not represent objective assessment may give the military and the system a requisite breathing space. It may well be that by the time the objective reality presents its stark face redeeming crucial advancements would have occurred. Secondly, it is conceivable that moderate skepticism engendered by long discontent with civilian governments and previous regimes may have led to a "negative development predisposition."[21] Consequently, "holding the line" in terms of objective overall performance or even satisfying reduced demands may constitute significant performance in the eyes of the citizens. No doubt, this presumes that the military has succeeded in establishing temporary or even conditional legitimacy. And in that case, a negative development or even a perception of development will give credibility to the government's capabilities and it will tend to solidify the military regime's legitimacy.

This is not to suggest that the regime can deceive all of its people all of the time. But to talk about the military's political and economic capabilities only in theoretical and objective terms is inadequate; it does not take skillful and shrewd political leadership into account. Nor does it take into adequate consideration, the tendency of more sagacious military regimes to promise less. I would like to advocate a distinction between legitimacy for a political system and legitimacy for a political regime. The former may take "prolonged effectiveness over a number of generations."[22] In the latter case, however, the time period can be significantly telescoped. I am in complete agreement that,

> "No groups of rulers can long base their claims for legitimacy on acrimony and memory of previous injustices. If the new military governors of African countries intend to remain in power for an extended period, they must seek to build the capacity of governing institutions, in terms both of legitimate organizational strength and skillful use of resources."[23]

However, we should not lose sight of the words, "remain in power for an extended period."

IV. Legitimacy Propositions

I will advance the following general legitimacy propositions:

1. That the legitimacy strategy used by the military regimes in Africa is partly dependent upon the circumstance of military takeover.

2. That the legitimacy strategy is partly dependent on the ambition and goal of the new military regime.

3. That the military regime's legitimacy strategies are not necessarily static. They are subject to re-examination depending on:

    (a) how established the military regime is;

    (b) the regime's clear minded perception of its mission and its resolve to pursue it;

(c) the coincidence or otherwise of its goals with the other sectors of society;

(d) the unity within the military organization; and

(e) the relative political strength of the various sectors of the society.

TWO TYPOLOGIES OF LEGITIMACY ENGINEERING AND COALITIONS UNDER MILITARY RULE

LEGITIMACY I

Where the military regime bases its legitimacy on the preservation of territorial integrity of the state and where it succeeds in selling the idea of a common enemy of the state, a temporary unity of state results. The successful engineering of this is likely to involve effective communications and contacts between the representatives of the local traditional establishments and those of the military regime. Because of low literacy, this will be brought about mostly through personal contacts with these traditional leaders (e.g. chiefs) and also to some extent, by radio. Such solidarity, if it develops, tends to weaken the traditional pockets of resistance to centralization and integration.

If violent confrontation results from the defense of the territorial integrity, modern weaponry and the need for reorganization of society to prosecute the war effectively call, at least temporarily, for fundamental restructuring of authority relations. All activities are subsumed or made subordinate to the goal of state survival which becomes the most important goal of society. Because traditional authority and organization belong to a different order in the face of modern military techniques and military capability, the traditional leaders and people, once they are agreed on the need to destroy the enemy, recognize the necessity for a modern organization and leadership pattern. Thus an alliance between traditional and military leadership is forged. At best, traditional authorities are partners. In a majority of cases, they are reduced to junior partners. They surrender some of their rights and privileges and bestow approval on new military leadership. The formal organizational characteristic of the military leaves its mark on the active participants in the conflict. If by a stroke of luck the war is fought with overall minimum financial sacrifice, the shape and/or composition of the economic and class structure of the system are fundamentally affected in ways which will bolster the military establishment.

If care is taken to ensure that in the perception of the traditional leaders, traditional authority's significance has not diminished, which is a distortion of reality in this case, and if the ability of the military leadership is not seriously undermined by their performances on the battlefield, fundamental reorganizations leading to the inevitable weakening of traditional authority result. After the war, new values and a new elite permeate the entire country. If the soldiers are demobilized, they find that they can no longer comfortably subject themselves to traditional patterns of authority. If they remain in the military, their increased wealth is conspicuously displayed everywhere and at any opportunity. Consequently, they become idols. New heroes and new myths develop. Traditional authorities will find it safer to support the new heroes as long as there is no attempt to withdraw their chiefly allowance or an attempt to refuse them their theoretical status. In reality, they have had their legitimacy and importance eroded by default. It will therefore be impossible for them to garner support to do battle. In the long run, not only do the traditional authorities in fact lose their people's traditional loyalty, but in due course they are viewed as extractive agents of central military leaders. This is particularly true in the instances where the war is costing a lot of money or where the military leadership chooses to wage the two wars--economic and military--concomitantly.

The academicians are theoretically committed to the idea of a nation. The preservation of territorial integrity of the states by violence is not likely to meet with their disapproval as long as all other avenues have been exploited unsuccessfully. It must be recognized that in developing states the intelligentsia is not united. They are anxious to be in powerful positions. The entry of the military into politics under the circumstance which we have been discussing offers them a number of opportunities. The military recognizes the need for academic courtiers as well as articulate minds who can attempt to present their cases before the international world in such a way as to neutralize antagonistic world opinion or even generate international support. Secondly, the military also recognizes that governmental functions must proceed and the bureaucrats who constitute part of the intelligentsia need to be courted. Because of the usual lack of governmental and political experience of the new military leadership and the desire for ideas and advice, the bureaucrats and academicians experience a period of unusual efficacy and the resultant high morale usually leads to high output and performance. Thus there is a coalition of the military, the technocrats and the idealists. However, as the brutality of war is revealed and as corruption manifests itself among the military, the intellectual idealists may become disenchanted. In that case the intelligentsia, once again is divided between the idealists in or out of power and those who crave or want to retain power. The latter is willing to concede necessary evils; even the restriction of freedoms. However, as the military leaders become sure-footed politically and as they judge the need for the services of the intelligentsia unnecessary or redundant, their reference for and tolerance of intellectuals diminish. In fact, there may develop a strong ambivalence about the intellectual. Since most of the institutions where intelligentsia can work tend to be "national in scope," and governmental in sponsorship, disaffected intellectuals may have only four choices:

(1) accept their junior partnership and benign neglect as long as they need their daily bread;

(2) leave their country and seek fulfillment in countries with a libertarian tradition;

(3)    stay behind to perform their self-appointed role of governmental critiques despite the maximum political risks involved;

(4)    turn inwards and resume their skeptical attitude towards politics.

As far as the bureaucracy is concerned, the top echelon remains important because of the disinclination of the African military bureaucracies to perform civilian administration as well as the inexperience of the military in the area of developmental administration.

Discussing the relationship between intellectuals and the military Shils writes:

> "They (military) are naturally patriotic, and their technical orientation gives a technocratic coloring to their conception of natural progress. If the modern intellectual class has a reasonable proportion of persons with technological education and experience, the military will tend to regard it as an ally."[24]

I feel that this typology tends to over-estimate the technological competence and fervor of the military at least in Africa. How does the military deal with politicians? Again, Edward Shil:

> "Their (military) education is technical, and efficiency is one of the standards which they have learned. They tend to be suspicious of flamboyant oratory and of the politics of negotiation, fixing and compromise. Their belief that they are under obligation to a more austere morality makes them disapprove especially of parliamentary politicians and cabinet ministers who traffic in import permits, foreign exchange licenses, government contracts and profitable appointments. This type of anti-political attitude does not make them more sympathetic with the oppositional activities of lawyers, journalists, and other intellectuals, whom they regard as part of the same repellent system. When they collaborate with them, the alliance is untenable."[25]

This portrayal needs considerable amendment. The military, it must be understood in this circumstance, has usurped the functional role of the politicians because the ruling political class is judged incompetent to deal with the societal problems. Political activities are proscribed, political parties are banned and political instrumentalities are revoked. However, since man is a political animal and in the face of the constant need to order societal activities, politics cannot be dismissed really. With the dismissal of the ruling parties in the interest of the consolidation of the military junta's position, politicians must be watched and resources available to them frozen so as to minimize their threat. Particularly in the new states, it is not easy to dislodge a man who has tasted power. In the interest of unity, the use of decidedly active opposition party members may be delayed. Politics is, for a while, presented as dirty and politicians as monsters or people who have sapped the energies and resources of the state to unproductive ends. Commissions of enquiries are set up to investigate their activities. But the inexperience of military leaders in the acts of politics and the discrediting of politicians therefore means that, as much as possible, the military regime needs to turn to intellectuals with the technical know-how and former politicians with little record of discredit but considerable support from key sectors of society. Since the goal is a united front and effort, united advisory councils may be formed. Various communities, within a restructured framework, will be represented on such advisory councils. These men help to engineer legitimacy for the military leaders by acting as brokers and also by acting as mentors. If they succeed, they become reduncant. Considerable conflict arises between them and the bureaucratic elite. As the military leaders become increasingly accepted as legitimate, and a general acceptable priority of goals is established, the bureaucratic executants, not the politicians, become more important. The loss of status and privileges traditionally associated with political advisers and the increase in the status and role of bureaucrats at the expense of political advisers may lead to jealousy and tension between the new pseudo-political and bureaucratic classes. A member of the former is then faced with five alternatives:

(1) attempt to maintain his status by improving his influence within the group he represents on the council;

(2) attempt to maintain his status by improving his relations with powerful members of the military establishment;

(3) attempt to maintain his status by improving his technical competence and knowledge on issues dealing with his ministry and other ministries;

(4) resign his position and bid his time;

(5) remain in his position with diminished status in the hope of remaining in public limelight.

The military will tend to look at labor with suspicion because, in the situation of war, demands for wage increase and traditional labor instruments of strikes are unsalutary. Every attempt is made to restrict or contain the labor union. Attempts are made to appeal to their patriotic spirit. However, given the inflationary process which is almost an adjunct of war and the ever-increasing tendency to curb labor's bargaining ability, labor usually falls out of grade in the long run. The labor leadership may find itself in a dilemma. If it should follow the government in the face of inflationary spiral, it will incur the disaffection of the rank and file union membership. If it should push the government, it may find its union proscribed and the leadership in detention. Moreover, because of the usual overall support given to the government "war efforts" by the various segments of society, labor can ill-afford a confrontation. Consequently, it may have to acquiesce in the hope that the war will soon be over. If the military junta decides to remain in power after the successful conclusion of the war, then it will have to view labor with greater suspicion. A marriage of convenience between labor, radical intellectuals, and ambitious politicians can be very potent if it finds support from a significant segment of the army. In the event that the military regime finds it necessary to continue after the end of the war, the warning of Welch becomes relevant. The sustenance of its legitimacy will depend on its performance.

## LEGITIMACY II

This typology represents military legitimacy engineering after a take-over from an essentially socialistic regime. If the most important reason for such

take-overs is the need to restore individual freedom and democratic government,
then the military leaders who take over under such circumstances labor under a
paradox. By professional training they are non-democratic and non-political, but
they have undertaken a self-appointed task of bringing about democracy--a situation
antithetical to the military chain of command. Shils writes:

> "By tradition, and perhaps by necessity, the military is a hierarchy and regards such an order as reasonable. It regards the unquestioning execution of decisive and unambiguous commands as right. It is impatient with the muttering of public opinion."[26]

By the use of force, or the threat of the use of force they have brought about a change
of government. They are quite aware that this is a non-conventional means to
bring about democratic change. Consequently, while the act in itself is perceived as noble, the posture of such military leadership tends to be apologetic.
They are aware of the need to be most restrained in their rule and they tend to
overcompensate for their soldierly background and the 'necessity' to use force.
Considerable energy is therefore spent on persuading both "friends" and "foes"
about the genuineness of the coup. Because socialistic regimes tend to be well
entrenched with the "Eastern bloc" nations, the military leadership in order to
consolidate its position feels the need to be vehemently anti-Eastern in its foreign
policy. Such a policy is salutary in two ways: First, societal aggression may
be chanelled towards the "communist outsiders" who in turn, have "misled" well
meaning nationals. This is an attempt to unify both supporters and enemies of the
deposed regime behind the new military take-over. Every attempt is made to deal
with deposed political activists within constitutional means. Otherwise, one is
haunted by the paradox. Secondly, within the framework of the cold war, this is
an effective tool to garner requisite support from the Western powers. The nature
of such support may have definite impact on the kind of government which the military leaders will have and the kind of government they would like to see after the
military exit. It would seem that this, rather than the "Western military training"
of the coup leaders, will better explain the particular Western biases that are

exhibited in such regimes. Parenthetically, I must say that Western trained military leaders have led anti-Western regimes. Given the circumstances in which such coups take place, the nature of the declared goal of the coup, and their pattern of Western international support, such military regimes find that their policies tend to be judged in terms of their impact on the freedom of individuals and other democratic ideals which often involves a laissez faire framework. The regime seeks to persuade rather than compel. It relies very heavily on lawyers, educated elite and Western private enterprise. Traditional rulers are seen as the spokesmen for the uneducated man. Consequently, very little is consciously done to undermine traditional institutions and authority. If, however, the previous regime has interfered with traditional institutions, attempts are made to engineer changes. These changes are perceived as representing a return to the original status of the traditional institutions.

In comparing underdeveloped countries which are 'socialistic' with those which are 'democratic,' one finds that, in the latter the educated tend to enjoy higher status and income. Quite apart from the intellectual preoccupation with freedom of thought and expression, the educated elite's self-interest dictates a preference for democratic order. They often feel uncomfortable under dictatorial regimes because very little respect is bestowed on those reluctant to compromise.*
The advent of the soldier bearing proclaimed gifts of democracy is most welcomed to this educated elite. They feel most at home and are very kindly predisposed to these military leaders. The educated elite which was once weak, divided, hesitant, aloof, may now form an active bastion for such a regime. Their advice will be sought, given even when not solicited, and taken into account in policy formation. This provides them with an opportunity to join the ruling class without the fear of losing their creed. Parenthetically, we should note that this activist posture, no matter the motivation, is pregnant with dangers. They write to show why the old regime failed, why the military is justified in taking over, and what must be

_____
*The agonies of Soviet writers and intellectuals attest to this point.

done to make sure that democracy is enshrined. As the military regime goes on and as the educated elite becomes more activist, the latter gets tired of playing "back room boys." It becomes impatient because it wants to see "true democracy in action." To them, a military regime, no matter how sincere, will never do as a substitute for a duly elected government of the people. The military rulers are constantly needled.

The constraints on this category of military leaders under the situation we have described is such that we may wonder how much of its output the regime is actually responsible for. They are haunted by the incongruity of their own circumstances, and perhaps the pressures of various "constituencies"--Western countries, educated elite, impatient former opposition members, budding politicians, and newly awakened citizens filled with great expectations.

In addition to the intellectuals and traditional authorities, the military regime relies upon some respected politicians poised in sustained opposition against the deposed regime. The political inexperience of the military leaders in the category and the fact that, by default, they usually share the same ideological predisposition with the opposition party, make the opposition politicians powerful. They are often eager to offer their services. In fact, it is possible that prominent former opposition members have proteges among the coup leaders. It is therefore natural for these politicians to seek to use their connection to juggle for the most advantageous position to get ahead before the civilian political race begins. The situation may be one of mutual dependence. However, in a politically sensitive environment, the suspicion of favoritism for certain political figures is dangerous because it may destroy the precarious solidarity of the military leadership.

Given its goal, such regimes are, *ipso facto*, transitional and corrective. By their nature, such regimes sow the seeds of their own destruction: If they succeed, they must go, if they do not succeed, they must immediately hand over to let "the people take care of the mess." Despite their limited freedom of action, such regimes evoke great hopes from the citizenry.

A relevant variable in the relationship of such regimes with governmental bureaucracy is the degree of penetration of the bureaucracy by the deposed regime. One can expect an inverse relationship. If the old socialist regime has fully penetrated the bureaucracy one may find only perfunctory dependence on the higher bureaucrats. If the reverse is true, one can expect a high degree of influence by this group. However, here more than in a situation of war, the rivalry between bureaucrats and political advisers and intellectuals is bound to be more spirited. However, the consequences of such rivalry are different. In the latter case the higher bureaucrats are bound to go back to the backroom while the educated elite and the new political 'advisers' are increasingly listened to. After all, technocracy is not democracy.

All in all, the problem of engineering legitimacy in this case is not difficult once the military leaders have effectively neutralized the ruling party activists, either by temporary detention or effective surveillance. It is sometimes difficult for this type of military regimes to use extra legal methods in dealing with them. Consequently, an effective and less conscience-tormenting way is to appoint commissions of enquiry to investigate every phase of activity and dealings of these activists. While these commissions are not extra-legal they perform the twin tasks of providing legitimacy for the regime by discrediting the deposed one over a carefully drawn out but legal procedure. These commission hearings receive the widest and most prominent coverage in local newspapers, radio and television. Government representatives at the local level work assiduously in order to remind the non-literate mass about the shady deals and bad political performances of the deposed regimes. A careful orchestration of the stage of institutionalization will ensure the relevant sectors of society that the military regime has not reneged on its self-declared path. Supporting the military regime therefore is supporting the day when participation and representative leadership will take over. This is a carrot for support. If, however, the military leadership should want to use the military force as a substitute for its legitimacy, opposition can be forthcoming from academicians, ex-politicians and even traditional rulers.

At the very best such regimes aim for a welfare state. But because of the psychopathological fear of socialism and the Eastern block as well as the pressure from the new benefactors, i.e. Western nations, classic capitalism may be pursued. The degree of irrationality in the political and economic policy depends on:

(1) the extent of the pervasiveness of socialist orientation and policies in the regimes they deposed. One may wonder whether one can succeed, in three years, in reindoctrinating a people subjected to ten years of antithetical ideology.

(2) the degree of influence exercised by the educated elite and the degree of the deprivation they experienced under the old regime.

(3) the degree and kind of cooperation given to the regime by Western countries.

FOOTNOTES

1. Samuel E. Finer, The Man on Horseback: The Role of the Military in Politics. (New York: Praeger, 1962), p. 7.

2. Robin Price, "Reference Group Theory and the Ghanaian Case," World Politics Vol. XXIII, 3, (April, 1971), p. 402. He argues that because the metropoles still represent the significant others for the military in the new states, a "paradoxical" situation is created--a military officer corps which tends to be non-nationalistic and non-puritanic.

3. Claude Welch, Jr., Soldier and State in Africa, op. cit., p. 37.

4. Samuel P. Huntington, Political Order in Changing Societies (New Haven: Yale University Press, 1969), pp. 221-222.

5. Samuel Huntington, Ibid.

6. Robin Price, op. cit., pp. 399-430.

7. Robin Price, Ibid., pp. 404-405.

8. Robin Price, Ibid., p. 406.

9. A. K. Ocran, A Myth is Broken (London: Longman's Green and Co., Ltd., 1968).

10. Ghana Time, May 1, 1972, p. 6.

11. Huntington, op. cit., p. 193.

12. Robin Price, op. cit., p. 403.

13. V. A. Olorunsola, "Patterns of Interaction Between Bureaucratic and Political Leadership, Journal of Developing Areas (October, 1968), pp. 51-65.

14. These propositions were extracted from Price, World Politics, op. cit., pp. 427-29.

15. Claude Welch, Jr., op. cit., p. 37.

16. Claude Welch, Jr., Ibid.

17. Claude Welch, Jr., Ibid.

18. Claude Welch, Jr., p. 38.

19. Claude Welch, Jr., p. 39.

20. Samuel P. Huntington, Changing Pattern of Military Politics (New York: Free Press, 1962), p. 40.

21. Fred Riggs, Administration in Developing Countries: The Theory of Prismatic Society (Boston: Houghton Mifflin, 1964).

22. Welch, op. cit., p. 47.

23. Welch, op. cit., p. 46.

24. Edward Shils, "The Military in the Political Development of the New States," in John J. Johnson (ed.) The Role of the Military in Underdeveloped Countries (Princeton: Princeton University Press, 1962), p. 40.

25. Shils, Ibid., p. 35.

26. Shils, Ibid., p. 28.

CHAPTER II
BACKGROUND

INTRODUCTION

The reason for taking a look at a country's past political framework and culture is that somehow these are salient for the understanding of the present and probably the future as well. To the extent that the military regimes tend to take over the mantle of power from civilian authorities as a result of purported malfeasance of duties on the part of the latter, the presumption is that the former feels more competent. A diagnosis of the reasons for the failure of civilian authorities is a prerequisite for the proper assessment of the potential of the military usurpers. Is the reason for the failure innate poor political leadership? Or, is it due to dissonance in the rhythm between the leadership and what we might call the temperament of the people? However this might be, a short and admittedly truncated investigation into the political tradition[1] and history in which the deposed politicians operated is necessary.

In this chapter, I intend to provide general background materials on each of two countries involved in this study. More specifically, I will discuss

1. the problems confronting each country;

2. the political tradition of each country;

3. the civil-military relations.

## NIGERIA

The examination of Nigerian political history suggests that the country is beset by a set of problems which must be faced squarely in the interest of successful political development. I do not claim that these problems are peculiar to Nigeria. On the contrary, most of them are common to the new states. Because I have dealt with them in greater detail elsewhere, no detailed discussion of these problems is envisaged here.[2] I shall outline the problems and discuss them as briefly as possible because I firmly believe that they are salient for the understanding and analysis of Nigerian political dynamics and the estimation of the achievement of the Gowon regime.

Briefly then, let me outline them:

1. the problem of differing political cultures among the various ethnic groupings in the country as well as the inability of those in authority to reconcile differing norms with one another;

2. the problem of differing impact of colonialism which manifests itself in uneven educational opportunities which in turn results in sharp differences in the rate of growth among various parts of the country;

3. the problem of ethnic based political parties which, for the selfish interest of maintaining themselves in power, accentuate sectional feelings and intensify primordial attachments;

4. the loss of idealism, the reckless pursuit of personal wealth by the fortunate few, and the widening of the gap between the haves and the have nots;

5. a sense of frustration by citizens regarding their future and fortune in the political order, (the issue of rigged elections and the absence of freedom to pursue economic activity anywhere in the Federation);

6. the politics of cultural sub-nationalism and the politics of regional security;

7. the apparent unwillingness to attack Nigerian problems at their foundation, (i.e. the preference for patchwork has led the country to develop a vicious cycle of crises);

8. the problem of making national institutions behave in truly national fashion.

Let me explicate further on some of these. The problem of heterogeneous political culture is the result of the British creation of the Nigerian state out of a conglomeration of ethnic groups with diverse political attitudes. The Hausa-Fulani, the largest ethnic group in the North, through a successfully executed *jihad* brought about the Fulani Empire. This was a large state form of political organization which did not differentiate between religious and political authority because the same Emir personified both. These Emirs came from royal families and were supported by titled officials and traditional offices hierarchically organized. The system has been described by Sklar and Whitaker as "despotic in form" because the commoner was at the mercy of the uncertain benevolence of his overlord.[3] In essence, then, the Hausa-Fulani traditional political system was a theocracy. Of course, in a theocracy the citizen's conceptions of his ruler, the ruler's legitimacy and role, and the citizen's right and obligations are quite different from the conceptions of a citizen from a democratic or parademocratic political system. Yet, this incongruity was the case in Nigeria. For example, the Ibos did not have large political organization. Political recruitment among the Ibos placed heavy emphasis upon the possession of achievement criteria with some sprinkling of ascriptive ones. One was almost under obligation to be aggressive and ambitious. The village chief was *primus inter pares*. Consequently, his power was quite limited and the citizen's conception of his role in the political process was an active and participatory one.

The Yoruba traditional political culture, on the other hand, fell between the two extremes discussed thus far. It was essentially gerontocratic. While the power of traditional authority was generally recognized, a strong and effective balance system operated.

Thus, by the declaration of a Nigerian state, the British juxtaposed theocratic, parademocratic and gerontocratic traditional political cultures. There were no successful attempts on the part of the British to reconcile these different political attitudes. Nor did the Nigerians succeed in fundamentally dealing with them to ensure the elimination of recurrent contraditions among the traditional political cultures and their reconciliation with the modern Nigerian political culture, which professes to be democratic.

The problem of uneven educational opportunities is a consequence of geography, an accident of history and a conscious British colonial policy. It is almost an axiom of colonial history that the areas geographically most removed from the coast are often the last to be reached by Western influences of education etc. In this respect, Northern Nigeria was at a disadvantage. Furthermore, it was a conscious policy of the British not to interfere with the Islamic religion. This meant that Christian missionaries who brought education to the country were discouraged from building schools since this would have the effect of undermining Islam. Thirdly, by accident, history created a situation in which Northern Nigeria was more oriented towards North Africa and the Sudanic states than towards the South. To a considerable extent, this made the rooting of Western influences more difficult. The net effect is that while the South was taking advantage of missionary schools, the North remained behind. This disadvantage led to uneven development in the country and to the uneven distribution of manpower resources. Thus, the North which claimed to have fifty percent of the Nigerian population had the least indigenous modern manpower resources and remains the least developed.

The protectionist attitude which the British had toward the North as well as the strength of the Northern traditional rulers meant that the birth of nationalism was delayed. Even when it emerged, it was in reaction against domination by the

Southern educated elite. The birth of a pseudo-political organization in the North was brought about by the few educated Northerners. Its infiltration by the traditional establishment of the North is well documented by Richard Sklar in <u>Nigerian Political Parties</u>.[4] Suffice it to say that it was committed to the maintenance of Northern regional security, a very gradual approach to change, and a conservative political ideology. A political party, the Northern Peoples Congress, (NPC) whose ethnic base was Hausa-Fulani, emerged.

The Action Group was formed in 1945 from an ethnic organization called Egbe Omo Oduduwa (Yoruba Descendents Union). The association was formally converted in 1956 into a political party. With the initial cooperation of the traditional rulers and through a careful exploitation of anti-Ibo sentiment, it managed to get control of power in the Western Region. Until the Western Regional crisis, it was in control of power in the Western Region. It remained essentially a party of the West until the Federal election of 1959 when its leader, Chief Awolowo, mounted a well financed campaign in the North and East. Unfortunately for it, the Northern establishment was determined not to allow it to make inroads. It met with less vicious but equally determined opposition in the East. This diligent national campaign netted the Action Group poor results. By 1962, in pursuit of personal interests and regional security, many of its successful Northern candidates in the Federal elections had switched sides to declare for the parties in power. The Action Group was soon plunged into an internal crisis. The question was really not an ideological one, but one that revolved around strategy. Which is the best way to protect Yoruba interest and Western Regional security--join the NPC coalition or remain in opposition? Akintola wanted the Action Group to join the NPC government. Awolowo insisted on remaining in opposition in the hope of teaming up with a more compatible political party (NCNC) National Council of Nigerian Citizens, to form the government the next time. Eventually, what I will call the first Western Regional Crisis resulted. Awolowo was accused of plotting to overthrow the Federal government and he was imprisoned. The Action Group was divided into two, Akintola and Awolowo factions, and a state of emergency was declared in the West by the federal government.

Despite its national orientational pretension, the NCNC was essentially an Ibo based political party. Like the Action Group, it claimed multi-tribal membership, but its general orientation when the chips were down was towards the preservation of Eastern regional security.

All Nigerian political parties despite their pretensions failed Nigerians through the pursuit of regional security and parochial interests. They exacerbated sectional feelings not adumberated them. They aided the use of corruption rather than stemming its tide.

The experience of Ibos, the AG, and the other opposition parties in the North; the experience of the Federal elections of 1959 and 1964, and particularly the Western election of 1965 and its after effect; all suggest that many Nigerians came to develop a skeptical attitude towards democratic institutions and a sense of frustration regarding their future and fortunes in the political order. The situation in the East was different only in the matter of degree.

The politics of regional and ethnic security manifested themselves in many ways. For example, the seeming inability of Nigerians to agree on how many Nigerians there were betrays mutual distrust; the fear that a tribe will inflate its population and thereby control power. Since Nigerian political parties were ethnically based and because the party with the most votes got the power, the census became a most important determinant. If the spoils belong to the victor, then the tribe with the victorious party has the plum of office. The zero sum game is ominous in a country where government is ubiquitous and where it constituted the pervasive employer. Those who perceive themselves as constantly out of power become frustrated, depondent or desperate.

Numerous commissions[5] of inquiry have confirmed what most Nigerians suspected. Politics came to be looked upon as the most financially rewarding industry.

Politicians extracted financial rewards from contractors as well as constituents. These "commissions" were demanded for the performance of normal duties as well as for illegal acts. The diminishing world cocoa prices, the rise in unemployment figures coupled with poor example from politicians created an atmosphere where people were frantically and constantly looking for short-cuts to wealth. With the possible exception of Northern Nigeria, political and economic power were concentrated in the same hands.

## CRISIS CYCLE

Following the split in the Action Group the forces opposed to Akintola's deputy party leadership and his premiership of the Western region tried to oust him. Pandemonium and fights broke out in the region. The Prime Minister declared a state of emergency in the region, dismissed the regional parliamentarians and their leaders, and appointed an administrator. The supporters of Awolowo saw the Federal government's move as a deliberate attempt to prevent a constitutional and legal ousting of Akintola from the premiership. It should be recalled that Akintola had advocated an AG-NPC coalition as the only productive strategy for Western regional security and Yoruba ascendency. The state of emergency meant that a vote may not be taken on the issue. When the state of emergency, declared in May, 1962, was lifted in January, 1963, Akintola was installed as the premier by the Federal government. Again many people in the region regarded this as yet another proof of the Federal government partisanship. A new election could have been called following the lifting of the state of emergency. This is one of the many cases which demonstrates a peculiar unwillingness of Nigerian leaders to attack problems at their foundation. Seemingly, the preference was always for patchwork.

The reinstatement of Akintola was followed by the birth of his party, the Nigerian National Democratic Party (NNDP). His party, which split from the AG, pursued a policy of active cooperation with the NPC. The informal coalition was soon formalized in time to conduct the 1964 Federal elections. The coalition party was called the Nigerian National Alliance (NNA).

The Federal coalition government of NPC-NCNC had drifted apart as a result of several factors including the controversies of the Nigerian census. It was clear that the powerful section of NPC would like to see the coalition dissolved and replaced, after the 1964 Federal election, with the NNA. The NCNC for its part, prepared to preserve the Eastern regional security by forming an alliance with the Action Group. The alliance was called the United Progressive Grand Alliance (UPGA). The stage was set for an UPGA-NNA confrontation in the Federal election.

The UPGA party complained of victimization and about obstructionist strategies which, they claimed, they were subjected to in the North and West. Ultimately, they decided to boycott the election. The elections were held despite the effective UPGA boycott in the North and in many parts of the West. The President of Nigeria, himself an Ibo and former member of the NCNC, refused to invite the Prime Minister to form the government. After a few days of grave crisis and the apparent support of the armed forces for the Prime Minister's position, the President gave way. In return, the Prime Minister made some concessions. One of the concessions was that a new Western regional election would be held soon.

The Western regional election was held in 1965. Although elections in Nigeria have never been without irregularities, this election witnessed the most numerous and flagrant abuse of the democratic process.[6] Unlike the past when the aggrieved, defeated candidates took to the courts to seek redress, their supporters took to the streets. Law and order broke down and it was clear beyond a doubt that Akintola's government was perceived as illegitimate. It should have been clear also that it would be difficult to impose this government upon the people of the Western state for any appreciable period. Chief Akintola partially understood this; his secret trip to the Sardauna a few days before the January elections suggests considerable apprehension and unease on his part.

These crises, the failure of Nigerian political parties, and the impotence of the Nigerian bureaucracy were construed by some as an invitation for the direct involvement of the army in Nigerian politics. Particularly, attention was given to the fact that instead of dealing with this second Western crisis with the same dispatch with which he dealt with the first one, the Prime Minister, as if under the spell of "Peter's law of incompetence" was busy playing host to a Commonwealth conference on Rhodesia. In some ways, his problem was that of a decision maker with extremely restricted decision latitude. We now know that this is a clear demonstration of the paradox of Nigerian political power; the Federal Prime Minister who is supposedly the most constitutionally powerful Nigerian, was restrained by a regional premier from doing what he would have liked to do to resolve this crisis.

## THE NIGERIAN ARMY

The Nigerian Army, like all its ex-British colonial counterparts, began out of the need for a pacification instrument; thus, we had the Glover's Hausas of 1863, Oil Rivers Irregulars of 1885, and the Royal Niger Constabulary of 1886, later known as the Northern Nigerian Regiment. These constituted the nuclei of the Nigerian Regiment of the West African Frontier Force in 1914. In response to the war needs, the regiment was enlarged and many of its soldiers saw action in German Camerun and Tanganyika. After the war, the army was demobilized so that it had only about four battalions. These battalions were used to collect taxes particularly in the area of the Middle belt.

World War II brought greater need for soldiers. Twenty-eight battalions were raised in Nigeria, ". . . 121,652 Nigerians served in the army, of which approximately 30,000 served abroad winning 86 decorations (8 D.C.M.'s, 58 M.M.'s,

20 B.E.M.'s) and 243 mentions in despatch."[7] They helped to liberate Ethiopia from the Italians and many of them saw action in the Burma campaign.

Recruitment into the army at this time was by the direct use of government propaganda machinery and through appeals to traditional authorities who sometimes used their influence to boost the number of army volunteers. Between World War I and World War II army recruits came predominantly from Northern Nigeria partly because the military authorities believed that certain tribes were more belligerent and therefore more desirable in an army of infantry and artillery. World War II saw some improvements in military technology. Therefore, the army needed greater technical competence; drivers, mechanics, and other tradesmen were in demand. Since most of these skills required greater Western educational competence which at the time was in very short supply in the North, Southerners had to be courted and recruited into these technical and clerical positions in the army. The Southerners tended to come from the minority areas of Southern Nigeria e.g. Calabar, Ika-Ibo and Ondo.

Unlike the police, the army did not have a minimum educational requirement. After the war, recruitment into the army continued to be based on good physique and a simple intelligence test.

NIGERIAN ARMY AND POLICE RECRUITMENT TABLE

| REGION | % OF POPULATION 1952 CENSUS | % OF ARMY RECRUITS 1946-1958 | % OF POLICE RECRUITS IN 1955 |
|---|---|---|---|
| North | 54.5 | 62.5 | 17.5 |
| East | 23.0 | 25.0 | 45.5 |
| West | 20.0 | 11.0 | 33.0 |
| South Cameroon | 2.5 | 1.5 | 4.0 |
| TOTAL | 100.0 | 100.0 | 100.0 |

This table needs to be qualified. The eleven percent in the Western column of army recruits is misleading because most of these came from minority areas.

In fact, in 1966, years after the quota system was introduced, there were only 700 Yoruba soldiers in the army. Similarly, some explanation is necessary for the Northern figures. The record of the Fifth Battalion taken after the Ibos had left the battalion indicated the following religious distribution:

| RELIGION | NUMBER |
|---|---|
| Protestant | 328 |
| Catholic | 233 |
| Animist | 36 |
| Moslem | 84 |

Given the very low percentage of Hausa-Fulani who are Christians, it can be presumed that the predominance of Christians here indicates that most of these soldiers came from the minority areas.

In 1958 the military population was put at 7,600. By 1965 it had grown to about 10,500. By 1971 it had rocketed to over 250,000. This dramatic growth from 1966 to 1971 reflects the military build up occasioned by the war. This time the Yoruba leaders made concerted, vigorous and successful attempts to recruit Yorubas into the army.

Although between 1959-1966 the rank and file growth was about 33%, the officer growth rate was almost 100% (283-508). Therefore, some officers might have been apprehensive about their futures. The impact of the quota policy upon the recruitment of officers is most revealing when we tabulate the regional background of the officers at various times: before independence, before the introduction of the quota system, and after the introduction of the quota system.

REGIONAL BACKGROUND OF NIGERIAN OFFICERS[10]

|  | North | | West & Midwest Not including Ika-Ibo | | East & Ika-Ibo | | South Cameroon | |
| --- | --- | --- | --- | --- | --- | --- | --- | --- |
|  | Number | % | Number | % | Number | % | Number | % |
| Pre-independence | 8 | 14 | 10 | 17 | 37 | 65 | 2 | 3.5 |
| Pre-quota system | 21 | 32 | 12 | 18 | 29 | 45 | 3 | 5 |
| Post Quota system | 104 | 48 | 46 | 21 | 66 | 31 | - | - |
| Total | 133 | 39% | 68 | 20% | 132 | 39% | 5 | 2% |

This table shows:

1. that before independence sixty-five percent of Nigerian officers came from the East and Ika-Ibo while only eight percent of the officers came from the North;

2. that after independence and before the introduction of the quota, the North improved its officer contribution to thirty-two percent while the East and Ika-Ibo contributed forty-five percent;

3. that after the introduction of the quota system, the North got almost half of the officer recruits (forty-eight percent) and the East and Ika-Ibo got about thirty-one percent;

4. that the contribution of the West and Midwest did not alter dramatically.

Before the January 1966 coup d'etat the overall composition of Nigerian officers was as follows:

| NORTH | | WEST & MIDWEST NOT IKA-IBO | | EAST & IKA-IBO | | SOUTH CAMEROON[11] | |
| --- | --- | --- | --- | --- | --- | --- | --- |
| NUMBER | % | NUMBER | % | NUMBER | % | NUMBER | % |
| 157 | 32.5 | 126 | 26.5 | 190 | 40.5 | 2 | .5 |

There were about twenty female nurse officers not included. We would guess that most of these came from the East and Ika-Ibo section.

Nigeria did not open its own Nigerian Military Training College (NMTC) until April 1960. Therefore, it had to send its recruits to Teshie for six months training after which the military authorities in Teshie decided who would go to overseas officer training colleges. There was, therefore, no room to influence the regional composition of officers beyond the confines of objective criteria. After the NMTC was created, and the need to go to Teshie eliminated, the Minister of Defence instructed that "where there are potential cadets of equal merit, consideration may be given by the board to the ethnic balance between regions."[12] This instruction resulted in some adjustment in favor of the North.[13] The officers from the other parts of Nigeria must have found this quota disconcerting. When the Nigerian Defence Academy was opened in 1964, it made it possible not only for Nigerian officers to be trained in Nigeria but also for a more rigorous quota system to be executed.

OVERSEAS TRAINING FOR NIGERIAN OFFICERS

| YEAR | NUMBER |
|---|---|
| 1959 | 12 |
| 1960 | 21 |
| 1961 | 42 |
| 1962 | 37 |
| 1963 | 96 |
| 1964 | 59 |
| 1965 | 35 |
| 1966 | 50 (first graduates from the Nigerian Defence Academy) |

Countries of training: U.S.A., Ethiopia, Australia, United Kingdom, Canada, Pakistan, India.

Although before the civil war, the Nigerian military, unlike the Nigerian police, had the reputation of being corruption free, the scoreboard was not perfect even during this period. In 1964, even when the British General Officer Commanding (GOC) was still in command there were three known cases of corruption in the military.[15] On the overall, however, its record in this respect was a good one if compared with the records of other Nigerian institutions.

Before the civil war, the army was by far the largest of the military establishments, the navy and the air force remained essentially embryonic. Within the army, the infantry constituted the overwhelming majority. The units requiring greater technical competence such as the medical and the engineering were small indeed. Furthermore, only a very negligible percentage of officers had university training.

The condition of service and financial remuneration of the military was poor for a long time, but by 1964 the conditions of service and salary had become comfortable. In fact, they compared most favorably to civilians' salaries. For example, a new lieutenant with fewer years and amount in educational investment got more than a university graduate.

All in all in terms of conditions of service, there were hardly many grounds for discontentment of the Nigerian military as an organization. But, the recruitment policies must have been disconcerting for non-Northerners. Furthermore, the use of the army was not very satisfactory to many officers. The latter point will be discussed presently.

CIVIL-MILITARY RELATIONS

According to Miner, a first attempt to overthrow the Nigerian government was around the day of Nigerian independence. Some junior officers of the First Queen's Own Nigerian Regiment of Enugu planned to seize the battalion headquarters. They obviously expected a domino effect in the other parts of the Federation. The plot was discovered and those involved were imprisoned for six months without publicity. They were returned to their posts upon the completion of their sentences.

Before and after this event, however, the army was viewed as a government show piece. For example, in 1959 during the Federal election campaigns the government ordered the Nigerian Army to go on parades in various parts of the Federation to "show the flag." It was assumed that this show of force would act as a deterrent to would-be agitators. This was also repeated during the 1964 Federal elections. How effective the military was in this respect is open to debate given the disturbances and disruptions rampant at least during the 1964 elections.

In 1960, the army was used to subdue the unrest in the Tiv division of the Northern Region. In 1964, another disturbance broke out and it was necessary to use the army again to subdue it. Some of the officers involved found the assignment distasteful. They felt that they were being used to repress innocent men and women. This is not to argue that the Nigerian military as an organization was alienated from the political establishment. However, it does recognize that there were many who were becoming apprehensive.

The Action Group plot of 1962 is another occasion which could have involved the military at least tangentially. Chief Awolowo, the leader of the Action Group and the leader of the opposition in the Federal House of Representatives was alleged to have been involved in a plot to overthrow the Federal government. At the treason trial, it was alleged that Awolowo suggested that Brigadier Ademulegun should be contacted. Surprisingly the prosecution did not make a public attempt to find out whether or not this was done. However, the fact that Brigadier Ademulegun was confirmed in his position is an indication either that he cooperated secretly with the government or that he was antagonistic to the plot.[16]

Following the Federal elections of December 1964, (see earlier discussion) Dr. Azikiwe refused to invite Tafawa Balewa to form the government. Rather, he invited the heads of the navy, police, and the army to ask if they would support him in his intention to take over the government given the situation in the country. The armed forces declined to give him their support because they could not accept him as the legitimate source of operational orders. A senior Nigerian army officer who claimed to have been consulted by his General revealed to the writer that their position was that as Field Marshall, Dr. Azikiwe was in fact a part of the armed forces. However, that might be, the heads of the services also consulted with the Prime Minister and the Attorney General. Without the backing of the armed forces, and following the friendly intervention of the judiciary on the side of Sir Abubakar Tafawa Balewa, Dr. Azikiwe gave way. The point here is that this was a case in which the armed forces were being lured into political participation. In retrospect, there were some army officers who were not satisfied with the manner of the resolution of the crisis nor with the "neutrality of the armed forces" in this case. No doubt some felt that the opportunity if taken would have prevented the country from sinking into deeper abyss and that this would have preempted later acrobatic rescue operations. The supporters of the neutrality felt that this was a clear signal to the politicians that the army would expect them to take care of their domestic political mess which they created. If that was the intention, the politicians did not get their message. The armed forces continued to be enticed into politics rather unwittingly by both sides. For example, when General Ironsi, an Ibo, was appointed by the Prime Minister as the Officer Commanding the Nigerian Army, the __Nigerian Citizen__ suggested that such a position should be tied to a political plum.

General Gowon in 1966 claimed that he was approached by Lt. Cols. Ojukwu and Banjo about the three of them taking over the country.[19] "The Nigerian Government Statement on the Current Situation," also claimed that a plan by an Ibo officer to assassinate most senior officers of the army existed as far back as 1964. It claimed that the plan was suspended because having been "tipped off" the most senior officers stayed away. But the validity of this plot is subjected to objective criticism by Miner.

Following the Western Regional elections, the validity of which was not accepted by most Western Nigerians, the Akintola government and the entire region witnessed what amounted to a revolt of the masses. It was alleged that Chief Akintola in conjunction with the Sardauna of Sokoto, the most politically powerful individual in Nigeria at the time, had planned at a meeting with BrigadierAdemulegun and Col. Largema, Commander of the Ibadan Garrison, to use force to repress this expression of violent disapproval. It was then argued that a preemptive coup was necessary so that the politicians would not use the army to repress people protesting against the denial of their legal right to vote a government out of power. In any case, on January 15, 1966, a group of army officers carried out a coup d'etat.

## GHANA

A Ghanaian political scientist in an exploratory but profound observation of Ghanaian politics has come up with some startling notes on the Ghanaian political tradition. He suggested that the colonial as well as the post-colonial Ghanaian history is compounded by these vital elements among others: (1) "despotism; (2) excessive hero worship and sycophancy born by subservience to persons in authority; (3) corruption; (4) cynical unconcern for the public weal--particularly on the part of public-office-holders; (5) exaggerated demands for respect for age and experience; (6) vindictiveness; (7) a genius for intrigue aimed at destroying the reputation of others; (8) liberalism; and (9) an excessively cantankerous and conspiratorial oppositionism (particularly from 1954 onwards, pre- and post-independence periods)."[20] He sees the Ghanaian political tradition as a product of a "parallelogram of certain potent forces, namely, the indigenous political and social heritage, colonial rule, the 'old' and 'new' nationalism of the period between the two world wars . . . , and the politics of industrialization of the "gap."[21]

Let me take the issue of freedom through Ghanaian history. I have taken this issue because of its preeminence among the goals of Ghana's first military regime.

Using the Akans as a paradigm, Drah argued that although the traditional political system was characterized by a few democratic features of a restricted kind, democracy was not consciously articulated as a philosophy of life. There were significant constraints which prevented the system from functioning democratically.

During the colonial rule, despotism and liberalism struggled for co-existence. Given the nature of colonial regimes, however, the tilt was to the side of despotism. Furthermore, the CPP (Convention Peoples' Party) era witnessed the easy triumph of despotic over liberal elements. In Drah's opinion the forcible removal of the Convention Peoples' Party regime was not a triumph of bona fide liberalism, but the triumph of an emasculated kind.[22]

It does appear, in the main, that Mr. Drah recognized the constitutional libertarian tendency of the Ghanaian intellectual. However, he seems to be suggesting that because of the bitterness of their experience under Nkrumah, the best of them probably might become subservient to that which they seek to eliminate. In the attempt to forbid the reinstatement of a dictator which one detests, one might become oblivious to other forms of dictatorial tendencies. This may become important when we examine the reaction of the academic community to the Convention Peoples' Party (CPP), the Progressive Party (PP) government, the National Liberation Council (NLC), and the National Redemption Council (NRC).

Again looking at Akans as a paradigm, David Kimble's nomenclature of democracy seems more apt than the term democracy, because in essence, "it is the rule by popular heroes of the people." How does one draw the line between the acceptance of rule by heroes and hero worship? Although the system of political recruitment and change stipulates that popular heroes who have lost their popularity must be divested of their office, there are important constraints on the ability of commoners to act against unpopular chiefs. For example, failure to substantiate allegations may lead to death.[23] Is this not manifested in the overall continuing reluctance to speak out against the government of the day?

Despite the claim of traditional emphasis on conciliation, consultation and compromise, the game of political leadership was a mutually exclusive one. Therefore, when a chief is destooled, the entire lineage goes down with him. This attitude, Drah contends, operated in traditional Ghana as well as in the Ghana of the CPP. We also wonder if by necessity, it did not operate under the NLC. But can a nation in dire need of maximum cooperation to raise itself out of the economic doldrums afford this zero sum game?

If Mr. Drah is correct, part of Ghana's difficult rests in its political tradition. To say this is not to argue that it cannot be modified or changed. Rather, it is to say that the political leadership whether it is by military, civilians, or intellectuals, must take infinite and calculated cognisance of this fact.

Now let me turn to Ghana's political history. The goal is not a detailed chronology of events because there are quite a number of excellent books on Ghana's political history. Rather, I would like to highlight some important points in the country's political evolution because I consider them relevant. First is the fact that the imposition of British rule over Ghana generated antagonism initially between the British and traditional rulers and later between the traditional rulers and their subjects. Second, the introduction of education and cash crops gave rise to a new class of people which demanded a role, indeed leadership, in the political frame of things. Third, World War II was an important catalyst.

> An anticolonial nationalism erupted at the end of World War II.
> Prior to then a small, bourgeois, merchant-professional class
> with aristocratic proclivities (partly comprising old coastal
> trading families) had emerged and promoted African advancement
> by constitutional reform in political competition with the
> chiefs. The post-World War II nationalism was precipitated
> by imminent expectations of change and the felt grievance of
> many groups: the merchant-professional class, denied commercial opportunity, social status, and political power (by
> the chiefs); the anguished cocoa farmers, whose trees,
> stricken by a contagious disease, were being cut, rural youth

> (commoner) associations, constrained by colonially supported
> traditional power; ex-servicemen, petty traders, and frustrated,
> alienated primary- and middle-school leavers (both graduates
> and drop-outs), educated to the opportunity but bereft of the
> possibility of social mobility and modern status within the
> confines of a colonially and traditionally structured society.
> The diffuse grievances of many groups were aggregated in the
> sentiment that things could only be put right under African
> rule. Throughout much of the colony and Ashanti, the legiti-
> macy of colonial authority and its agents--the chiefs--was
> discredited and spurned, and legitimacy passed to those who
> recognized, demanded, and incarnated the right of African
> rule.[24]

Fourth, the constitutional liberalists of the Danquah-Akufo-Addo-Busia school began not only to challenge the national right of chiefs to rule but also the very basis of colonial rule. Soon the cry would be against indirect rule in favor of self rule. It is under these circumstances that Kwame Nkrumah returned home in 1947 after ten years of absence, at the request of the United Gold Coast Convention which offered him the post of secretary.

Nkrumah seemed more perceptive than these constitutional liberalists in that he forsaw difficulty in their relationship. His immediate reaction on receiving the letter of invitation from the United Gold Coast Convention (UGCC) was that it would be

> ". . . quite useless to associate myself with a movement backed
> almost entirely by reactionaries middle class lawyers and merchants,
> for my revolutionary background and ideas would make it impossible
> for me to work with them."[25]

As a matter of strategy, he thought he would accept the invitation "fully prepared to come to loggerheads with the Executive of the UGCC if I found that they were following a reactionary course."[26]

From the beginning, therefore, the ideological orientations of the UGCC and Nkrumah seems to be at poles. When Nkrumah started to use certain ideological terms such as 'comrade', certain members of the executive of the UGCC were uneasy. However, this did not lead the UGCC to a serious disengagement from Nkrumah.[27] Nkrumah seemed to be bent on divesting the UGCC from the course of its leadership. He used his popularity with youth societies to pressure the UGCC to the left. The demands of the youth societies became burdensome on the UGCC and the leadership felt that Nkrumah was responsible for engineering a good deal of this pressure. Because of Nkrumah's popularity, it was difficult for the leadership to effectively deal with him. Eventually, the leadership felt it had no option but to suggest his removal from his post. Nkrumah became a martyr and the Committee on Youth Organization, which was a large section of the UGCC, insisted on his reinstatement. Finally, on June 12, 1949, Nkrumah announced the formation of the C.P.P.[28] versus UGCC, or "positive activism" versus "constitutional liberalism."

The profile of the UGCC was that of a political organization led by a small, merchant-professional class. It began as a proto-party to aggregate both its class grievances against chiefs and colonial structure, and nationalist sentiment, and it was led almost entirely by lawyers. Moreover, it was elitist and reformist in orientation. The inclusion of Nkrumah in its leadership cadre and the existence of certain economic discontent during the colonial period forced the UGCC to broaden its membership to include smaller associational groupings.[29] Unfortunately, its leadership allowed itself to be pictured as anti-democratic because of its failure to subject itself to open democratic election by the entire membership.

The 1948 strikes pressured the British government to relinquish part of its control of the Gold Coast. This put the UGCC in a uniquely advantageous position as the only political party. In effect it tantamounts to yielding the relinquished power to the UGCC. Unfortunately, the party was not as generous as the British in dealing with their own rank and file. They refused to allow the uneducated man to participate in elections of party officers. This was promptly interpreted as an attempt of UGCC leadership to retain power on behalf of and use for the benefit of their social class to the detriment of the common man and workers who had been the effective tools of the reluctant British concession. Nkrumah, by supporting the demand of these "common men" against the UGCC leadership projected himself as the man of the people.[30]

On the other hand, the CPP at least in the beginning, was populist, anti-traditional authority, anti-colonial, anti-professional. It was "extraparliamentary in inception and spirit, populist in ideology, and chiliastic in vocabulary." Its record of militant nationalism later became a legitimization instrument. After all, it was "the party of the commoners in whose behalf it facilitated and legitimated a social and political revolution which was already occurring at grass roots."[31] It sought the coalition of the urban and the rural. The party was later maintained by Nkrumah's charisma which became less functional and efficacious as economic hardship starkly eroded it. The reduction in governmental economic delivery and redistributive function led to a decline in charisma. This ultimately meant that increasingly coercion was necessary as a basis of legitimacy.

The dependence on coercion for legitimacy reduced to a minimum the chances of an accurate feedback to decision makers. Increasingly, the leader seemed further alienated from reality and his corrective measures were bound to be unrealistic. It became extremely dangerous to volunteer adverse, but honest, reactions to governmental programs--partly because truth tended to be heretical in the circumstances and also partly because of considerable unpredictability of the leadership reaction. In any case, the CPP regime found itself in a situation in which conspirational oppositionism seemed to many to be the only alternative despite the escalation of risk to the opposition. Thus, Busia and his exiled colleagues, some members of the traditional elite, some members of the minority tribes, the police, and finally the military, escalated their "clandestine" negative reaction. While, by and large, the academicians held Nkrumah in disdain, they did not demonstrate their dislike in ways that Nkrumah objected to very seriously. (There was no *Legon Observer*) In any case, Nkrumah's plan was to destroy the elitist orientation of the university and to inject into the new recruits considerable ideological commitment. Ironically, this appears to be the thrust of the National Redemption Council's strategy. This then is the stage and context of the coup of February 24th, 1966.

Between February 24, 1966, and September, 1969, Ghana was ruled under the military council of eight men (four police and four army) which called itself the NLC. Later in this book, I will examine the nature and performance of this regime in detail. For the moment, however, suffice it to say that it eschewed radicalism and the mobilization approach to development. It depended largely on the anti-CPP forces for advice. In short, it looked for anti-CPP credentials.[32]

The NLC handed over power to the Progress Party led by Dr. Kofi A. Busia. The nature and performance of this civilian regime as well as that of the NRC which overthrew it on January 13, 1972 is a matter of central concern to my endeavor. In some respects, the orientation of the Busia regime is as different from that of theKnrumah regime as that of the NLC from the NRC.

## CIVIL-MILITARY RELATIONS

The Gold Coast Regiment was developed during the period of British pacification. It relied on Fantis for its troop supply from 1807-1873. After this time, it recruited from Nigeria. In response to Ashanti belligerence and the French threat, the British established the West African Frontier Force (WAFF) which recruited 2,000 African soldiers commanded by 100 British officers and noncommissioned officers. The units established in Sierra Leone, Gambia, Nigeria, and the Gold Coast Regiment were incorporated as part of the W.A.F.F.

Although during World War I recruitment was intensified and many African soldiers saw action, there was no African military officer until World War II. By this time, the W.A.F.F. had grown from a force of 6,500 to that of 176,000 men.[33]

The advancement of some Africans to officer class improved the general morale and performance of African soldiers. The opportunity to travel to other lands and have exchange of ideas with different people must have broadened the outlook of the African soldier. The British recruitment policies encouraged consciously more seemingly warlike tribes, illiterates, and people from the hinterland. People with requisite tools for performance in civilian institutions did not initially find the military institution attractive. In the case of the Gold Coast, the Ashantis were discouraged by the British because of the lack of trust of the colonial authority, but the northern tribes were attracted because the military offered them the brightest prospects. The coastal peoples were usually reluctant to join because they had other avenues for economic and social advancement. The Ghana Navy and Air Force which were established in 1959 as support services were popular with the southerners, however. As a whole, the Volta Region is the region with the heaviest representation in the officer class of the Ghana Armed Forces.

Africanization proceeded at fast pace in the Ghana Armed Forces. For example, when the Gold Coast Regiment was changed to the Ghana Army in 1957, it had only twenty-five Ghanaian officers as opposed to 220 British officers. By 1961, however, this number had grown to 160. Although the Ghana Military Academy was established at Teshie in 1960, it did not reduce overall overseas military training for the Ghana armed forces because advance military training abroad continued.

The first direct indication of military involvement in politics occurred in December, 1958, when Major Benjamin Awhaitey, the Ghanaian commander of Giffard Camp, was found guilty of failure "to report 'conspiratorial conversation'" which members of the United Party led by R. R. Amponsah had with him.[34] This incident demonstrated the vigilance of Nkrumah and his suspicion of the army. By the way, the prosecution witness was a man who later became the Chief of Defense Staff,

Major General Nathan Aferi, in succession to Major General Otu who together with Major General Ankrah were forced to retire.

Major General A.G.V. Paley, who had been Ghana's Chief of Defense Staff since 1958, was replaced by another British officer, Major General H. T. Alexander. Both of these officers had attempted to keep the military and the political institution separate and autonomous, each operating within its constitutional bounds. In the end, the replacement of General Alexander and of the two successive Chiefs of Defense Staff was interpreted by many as a frantic search by Nkrumah to have a Chief of Defense Staff pliable to the wishes of the President. The dismissal was seen by many as civilian interference in military affairs.

It must be added, parenthetically, that Nkrumah coupled the replacement of General Alexander with the replacement of eighty British officers who were in the Ghana army. Thus, it was not clear to some officers, at that point, whether the step was not motivated by military nationalism rather than by interventionist predisposition per se. One must seriously entertain this thought particularly since Nkrumah replaced Alexander with Brigadier Otu.

In any case, under Major Generals Paley and Alexander the Ghanaian military operated a British model which separates the political from the military role. Major General Paley outlined this code of conduct thus:

> After 1st July, 1956, when Ghana, though not yet independent, was paying for the whole cost of her army and was gradually being led to assume complete control, there were suggestions in certain irresponsible quarters that the army could be a useful means of crushing political opposition. It was my duty on this occasion to explain that in a democracy an army was not a political weapon and could only be used in accordance with the law and not in accordance with political desires. This was not fully understood by all responsible politicians whatever their party.
>
> At the same time, and more so as internal security was the primary role of the army, the officers of the army had to be educated on the correct use of the army for internal security and on the extreme undesirability of being mixed in politics. The first of this task is part of the normal military training of officers anywhere, though it was of particular importance in Ghana at that period both on account of local conditions and

because the inflow of Ghanaian officers was becoming appreciable . . . .

The only other persons in the political sphere (besides friends) with whom officers and soldiers should discuss military matters, except in the most general terms, are the Minister responsible for Defense, the Minister of State concerned and the Parliamentary Secretary, and their conversations would normally be in the presence of their Commanding Officer or at once reported to him.

Although . . . by all means be friendly with individual politicians . . . use your common sense; keep off military or political matters and do not be so friendly with any individual politician to such an extent as to cause suspicions of your brother officers or of other politicians. Politics amongst the military will wreck the army; the army in politics will wreck the state.[35]

Under the pretext of presenting a code to prevent military intervention in politics, Major General Alexander, Major General Paley's successor, was probably warning the politicians about the danger of politicizing the military. He warned that there are three reasons which provoke military interventions: (1) the Head of State interfering in the appointments or promotion of nepotism, or any other means of favoritism, (2) the swindling of the military over supplies or military barracks, and (3) a corrupt and inefficient administration in either the military or civilian sphere.[36]

In pursuance of his exposition of a code for the separation of the political and military order, Major General Alexander argued that it was the duty of every soldier of Ghana to remain loyal to the state. He reminded officers that while they may be well qualified to hold the position of leadership in the armed forces, the political realm represents a completely different order within which the officers were not trained to operate. Thus, it was assumed that it would be preferable for a corrupt civilian official to remain in a capacity where he had at least some competence than to replace him with a competent military officer-- even if the military officer was trying to save the nation. He simply just did not know how to go about the task of establishing an effective civilian government.[37]

Between 1959-1960 Nkrumah sent the Ghana Army into the Congo. As events later proved, this was a costly error for Nkrumah because it increased the army's confidence in itself and its role. At the same time, their bitter experience seemed to have alienated the military from Nkrumah. This alienation is well documented in General Afrifa's book.

As the assassination attempts increased, Nkrumah withdrew more and more and relied increasingly on repressive methods and institutions. However, when a warrant officer became implicated in an assassination attempt, Nkrumah distrusted the bona fide armed forces institutions and created his special guard. This special guard was called the President's Own Guard Regiment. Thus, an essentially ceremonial unit created as part of the regular army, on October, 1960,[38] was detached from the regular army in 1965 after the January, 1964, assassination attempt and was given its own name.[39] This was an attempt to create a counterpoise to the regular military and police units whom he felt he could no longer trust. The new Nkrumah plan called for two regiments to be detached from the regular army and given special training and privileged status, pay, and better equipment. Each regiment was to have 1,142 men and fifty officers. By 1966 however, only one of these regiments had been formed and the other was still in training.

This decision was quite unpopular with the top brass of the Ghana armed forces. The Chief of Defense Staff, S. J. A. Otu, and the Army Chief, J. A. Ankrah, protested to the President who promptly relieved them of their posts. The dismissal of these men was very unpopular with the army because these men were Ghanaian officers held in very high esteem by the Ghanaian soldiers. This was clearly seen as an intrusion into army affairs. It was one thing to dismiss Alexander under the pretext of indigenization, but it was quite another thing to dismiss the highest ranking and respected Ghanaian officers.

The general state of the economy was fast deteriorating, and the economic depression which afflicted most Ghanaians soon reflected itself in the regular armed forces with stark reality. Thus Major General Ocran revealed *ex post facto* the thinking of the Ghanaian military when he wrote: "Nkrumah, in his desire to find money for his own pocket, his grandiose schemes, and his many ever-demanding girl friends, and his hangers-on, ordered the immediate withdrawal or curtailment of the small amenities and benefits enjoyed by civil and public servants including members of the Forces."[40] "One day they were to pay for their electricity; the next day they were to lose their training allowances; the following day they were to lose their traveling facilities. We all wondered what was happening to us."[41] "By late 1965 the going was getting tough for most senior officers. The salaries introduced in 1957 meant little in 1965. They were worth only a third of their value.[42] If almost every officer was in the 'red', the plight of the rank and file could well be imagined."[43]

The poor economic conditions reflected themselves not only in the standard of living of the army, but also in the military norms of the army. What is the commander to do with "the soldier who turned out for parade in torn uniforms, with underwear showing underneath their shorts or trousers?" Apparently, some soldiers came to parades either without polishing their boots or with holes in their shoes. These violated the army dress code.[44]

What seemed to bother some officers more than the hardships is that the cancellation of these amenities was made unilaterally by circulars without consultation with the National Defence Council (NDC) who alone had the authority to amend these conditions.[45] Again, as the officers saw it, the autonomy of the armed forces had been trampled upon by the politicians. The NDC had become a moving sepulchre. It met only once between 1961-66.[46]

The soldiers lamented the loss of their own hospital to the politicians. Thus, concluding the list of military grievances against Nkrumah's political regime, Ocran wrote:

> In accordance with military practice, and for operational reasons, the military have their own hospitals designed for the requirement

> of war . . . Nkrumah grabbed the hospital too, where he sent his close and distant relations, friends, and Ministers, party boys and servants and his security officers. Invariably, these patients so extended the net that in course of time and, more precisely by 1964-65, the hospital had become a civilian hospital, the military personnel having been relegated to second, sometimes, third, priority.[47]

Even if we make allowance for some partisanship in General Ocran's account, the overall picture suggests that Nkrumah and his political associates were bent on a gradual neutralization of the regular military and its replacement with another military more responsive to the political machinations of the party. The military seemed demoralized and alienated from the party and its leadership.

FOOTNOTES

1. What is political tradition? In the Hegelian conception, it is a concrete universal: "a concrete entity which, like the historical individual, continues in some sense the same through all the changes it undergoes, as the acorn becomes the tree, as the child becomes the man; each is different in its various phases and yet identical."

As Michael Oakeshaft sees it, it is "the diffusion of authority between past, present and future; between the old, the new and what is to come. It is steady because though it moves, it is never wholly in motion; and though it is tranquil it is never wholly at rest."

2. V. A. Olorunsola, Politics of Cultural Subnationalism (New York: Doubleday, Inc., 1972).

3. M. G. Smith, Government in Zazzau 1800-1950 (London: Oxford University Press, 1960).

4. Richard L. Sklar, Nigerian Political Parties: Power in an Emergent African Nation (Princeton: Princeton University Press, 1963).

5. Commissions Tribunal into the Lagos Executive Development Board Proceedings, Lagos, 1967, 90 volumes; Report of the Tribunal of Inquiry into the Affairs of the Nigerian Port Authority, Lagos, 1967; Tribunal of Inquiry into the Affairs of the Nigerian Railway Corporation Proceedings, Lagos, 1967, 6 volumes; Report of the Electricity Corporation of Nigeria Tribunal of Inquiry, Lagos, 1967; Committee of Enquiry into the Affairs of the Northern Nigeria Housing Corporation: Government White Paper on the Report of the Committee, Kaduna, 1966.

6. Olorunsola, op. cit.

7. N. J. Miners, The Nigerian Army 1956-1966 (London: Methuen & Co. Ltd., 1971), p. 14.

8. Miners, Ibid., p. 25.

9. The Observer, October 23, 1966.

10. Miners, op. cit., p. 118.

11. Miners, op. cit., p. 119.

12. See House of Representatives Debates, 18 April 1967. Quoted from Miners, op.cit., p. 116.

13. In 1960 only six out of sixteen graduates of the Nigerian Military Training College were from the North. In March, 1961, only five out of seventeen came from the North while nine of the graduates were Ibos. Consequently, a sterner intruction of rigid quota was given--"In future fifty percent of all cadres must be from the North, and this is to apply both to the initial selection board and the final pass list whatever the order of merit." Miners, op. cit., p. 116.

14. Miners, p. 124.

15. See Miners op cit. and Robin Luckham (London: Cambridge University Press, 1971). Lt. Col. Imo was court martialled for corruption. Lt. Okafor stole ₤2,500 from the army. Three British officers were court martialled for embezzling ten percent of the naval estimate.

16. Richard Sklar, "Nigerian Politics: The Ordeal of Chief Awolowo, 1960-65," in Politics in Africa, Gwendolen Carter, ed. (New York: Harcourt, Brace & World, Inc., 1966).

17. Nigerian Citizen. 3 March 1965.

18. West Africa. 13 January 1968.

19. Miners, p. 146.

20. Yaw Drah, Ghana Journal of Sociology, Vol. 6, No. 1, Feb., 1970, p. 4.

21. Yaw Drah, Ibid.

22. Yaw Drah, Ibid., pp. 4-5.

23. Yaw Drah, Ibid., p. 18.

24. Jon Krause, "Arms and Politics in Ghana," in Claude E. Welch, Soldier and State in Africa, (Evanston: Northwestern University Press, 1970), pp. 157-58.

25. Kwame Nkrumah, Autobiography of Kwame Nkrumah (Edinburgh, New York: Thomas Nelson & Son, 1957), p. 62.

26. Nkrumah, Ibid.

27. Krause, op. cit., p. 160.
Also, Jon Krause, "Ghana, 1966" in The Politics of the Coup d'etat: Five Cases, (New York: Van Nostrand Reinhold Company, 1969), pp. 92-93.

28. Krause, Ibid., The Politics of Coup d'etat, pp. 93-96.

29. Krause, Ibid., Soldier and State, pp. 159-60.

30. Krause, Ibid.

31. Krause, Ibid., p. 160.

32. Erick Ayisi, Political Quarterly, Vol. 41, Oct.-Dec. 1970, p. 434.

33. F. M. Bourret, The Gold Coast (Stanford University Press, 1952), p. 151.

34. Dennis Austin, Politics in Ghana, 1946-1960 (London: Oxford University Press, 1964), pp. 380-382, and Ernest W. LeFever, Spear and Scepter: Army, Police and Politics in Tropical Africa (Washington: The Brookings Institution, 1970), pp. 42-43.

35. A. K. Ocran, A Myth is Broken (London: Longmans, Green & Co., Ltd.), pp. 1-2.

36. Ocran, Ibid., p. 3.

37. Ocran, Ibid., pp. 3-4.

38. General Ocran reported that it was called Guard Company. The idea of such a company came from the military itself, and it was never intended to be a separate unit from the regular army. Rather it was to serve at VIP receptions, guard air craft and state house, perform general police duties, and free infantry battalions for field training. (Ocran, p. 28)

39. Krause, in Soldier and State, pp. 184-85.

40. Ocran, Ibid., p. 42.

41. Ocran, Ibid., p. 43.

42. Ocran, Ibid.

43. Ocran, Ibid., p. 44.

44. Ocran, Ibid.

45. Ocran, Ibid., p. 42.

46. Ocran, Ibid., p. 48.

47. Ocran, Ibid.

# PART II

## THE ECONOMIC PERFORMANCE

CHAPTER III

INTRODUCTION

This chapter is concerned with the conomic performance of the Nigerial military regime. First, I will examine the regime's economic goals and the method through which the leaders expect to achieve these goals. In this examination, several questions arise: What are the economic goals? How are they to be achieved? How realistic are these goals in the face of limited resources? Are there internal contradictions in these goals? Fortunately, the <u>Nigerian Second Development Plan</u> spells out in detail the economic goals. Thus, we can deduce the economic philosophy and rationale of the military regime. Second, I will investigate the perception of the military regime regarding its own economic performance. Third, I will critically analyze the economic performance claims. How does one characterize actual economic performance within the framework of the economic performance propositions? These propositions are as follows:

    1. Military governments of an ex-colonial army would behave in non-nationalistic fashion and would often give high priority to their identification with reference groups connected to another political community. Thus, there would be an absence of economic nationalism.

    2. Military rulers will not necessarily introduce rationality and pragmatism into economic policy making. Military officers trained in the 'West' will behave in just as irrational and unpragmatic ways towards the "Eastern bloc" economic interest as many left leaning nationalistic leaders are alleged to behave towards Western economic interest.

    3. When military officers have governmental control, they will be unconcerned with the realization of economic change and reform. Moreover, where there are civilian organizations or groups pressing for such economic changes these military officers will oppose them.

The citizens' perceptions of the regime's performance is deferred for later consideration.

One of the ways to assess the potential performance of a given on-going regime is to investigate the blueprints of the regime and to determine if the goals can be achieved at all in the light of the method advocated or in the face of hidden contradictions or unresolved ambiguities. In this respect, it is fortunate to have the <u>Nigerian Development Plan 1970-74</u> which spells out the goals of the Federal Military Government for the period of the Plan.

The crucial difference between this Plan and the previous one is that it was formulated by Nigerians for Nigerians. During the war years, the legitimacy of the Federal Military Government (FMG) was predicated essentially upon winning the civil war. Therefore, for over three years (1967-70), all resources were concentrated on the civil war. It may well be that this fact made the Federal Military Government desperately aware of the hiatus in economic planning.[1] At any rate, it became apparent once the military leadership informally decided not to go back to the barracks immediately after the end of the civil war that new goals had to be set to prevent the erosion of the regime's legitimacy. The Economic Development Plan easily provided such a harmless instrument. This point came through clearly in General Gowon's October 1, 1970, Independence Day broadcast in which the intention of the Nigerian military to remain in power was announced.

Five principal objectives which the FMG hoped to accomplish through this Plan were outlined:

1) a united, strong, and self reliant nation;

2) a great and dynamic economy;

3) a just and equalitarian society;

4) a land of full and equal opportunities for all its citizens;

5) a free and democratic society.[2]

The FMG proclaimed the establishment of a hierarchy of priorities. The highest order of priority was given to agriculture, industry, transportation and manpower development. Second in the order of priority were social services and utilities

such as electricity, communication and water supplies. The third order of
priority consisted of "other services." Significantly, defense and security were
placed in a class by themselves. Hence, by refraining from ranking defense and
security, deliberate ambiguity was written into the Plan.

The refusal to rank these two items is very problematic because it makes it
difficult for one to examine, objectively, the overall performance of the FMG.
For example, one cannot specify or anticipate the full amount or degree of direct
economic and political input of the Nigerian Armed Forces into the system during
the Plan period. It is also difficult to assess, with complete accuracy, the
degree of realism which the Plan contains.

Let me examine two of the five principal objectives of the FMG. These are
to establish Nigeria as a just and equalitarian society and as a land of full and
equal opportunities for all its citizens. By the government's own declaration,
these would necessitate the reduction of glaring differences in interpersonal
incomes and the promotion of balanced development among the various communities
in the Federation to ensure "that there is no oppression based on class, social
status, ethnic group or state."[3] What evidence do we have of the FMG's serious
intent to achieve these goals?

If one objectively compares the total effort envisaged in the 1970-74 Plan
with that of 1962-68 one will find the following:

1) that the total social-economic budget showed an increase of 3.5 percent;

2) that the education budget was increased by 3.2 percent;

3) that the health budget grew by 2.7 percent;

4) that the information budget was raised by 9.6 percent;

5) that water and sewerage was increased by 1.4 percent.

However, one should note that labor and social welfare suffered a decrease of .1 percent
while town and country planning was reduced by 4.3 percent.

TABLE 1[4]

|  | 1970-74 Plan |  | 1962-68 Plan |  |
| --- | --- | --- | --- | --- |
|  | N/Million | As % of Total | N/Million | As % of total |
| Social-Economic | 286,380 | 27.9 | 165,167 | 24.4 |
| Education | 138,893 | 13.5 | 69,763 | 10.3 |
| Health | 53,811 | 5.2 | 17,076 | 2.5 |
| Information | 10,931 | 1.1 | 3,662 | 0.5 |
| Labour and Social Welfare | 11,973 | 1.2 | 8,662 | 1.3 |
| Town and Country Planning | 19,075 | 1.9 | 41,746 | 6.2 |
| Water and Sewerage | 51,696 | 5.0 | 24,258 | 3.6 |
| Total (Public Sector) | 1,025,369 | 100.0 | 676,800 | 100.0 |

This is a mixed 'projected performance' profile. Labor, social welfare, town and country planning showed decreases. If one takes inflationary factors into account, however, anticipated increases in an absolute weighted sense are far from being outstanding. In fact, in the opinion of some scholars, "the provision of social services has been accorded a low priority in the plan."[5] To evaluate the FMG's efforts in bringing about a basic change in Nigerian society, an understanding of the existing class structure may be useful.

A Nigerian sociologist in an impressionistic analysis of contemporary Nigerian society argued that the present distribution of privileges takes a pyramidal form. A small high-privileged group consists of prosperous merchants, transporters, property developers, academicians, higher civil servants, company managers, army officers and graduate teachers. He contended further that the status of these men is a derivative of their superior educational opportunity, good employment, and business connections with expatriate companies. Many of the elite live in high quality residential areas at subsidized rents and have access to medical facilities and other amenities. Below this group is a large percentage of clerks, artisans, craftsmen and peasants who live in overcrowded urban areas and have little access to the opportunity structure in Nigeria. Finally, there are those who live in rural areas in abject poverty.[6]

This is an irrefutable observation of the opportunity structure in Nigeria. Therefore, if the FMG is very serious about reducing the irregularities in interpersonal incomes and in establishing social justice, one would expect considerable changes in the opportunity structure and an emphasis on income redistribution.

One of the indicators which dampens one's optimism in this regard is the minimum resource allocation given to the "gigantic" problem of housing. The Plan eloquently demonstrates the need for housing.

> One of the factors that gives rise to workers' agitation for wage increases is the rising cost of accommodation, that is to say, rent. This phenomenon is due at least in part to the rising cost of dwelling construction. As a means both of assisting the households in their building activities, as well as exerting a downward pressure on the general cost of living, it is an objective of public policy to break existing and new bottlenecks in the production of vital building materials like cement and iron rods. . . . Meanwhile, government will also arrange to bridge the gaps between domestic production and domestic demand through easier importation facilities for essential building materials. During the plan period, substantial expansion in investment in the building industry is expected to be carried out by both public authorities and private sectors.[7]

Despite this eloquence, the Plan only established a capital expenditure of N₤1.317 million on housing. The state of Lagos which is hardest hit by this problem, was allocated only N₤.5 million in the estimates. The total expenditure on housing for the Plan period is N₤45 million.

However, it would seem unfair to argue that the FMG Plan puts emphasis on the Nigerian economy achieving a high rate of growth without any concern for some income redistribution.

Performance Projected Growth

|  | 1970-71 | Per Capital Gross National Product 1971-72 | 1972-73 | 1973-74 |
|---|---|---|---|---|
| Population (million | 66.4 | 68.4 | 70.3 | 72.4 |
| GNP ( £ million) | 1781.8 | 1936.2 | 2092.1 | 2299.6 |
| Per Capital GNP (£) | 26.3 | 28.3 | 29.8 | 31.8 |

As the projected per capital gross national product shows, there will be an increase. The real question is who will be the beneficiaries of this projected growth.

Social justice as defined by the FMG in the Plan demands that those on the lower steps of the ladder should be the beneficiaries. In the area of housing, the workers and low income urban dwellers are bound to be disappointed. Furthermore the government's general attitude toward labor as betrayed in the Plan is not encouraging.

> Even the poorest-paid industrial worker is far better off than the average peasant farmer and infinitely better than the urban unemployed. This is not often appreciated by the self-seeking trade unionist. What is, however, important in the development context of post-war Nigeria is how to formulate labour and social welfare policies consistent with the overall national objectives and priorities, as well as the wise husbandry of the limited resources at the disposal of the community.[10]

O'Connell captures this attitude when he wrote: "Military rulers (including the bureaucrats who actually control government operations) tend to assume that labour trouble is illegitimate and sometimes hasten to ban such trouble and to remove those who forment it." After noting that there is no tidy way for all to share in the Nigerian annual economic growth of about six percent. He concludes; "Hence, it makes sense within the limits of public order to let the normal strategy of labour bargaining be followed. The alternative is to politicize pay claims excessively, turn every strike into a revolt, and polarize wage-earners against the regime."[11] Later on in this book I will return to the relationship between labor and the government. (See Chapter X)

I seriously doubt that the preceding government statement was intended as a slap in the face of Nigerian labor. Quite probably, it was meant to indicate the government's sharp awareness of the plight of the farmers, the primacy of the agricultural sector as well as the dire needs of the rural areas. Nevertheless the fact still remains that a study of urban versus rural investment of the Nigerian government in the 1970-74 Plan still shows a very considerable lag.

TABLE 3[12]

|  | Total Planned Investment £ million | Urban Investment £ million | % | Rural Investment £ million | % |
|---|---|---|---|---|---|
| Industry | 86.1 | 77.7 | 91.2 | 8.4 | 9.8 |
| Electricity | 45.3 | 40.3 | 89.0 | 5.0 | 11.0 |
| Water & Sewerage | 51.7 | 42.2 | 71.6 | 9.5 | 18.4 |
| Town & Country Planning | 19.1 | 18.0 | 94.3 | 1.1 | 5.7 |
| Education | 138.9 | 98.4 | 70.9 | 40.5 | 29.1 |
| Health | 53.8 | 45.2 | 84.0 | 8.6 | 16.0 |
| Social Welfare | 12.0 | 11.0 | 91.7 | 1.0 | 8.3 |
| TOTAL | 406.9 | 322.8 | 81.8 | 74.1 | 18.2 |

This table does not seem to represent social justice for the people who live in rural areas. Neither does it offer very bright opportunities for the rural dwellers.

The FMG declared agriculture and industry as highest priority areas. Yet, estimated governmental inputs do not seem to be consonant with this high priority. Although the agricultural sector is expected to show an eleven percent growth during 1970-74, in the real sense what is probable is a widening not a narrowing of the gap between rural and urban areas. Indeed, if we allow for population growth of 2.8% per annum during the Plan period, the actual agricultural growth is minimal. O'Connell correctly observed that, in comparative terms, the farmer will benefit less than the industrial worker. The Adebo interim award of December 1970, has already made the narrowing of the gap impossible.

Moreover, as the table above indicates, only eleven percent of the total government electrification and sixteen percent of the total governmental health investment are to be spent in the rural areas. Similarly, water supply is given low priority. Therefore, it appears that the improvement in the lot of rural dwellers can only come if there is a rise in domestic producer prices coupled with high cash crop export prices. (The latter is erratic and therefore not dependable.) Although farmers may find this consoling, it is not good news for the entire political system. But even then, farmers must realize that increases in their financial resources are neutralized by overall inflationary pressures. In addition, one cannot really ignore the poor financial posture of state governments and their understandable reluctance to forego the revenue from marketing boards, a substantial income source for state government, without Federal Government subvention.[13]

A Nigerian agricultural economist has charged that the agricultural program envisaged in this Plan represents, in essence, extension of the old colonial policy of an agricultural sector primarily geared toward the production of raw materials for overseas markets. He suggested that cocoa, palm oil, ground-nut production, should have been increased to promote the domestic processing of larger quantities of these commodities for overseas and local markets. This would have contributed more to the goal of self-reliance.[14]

The following table is revealing.

TABLE 4[15]

Proposed Expenditure on Some Important Agricultural Projects (£M)

| State | Food Crops | Export Crops | Research | Extension Services | Farm Mechanization |
|---|---|---|---|---|---|
| Federal | - | - | 4.362 | 17.000 | - |
| Benue Plateau | 0.442 | 0.100 | - | 2.026 | 0.071 |
| East Central | 2.299 | 5.480 | 1.160 | 0.550 | 0.100 |
| Kano | 0.709 | - | - | 6.927 | 0.742 |
| Kwara | 0.359 | 0.076 | - | 1.110 | 0.135 |
| Lagos | 1.500 | 0.245 | 0.240 | 0.315 | 0.300 |
| Mid-West | 1.673 | 1.989 | 0.172 | 0.226 | 0.040 |
| North Central | 0.266 | 0.185 | - | 1.560 | 0.232 |
| North Eastern | 0.370 | 0.093 | - | 1.373 | 0.150 |
| North Western | 0.216 | - | - | 1.301 | 0.176 |
| Rivers | 1.480 | 0.589 | 0.181 | 0.071 | 0.244 |
| South Eastern | 0.683 | 2.231 | - | 2.267 | 0.974 |
| Western | 2.992 | 3.735 | - | 1.165 | 1.606 |
| TOTALS | 12.989 | 14.723 | 6.115 | 32.881 | 4.770 |
| % of total investment on Agriculture, Fisheries & Forestry | 9.79 | 11.10 | 4.61 | 24.78 | 3.60 |

Admittedly, the government recognized the need to increase food production and protein and caloric intake. Nevertheless only 9.79% of the budget was devoted to this. In theory, the government was committed to increased productivity of the farmer through the use of cheap, simple hand operated, small motor powered, and animal drawn implements. Yet, ironically no budget allocation was made for the designing and testing of this equipment for use on Nigerian terrain. The whole area of "research" was inadequately funded. Indeed, as the chart above indicates, there are many states where no provision is made for this crucial item.

Within the agricultural sector itself, there are discrepancies between the apparent priority which government words give to some items and the actual allocations. For example, despite the declaration of high priority given to increasing the animal protein in the Nigerian diet, only 9.23% of the proposed expenditure is given to livestock development.

Another principal objective of the Development Plan is the creation of a united Nigeria. In the past, this problem has revolved around the determination of an acceptable principle of equity in the distribution of scarce resources and opportunity structures among the various peoples and sections of the country. If we take the area of education, the FMG Plan calls for the reduction of the gap between the states by giving highest financial assistance to states with low educational enrollment ratio. However, we find that the West which already is head and shoulders above the rest of the country was allocated £24.5 million for education while Kano and North East states were budgeted for £8.1 and £4.4 million respectively. At best, the Federal government can only make a beginning in its goal to narrow the gap.[16] In any case, it is difficult for a balance to be maintained in this arena. The FMG has now assumed full responsibility for the universities. The possible implication of this is yet unknown.

The basis of revenue allocation among the states remains essentially unchanged. The status quo is followed, and the Dina Report which recommended certain changes which would have been more in keeping with national unity, equity, and even development predispositions is shelved. Thus we have a situation in which estimated revenues show the Rivers state with £67 million; North West with £47.7 million; Midwest with £104.4 million; North East with £59.2 million; Benue Plateau with £63.3 million; and East Central state with £147.4 million. When these figures are computed on the basis of per capita revenue estimate, we find that the Midwest's allocation is three times greater than the West's and four times greater than the North West's; the Rivers state allocation is four times greater than East Central's and five times greater than the North East's.[17]

The new industrial policy of the FMG calls for the promotion of even development and fair distribution of industries in all parts of the country. Yet the Plan clearly stipulates that the correction of regional disparities will be reduced not at "the cost of stagnation in areas which are presumed to be relatively more developed. To do so would be to slow down the rate of development for the national economy as a whole."[18] Furthermore, the FMG states that it wants the "promotion of balanced development between one part of the country and another."[19] Elsewhere, it states that "industries sponsored by the Federal and State Governments will . . . be sited purely on economic consideration."[20] There is some contradiction in these two statements because private industrial developments tend to concentrate in areas of minimal cost. Urban sectors are more favored than rural sectors when it comes to the possession of infra-structures which are sine qua non for the location of industries. Consequently, more urban states and Lagos will remain privileged. Unless the FMG is willing to invest in infrastructural development in the less developed areas of the country, even development and fair distribution of industries will remain an unobtainable goal.

Now let me turn to the general characterization of the economy envisaged by the FMG. The question is whether it is pro-West, pro-East, or nationalistic. The FMG declared that "as a matter of general policy, the Government will encourage nationwide equity participation in all manufacturing industries. Shares will be allocated to the Federal Government, the state in which a particular industry is located, other states, and to Nigerian nationals willing to participate in industrial development."[21] Furthermore, it announced that the Government will hold at least 55% of the shares in iron and steel bar complex, petro-chemical industries, fertilizer production, and petroleum products. The Government "wants to minimize foreign control over the commanding heights of the Nigerian economy."[22]

Finally, the Government flatly declared that the "uncompromising objective of a rising economic prosperity in Nigeria is the economic independence of the nation and the defeat of neo-colonial forces in Africa."[23]

These assertions have led somebody to observe that if one were to take seriously the intentions which the government outlined in this plan, they would involve the following processes:

1. growth of the public sector to the point where it dominates the private sector;

2. extensive participation by government in directing growth-producing projects in industry and agriculture;

3. detailed control over the decisions of the private sector;

4. extensive development of the infra-structure by government--roads and communications, education, health, etc.;

5. technical description of how objectives are to be achieved;

6. consultation on projects at the level of the smallest social units-- villages and clusters of villages.[24]

In short, on the face of it, the FMG seeks to become a mobilization system, dedicated to the achievement of economic nationalism. Given the validity of the discussion on the Nigerian political system in Chapter II, it should take herculean efforts and extraordinary success to achieve a mobilization system. The political style of the Nigerian military regime does not strongly suggest this approach. I will deal with this in another chapter. Of course, the attainment of economic nationalism is another matter. Let us take a closer look.

Unlike the 1962-68 Plan, the 1970-74 Plan projects that 57.7% will come from domestic sources such as surpluses on the recurrent account from increased revenues, increased taxes, and more efficient tax administration. No doubt this distinction between the 1962-68 Plan and the 1970-74 Plan is due to the confidence engendered by the unanticipated elasticity of the governmental extractive capability during the civil war period. In terms of ideology then, one can refer to this, at least in part, as an enunciation of a policy of economic nationalism. It may stem out of ideological conviction, or it may represent attempted reconciliation with reality--a sort of economic pragmatism. Before one can declare that the Nigerian economy and Nigerian military leaders are meaningfully dedicated to economic nationalism, one needs to look at other factors.

It is necessary to examine the degree of realism in this projection; for, it does no good if, despite its declared goal, the government has to revert to the policy of very heavy external financing as a result of grossly exaggerated and unrealizable prognostication of domestic financial capability. The table below casts a disturbing picture in this regard. This table shows the projected revenue surplus of 1970/71 along side of the estimated revenue surplus. The Plan projected a £32.7 million surplus. In actual fact, the total approved budget estimate for this period of 1970/71 showed only a £3.4 million surplus. This is only about eleven percent of the projected surplus.

TABLE 5[25]

Projected and Estimated Revenue Surplus 1970/71

£ million

| Government | Plan Projection | Approved Budget |
|---|---|---|
| Benue Plateau | + 1.8 | + 0.2 |
| East Central | -20 | -15.4 |
| Kano | + 6.6 | .048 |
| Kwara | - 0.7 | - 0.2 |
| Lagos | + 4.7 | + 0.6 |
| Midwest | + 3.5 | + 6.2 |
| North Central | + 2.2 | + 0.1 |
| North West | + 2.5 | .037 |
| Rivers | + 5.4 | - .6 |
| South East | +24 | - (c) statistically insignificant |
| West | + 6.6 | + 2.2 |
| Federal | - 2 | +10.2 |
|  | -24 |  |
|  | +32.7 | + 3.4 |

Based upon the past behavior of the economy (1960-68), there is little reason to be optimistic. The 1962-68 Plan called for a total of £263 million as opposed to £450.2 million projected under the 1970-74 Plan to come from these domestic sources. However, in the two fiscal years before the civil war, only about one-third of the expected annual revenue of £44 million per annum was realized. Consequently, Nigeria's internal public debt rose from £49.43 million to £131.57 million during the 1962-68 Plan period.[26] One is almost propelled towards a pessimistic prognosis given the present spiraling inflation (estimated at between 14-20% in the cities) and the seeming inability of the military leadership to curtail it.

There is also a pattern of diminished dependence on the private sector for revenue.

TABLE 6[27]

|  | 1962-68 | (Revenue Source) 1970-74 |
|---|---|---|
| Private | 60.1% | 47.5% |
| Public | 39.9% | 52.5% |
| TOTAL | 100.0% | 100.0% |

The private sector is expected to supply 47.5% of the revenue in the 1970-74 Plan while in the 1962-68 Plan it provided 60.1% of the revenue. Is the public sector prepared to assume this new role? There is also the question of the ability of public corporations and the marketing boards to behave in such a way as to make this 1970-74 projection a reality. About £108 million is expected from this source. The political sagacity as well as the reality of such a projection, especially if it involves direct or indirect taxation, may be questionable in view of the tax riots in Western Nigeria.

Other signs of the theoretical commitment of the FMG to economic nationalism are evident on page 318 of the Plan. Here the Plan calls for the reconstitution of the Nigerial Council for Management Education and Training which will:

1) coordinate and obtain agreement on future programs of management education and training;

2) maintain a catalogue of all available programs; and

3) provide means for the exchange of relevant ideas and information.[28]

The FMG stated this economic nationalism predisposition categorically when it wrote: "Government will restrict the entrance of non-Nigerians into private partnership of Architects, Accountants, and Auditors, etc. . . . and measures would be taken to phase out expatriate or non-Nigerian partnerships and firms in these professional and occupational groups . . . in administrative and managerial grades . . . (and in) construction industry."[29] A decree (The Nigerian Enterprises Promotion Decree of Indiginisation Decree) has been promulgated to this effect.

Of course, there is the problem of capable executants. This is what the government had to say about its public corporations.

> The difficulties and inefficiencies of many public enterprises in Nigeria are evidenced by the series of Tribunals and Commissions of Enquiries which have reported on their activities over the last decade at both Federal and State levels. Many of these were fact finding; but some of them . . . were established for specific policy reforms. It is clear that many of the public enterprises were not responsive to the changing requirements of a growing and dynamic economy. Some do not possess the tools of translating into reality the hope of successful commercial operations. The level and quality of personnel are sometimes mediocre and reflect the worst traditions and rigidities of civil service. Being mostly monopolies, the worst of all possible worlds are thus compounded since they do not seem to enjoy the competitive benefits of private enterprise operations. Many of them suffer from over-capitalization and poor managerial effectiveness. Considerations other than operational efficiency also sometimes get in the way of Government in trying to exert corrective measures on erring Boards of Directors and Management. The principle of insulation from partisan political pressure and sectionalism is more remarkable for its breach than for its observance.[30]

To the extent that the Plan mirrors the sincere desires of the FMG, one can say that in Nigeria the military regime:

1) is interested in bringing about decreasing foreign participation and control of their economy;

2) has embarked upon increased mobilization of indigenous resources both human and material;

3) is prepared to make a beginning in the direction of economic=change and reform;

4) is indisputably concerned with economic nationalism more than any Nigerian civilian regime;

5) is enlarging the public sector by promoting new public ventures and by nationalizing, not indiscriminately, certain enterprises.

On balance, one important factor must be remembered. Nigerian oil and gas outputs have been on the increase. In fact, more revenue is being collected from this source than was anticipated in the Plan.

This increase may compensate for the lag in other sectors of the Nigerian economy. Let me cite some optimistic economic indices. Nigeria's exports during the first half of 1972 rose by about six percent over the corresponding period of 1971. The rise was due to an increase in the export of crude petroleum which was twenty-six percent higher than in the corresponding period of the previous year. During the first quarter of 1972, industrial production in Nigeria rose twelve percent over the production for the same period of 1971. The Central Bank noted an improvement in the government financial posture which led to drastic reductions in government borrowing from the banking system.[31] If this continues, then it is probable that money will be available for the projects outlined in the Plan. Of course, this is just the Plan. All I have done here is to critically evaluate the possibility of the Plan being realizable in the light of probable resources, the internal logic of the Plan itself and the expressed goals of the FMG.

GOVERNMENT'S PERCEPTIONS OF SHORTCOMINGS IN ITS ECONOMIC PERFORMANCE

The government is unhappy with its own performance in the area of agricultural development. It writes: "In the area of agriculture, there was stagnation. Food prices continue to skyrocket as a result of under-production. The export agricultural output actually suffered a substantial decline."[32] Due to inadequate agricultural inputs, the agro-allied industries did not attain the anticipated level of growth.

The government's greater concern is indicated in its own progress report which states that "steady growth of the economy will, to a large extent, depend upon what is happening to the agricultural sector."[33] Therefore this is a failure of considerable importance. The First Progress Report also indicated that the needs, and continued existence of marketing boards as well as their present power and function will be reviewed. It suggested that "the indications show that the system as presently operated discourages increased efforts and production by the farmers. The stagnation in the output and export of some cash crops is attributed to the marketing board system."[34] It should be interesting to see how the FMG goes about the task of this reexamination and that of persuading the state governments to incorporate the recommendations if and when they are made.

In the meantime, it appears that the state commissioners of economic planning have started the ball rolling on this score. It has been reported that they have recommended a new marketing board system which will no longer constitute the revenue earning sources of the state governments. In addition, the produce purchase tax will be scrapped. As a correlate, they ask the Federal Government to pay subvention to the states to cover the revenue losses.[35]

There are also problems with the governmental executing agencies. The report claims that some government officials are not conversant with their responsibilities. In addition, there seems to be inadequate executive capability. The government admits this fact. It wrote:

> It has become evident that in many areas executive capacity is still a big problem. There is a shortage of technical staff to conduct initial studies and carry out the necessary preparatory work without which projects cannot be implemented whether with domestic or external finance. The real bottleneck is inability

to prepare projects. In states where finance is a problem, there
is a scheme whereby they can be given Federal loans to implement
their capital programmes, provided the stateiis following the
spirit of the plan. State Ministries of Finance are aware of
this. In the light of this, finance can no longer be regarded as
a serious cause of low performance in plan implementation."[36]

In addition, the government admits its failure in the area of unemployment. It declares, "In spite of the large number of paid jobs created during the first phase of the plan, they were sufficient to absorb only a small proportion of those seeking such employment. Thus the overall picture is one of rapid progress in job creation but continuing serious imbalances in the labour supply-demand situation, aggravated by the structural imbalances between the kinds of jobs desired by young workers and the needs of the economy."[37] The Plan envisaged about four percent unemployment, but the unemployment figure of 7.8 percent was disappointing. It is doubtful that this figure includes the 800,000-1,000,000 unemployed of the East Central State. Coupled with this overall unemployment problem is the drifting of population from the rural to the urban centers.

The failure of the government to curb inflation is admitted. Instead of the 1.5 percent rate of inflation anticipated and despite the rituals of government concern and activity, inflation was said to be six percent in 1970-71 and 6.5 percent in 1971-72. The Federal Commissioner of Economic Planning admitted this defeat in presenting the Progress Report. In the urban centers of Lagos, Kaduna, and Ibadan, inflation probably ranged from sixteen to twenty percent in 1971.

Apparently, some state governments likewise were not completely satisfied with many crucial aspects of the Federal Government performance. For example, the Governor of Kano State, a progressive, has expressed dissatisfaction with the continued lack of dialogue between the various governments during the preparation of the 1970-74 Plan. He declared: "This glaring oversight sometimes resulted in wrong decisions at the federal level because those concerned are not aware of the local situation or the circumstance of the project involved."[38] The problem of coordination is very important in the political and economic context. The military Governor pointed out also that the purpose of the Progress Report was "to see how the plan was going on and to initiate action to remove bottlenecks." He asserted that the states have discovered that "many financial and technical problems that require internal and external loans, Federal Government grants, and technical assistance have not been met by the Federal Government despite repeated requests."[39]

What Governor Bako said could be interpreted as showing either a lack of responsiveness of the Federal Government to State governments or the lack of responsiveness of the Federal bureaucracy to the State governments. Alternatively, it could be interpreted as an effort on the part of the Federal bureaucracy to sabotage the goals of the Federal Government. Finally, it may simply manifest a considerable incompetence on the part of the Federal bureaucracy. No matter how it is interpreted, it does no credit to the performance of the military regime. Governor Bako hoped that "the misguided publicity given to the so-called performance ratio (of the Development Plan implementation) will not be repeated." Apparently, he feels that this has made it difficult to derive maximum benefit from the Progress Report.[40] Since Governor Bako is a member of the Supreme Military Council of the FMG, his criticisms are of particular interest and significance.

Dr. Adedeji, the Federal Commissioner for Economic Planning, said that the Federal Government has set up two standing committees to examine the Federal Government's economic and social policies and that the Doxiadis Association International has been commissioned to study the needs of the Nigerian major urban centers.[41] This suggests that the Federal Government is determined to continue to examine its performance and modify its policies in the light of new information. If this is so, then it augers well for the country. However, if this is designed only to stem criticism and pacify vocal critics without serious commitment on the part of the Federal Government, then it will be unfortunate.

For their part, the Federal officials were unhappy with the overall performance of the states. The Report indicated that only the Midwest and the Benue Plateau State exceeded their national targets. On the other hand, the Rivers, South East, East Central, North East and Kwara states all fell below their established goals.

## GOVERNMENT'S PERCEPTION OF ITS ECONOMIC ACHIEVEMENTS

The government was elated about the fact that the private sector investment exceeded expectations. Although the Plan envisaged a £165 million investment in this area, the final figure for 1970-71 was about £250 million. It was further encouraged by the fact that the bulk of this investment was in the "incorporated enterprises." It claimed that existing firms expanded their capacities, new businesses sprang up, and the enterprises in war affected areas were rehabilitated. It was pleased that the gross domestic product for the years 1970-72 exceeded their estimates substantially.[42]

The mining and quarrying industries produced the most impressive rate of growth. Oil exports were very impressive also. Although the anticipated oil revenue was £329.5 million, the actual revenue was £580 million. Part of this increase was due not so much to increase in the volume of oil but to the increase in the price of Nigerian oil.[43]

The government seems fairly happy with its industrial performance. It claimed that:

> . . . existing industries have been expanding their productive capacities in response to the bouyant demand and a large number of new ones are being established. Industrial expansion has continued to follow mainly the traditional path of import substitution led as before by the textile industry now producing an impressive range and variety of goods. In this industry, however, some progress is being made in the development of integrated progress as envisaged by the Plan. Apart from import substituting consumer goods, industries (like textiles, drinks, cigarettes, soaps, etc.), considerable growth is also evident in a few intermediate goods' industries particularly those producing building materials like roofing sheets and paints and packaging. But

because of the large amount of building and reconstruction work being undertaken, capacity is still much below demand and this is particularly evident in the case of cement which still has to be imported in large quantities."[44]

## RESTORING THE BALANCE

To restore the balance, certain points need to be made with regard to government claims. The government methodology was to take the percentage of expenditure of funds allocated as the measure of success. Consequently, it was argued that in 1970-71, sixty-three percent of the annual Plan was accomplished and that in 1971-72, seventy-two percent of the annual Plan was completed. But this is misleading because it does not take into account the practice of some ministries to overspend their budget allocation. One suspects that this is what Governor Bako had in mind when he was talking about the "so-called performance ratio." The Ministry of Defense has formed a habit of overspending its budget since the civil war. In some cases, it had done so very blatantly and outrageously. One must also note that although the country's overall growth rate in 1971-72 was about twelve percent, almost half of this came from oil--a "wasting asset." During this same period, the overall industrial contribution to the Gross Domestic Product was only fourteen percent as opposed to twenty percent during the civil war. Moreover, if one accepts the government's "performance ratio," one is negatively impressed by the fact that only N₤5 million of the N₤18 allocated for industry was actually spent.

It is therefore fair to note that since the growth rate of agriculture fell far short of expectations (only two percent), the government agricultural performance is at best mediocre. Given the high unemployment rate and the probability that it might become worse, the government performance here does not represent a passing grade. In the industrial sector a growth rate of 1.2 percent was achieved. However, this must be put in proper relief by the fact that it contributed only fourteen percent of the GDP. What will be crucial in the year ahead is how the government can use its resources from the "wasting asset" to engender labor absorbing enterprises and to accelerate the retooling of manpower resources for maximum utility and productivity. The government is increasing its pressures to bring about economic nationalism. The Nigerian Oil Corporation's successful negotiations with SAFRAP, a French state-owned oil company, AGIP, and Phillips, and its insistence on sixty-five percent ownership of Nigeria's only refinery with a 55,000 barrels per day capacity, as well as the Nigerian indiginization decree are a few examples of government activities in this regard. It is in this sense that one is heartened by the FMG's initiative to invite an objective assessor (Doxiades Association International) to see what modifications are necessary in its urban policies.

## CONCLUSION

This chapter demonstrates beyond any reasonable doubt that although the Nigerian military government is an ex-colonial army (See Chapter II), its economic policies and declarations show marks of strong economic nationalism.

It is necessary to note that the foreign and trade policies of the civilian governments that preceded it were anglophilic. For example, there was neither diplomatic relationships nor trade agreements between the Nigerian civilian governments and the government of the Peoples Republic of China. On the other hand, the Nigerian military regime has exchanged diplomatic envoys with this country. Furthermore, it is common knowledge that there have been increased educational and cultural exchanges between the FMG and the Soviet Government. Since 1968, Nigeria and USSR have been interested in the sale and purchase of commodities, both military and non-military. United Arabic Republic, Algeria, Morrocco and Nigeria are the four African countries with which the Soviet Union conducts the largest volume of trade. As Table 7 illustrates, the volume of trade between Nigeria and the

Communist Block has skyrocketed during the military regime. Nigerian export to the Communist Block jumped from $9 million in 1966 to $21 million in 1967 and $28 million in 1968. The import from the Communist Block increased from $27 million in 1966 to $38 million in 1967.[45] Indeed in 1972 alone, the Soviet Union sponsored two trade exhibits in Nigeria. At one of these exhibits, the Nigerian Trade Commissioner expressed satisfaction with the improved trade relations between Nigeria and the Soviet Union.

TABLE 7[46]

Nigeria's Foreign Trade, 1960-1970 (in millions of U. S. dollars)

|  | 1960 | 1966 | 1967 | 1968 | 1969 | 1970 | (1st 7 mo.) |
|---|---|---|---|---|---|---|---|
| Exports to: |  |  |  |  |  |  |  |
| 1. United States | 45 | 63 | 53 | 49 | 112 | 71 |  |
| 2. United Kingdom | 226 | 295 | 199 | 174 | 246 | 211 |  |
| 3. Netherlands | 60 | 73 | 87 | 76 | 120 | 111 |  |
| 4. Germany (Fed. Rep.) | 36 | 78 | 71 | 50 | 54 | 45 |  |
| 5. Communist bloc | 2 | 9 | 21 | 28 | 29 | 25 |  |
| Imports from |  |  |  |  |  |  |  |
| 1. United States | 32 | 116 | 78 | 62 | 82 | 77 |  |
| 2. United Kingdom | 256 | 214 | 181 | 168 | 242 | 179 |  |
| 3. Japan | 78 | 41 | 53 | 20 | 26 | 33 |  |
| 4. Germany (Fed. Rep.) | 43 | 77 | 71 | 59 | 74 | 50 |  |
| 5. Communist bloc | 11 | 27 | 38 | 33 | 38 | 28 |  |
| Totals: |  |  |  |  |  |  |  |
| Exports | 475 | 793 | 587 | 905 | 1,235(est.) |  |  |
| Imports | -604 | -718 | -541 | -696 | -1,100(est.) |  |  |
| Trade balance | -129 | 75 | 46 | 209 | 135 |  |  |

TABLE 8[47]

Export of Nigerian Cocoa 1971-72

| Countries | Tons |
|---|---|
| USA | 96,081 |
| USSR | 54,750 |
| West Germany | 54,550 |
| United Kingdom | 36,805 |
| Holland | 34,705 |
| Japan | 27,325 |
| Yugoslavia | 24,185 |
| Kenya | 600 |

Table 8 also shows attempts to diversify the Nigerian export market.

Recently, the Federal Commissioner of Economic planning led a high-power delegation to Red China. This delegation concluded two agreements, one was a trade agreement and the other was a technical agreement. Commenting on the agreements, the commissioner said that it would lay a "solid foundation for cooperation" between both countries.[48] Chinese Economic Missions have also visited Nigeria. Moreover, Nigeria has attempted to increase the volume of trade between it and Japan. In fact, Japan is now the fourth largest exporter into Nigeria, and has only recently extended a $24 million dollar loan to Nigeria.[49] Finally, Japan is now involved in trade in Nigerian oil, and Nigerian demand for Japanese cars is on the increase. All of these indicate a genuine desire for and considerable success in the diversification of Nigerian trade. The net effect of this is to make sure that Nigerian economic fortune is not totally tied to the West.

It is significant that despite diplomatic initiatives on the part of the United Kingdom to encourage the Nigerian Head of State, General Gowon, to pay a visit to England, such a visit only took place in the middle of 1973, three years after the initial moves. On the other hand, the Head of State has visited most African states. A majority of these visits have been tied with attempts to foster African economic communities.

The evidences amassed in this chapter demonstrate that like economic performance proposition 1, the economic performance proposition 2 is not borne out. Although Nigerian military leaders were trained in the West, they differ from their civilian counterparts in that they have not been irrational with the Eastern bloc where Nigerian economic interests, as they perceive it, are involved. To say this is not to say that they are socialists.

Finally, the evidence in this chapter does not support the proposition that the Nigerian military leaders are unconcerned with economic change. In fact, the reverse would seem to be the case. The *New Nigeria*, a Northern Nigerian newspaper, cautioned the Nigerian military governments, "before commercial bug bites too many governments," against excessive involvement in the economic sector. A prominent Nigerian businessman expressed fears over what he regards as signs of over-enthusiastic governmental activism in the economy.[50] The contention is not that Nigeria has become a mobilization system. Rather, the contention is that the military regime has not consciously sought to sabotage civilian desire for economic reform. I suspect that many Nigerians do feel that the government is not doing enough in the area of economic redistribution. On the other hand, many Nigerians feel that too much economic change has been instituted already. The citizens' perceptions will be discussed in Chapter XI.

## FOOTNOTES

1. James O'Connell, <u>The Quarterly Journal of Administration</u>, April, 1971, p. 313.

2. <u>Second National Development Plan 1970-74</u> (Lagos: Federal Ministry of Information, Printing 1970), p. 32, and General Gowon's broadcast to the nation, October 1, 1972.

3. <u>Second National Development Plan 1970-74</u>, p. 32.

4. First and Second Development Plans (Lagos: Federal Ministry of Information, Printing), quoted in <u>The Quarterly Journal of Administration</u>, April, 1971, p. 295.

5. Dupe Olatunbosun and S. O. Olayide, <u>The Quarterly Journal of Administration</u>, April, 1971, p. 298.

6. Francis Okediji, <u>Ibid.</u>, p. 287.

7. <u>Second National Development Plan</u>, 1970-74, p. 294.

8. Okediji, Olatunbosun and Olayide are also critical of this. See <u>The Quarterly Journal of Administration</u>, April, 1971, pp. 288 and 298.

9. Source is the <u>Second National Development Plan</u>, 1970-74, p. 54.

10. <u>Ibid.</u>, p. 259.

11. <u>The Quarterly Journal of Administration</u>, Op. cit., p. 323.

12. Adapted from <u>Ibid.</u>, p. 282.

13. See the resolution passed by the Commissioners for Economic Planning at their Kaduna meeting. Reported in <u>West Africa</u>.

14. A. A. Adegbola, <u>The Quarterly Journal of Administration</u>, April, 1971, p. 359.

15. Source is <u>Ibid.</u>, p. 36.

16. See also O'Connell in <u>Ibid.</u>, pp. 315-17, for a sceptical view on this score.

17. <u>Ibid</u>.

18. <u>Second National Development Plan</u> 1970-74, p. 34.

19. <u>Ibid</u>.

20. <u>Ibid.</u>, p. 36.

21. <u>Second National Development Plan</u>, 1970-74, p. 145.

22. <u>Ibid</u>.

23. Second National Development Plan, 1970-74, pp. 32-33.

24. James O'Connell, Nigerian Journal of Economic and Social Research, Vol. 13, March, 1971, pp. 41-42.

25. Compiled by Adedeji and Teriba in The Quarterly Journal of Administration, April, 1971, p. 340.

26. Adebayo Adedeji, Nigerian Federal Finance (London: Hutchinson, 1969), p. 215.

27. Second National Development Plan, 1970-74, p. 275.

28. Ibid., p. 318.

29. Ibid., p. 318.

30. Ibid., p. 289.

31. Daily Times, October 29, 1972, p. 3.

32. West Africa, 9th June, 1972, p. 719.

33. Ibid.

34. Ibid.

35. West Africa, October 30, 1972, p. 1463.

36. West Africa, June 9, 1972, p. 719.

37. Ibid.

38. West Africa, October 30, 1972, p. 1463.

39. Ibid.

40. Ibid.

41. West Africa, October 30, 1972, p. 1462.

42. West Africa, June 9, 1972, p. 719.

43. Ibid.

44. Ibid.

45. U.S.A.I.D., Economic Data Book, Africa. Revision No. 257, April, 1971, p. 6.

46. Ibid.

47. West Africa.

48. West Africa, September 29, 1972, p. 1305.

49. Le Monde, December 2, 1970, The New York Times, April 9, 1971.

50. Chief Fajemirokun, President of the Nigerian Chamber of Commerce, West Africa, July 28, 1972, p. 986.

CHAPTER IV

INTRODUCTION

The more specific treatment in this chapter deals with Ghana. Here, the economic performance propositions suggested by the reference group theory were applied to the Ghana Military Regime of the National Redemption Council (NRC). In short, this chapter examines the economic problems facing Ghana, the economic goals and priorities of the ruling military regime and the regime's perception of its economic performance. Finally, it applies the following economic performance propositions of the reference group school to the NRC regime:

1. Military governments of an ex-colonial army would behave in non-nationalistic fashion and would often give priority to their identification with reference groups connected to another political community. Thus there would be absence of economic nationalism.

2. Military rulers will not necessarily introduce rationality and pragmatism into economic policy making; military officers trained in the "West" will behave in just as irrational and non-pragmatic ways towards the "Eastern bloc" economic interest as many left learning nationalist leaders are alleged to behave toward Western economic interest.

3. When military officers have governmental control they will be unconcerned with the realization of economic change and reform. Moreover, where there are civilian organizations or groups pressing for such economic changes these military officers will oppose them.

Let me say that my concern here is not with Nkrumah regime's economic performance although occasional references will be made to it. The reader interested in this subject should read Elliot J. Berg and R. H. Green, Ghana and the Ivory Coast (ed.) Phillip Foster and Aristide Zolberg; John D. Essek's "Political Independence and Economic Decolonization: The Case of Ghana under Nkrumah," Western Political Quarterly, XXIV (March 1971), pp. 53-64; Bob Fitch and Mary Oppenheimer, Ghana:

End of an Illusion (New York: Monthly Review Press) 1966; Jon Woronoff, West African Wager: Houphouet Boigny or Nkrumah, (New Jersey: The Scare Crow Press), 1972.

## THE WEAKNESSES OF GHANA'S ECONOMY AND THE PROGRESS PARTY STRATEGY

The Ghana Economic Review 1971/72 aptly identified three structural weaknesses of the Ghana economy. These were:

(1) the domination of production by a single agricultural crop, cocoa, which accounts for about sixty-five percent of the foreign exchange;

(2) the overwhelming burden which foreign debt has imposed on the economy following the intensive infrastructural and industrial development of the 1950's and early 1960's; and

(3) the impressive population growth rate juxtaposed with the unimpressive economic growth rate.[1]

More specifically in terms of economic indicators, the Economic Review asserted:

(1) that between 1960-69 the population growth rate was three percent but Gross Domestic Production in real terms was about 2.5 percent. This represents a decline in real income;

(2) that national savings dropped from 16.5 percent of GNP in 1960 to about eleven percent in 1970;

(3) that investment fall was more precipitous because in 1965 it was 22.3 percent of GNP but by 1970 it had fallen to fourteen percent of GNP;

(4) that export remained at the same level as 1960;

(5) that although the manufacturing industries showed some encouraging signs, the problem of very high cost of agricultural inputs plagued it;

(6) that ten percent of the labor force remained unemployed;

(7) that at the time of the writing of the review, prospect for self sufficiency in food production was bleak. The review declared: "There is no evidence now to

suggest that agricultural production is sufficient to cope with the rapidly rising demand for food. In 1970 alone, Ghana spent about $180 million on the importation of food and raw materials."[3]

On the whole, the review flatly stated "the situation now is only one of inflation, continued strain on the balance of payments, difficulties with servicing of the external debt and the further misallocation of resources."[4]

Basically, the Busia government believed that the economic plight of Ghana was a result of "the regime of controls and the extreme centralization under which the economy has been functioning for the past ten years or so."[5] Consequently, his government's solution was to liberalize the external trade sector, decentralize the economic decision making apparatus and rely on market mechanisms.

On the face of things, Dr. Busia was very concerned about the disparity in the allocation of resources in terms of the rural/urban dichotomy; the urban population which in 1970 was 28.6 percent of the total population[6] was favored disproportionately in most things. This disparity was not due to deliberate neglect of the rural area on the part of pre-Busia government. Rather, it was because ". . . the choice of development strategy so far adopted has a built-in tendency to favor the economically already developed parts of the country which has meant the urban areas."[7] Although Table 1 below notes only the discrepancies in the distribution of electricity and water, there are other areas which underscore this theme of disproportional distribution of amenities.

The Busia government set itself the task of providing balanced development in the distribution of health, water and transportation facilities. Its effort to remedy the imbalance is evidenced in its emphasis on feeder roads, rural health ervices and rural water supply.[9]

The Busia government also attempted to increase the productivity of the agricultural sector of the economy. For the 1970-71 fiscal year, the specific agricultural ɔals of the Busia government were (1) increasing domestic production of the staple

TABLE 1

| Region | Population Number | Percentage | % of population served Water | Electricity |
|---|---|---|---|---|
| Ashanti | 1,477,390 | 17.3 | 32.3 | 17.5 |
| Greater Accra | 848,825 | 9.9 | 85.9 | 43.2 |
| Brong Ahafo | 762,670 | 8.9 | 28.2 | 2.6 |
| Central | 892,590 | 10.4 | 29.2 | 9.0 |
| Eastern | 1,262,880 | 14.8 | 29.4 | 11.8 |
| Western | 768,310 | 9.0 | 40.9 | 6.8 |
| Northern | 728,570 | 8.5 | 26.2 | 5.0 |
| Volta | 947,000 | 11.1 | 30.4 | 3.0 |
| Upper | 857,295 | 10.0 | 13.4 | 1.1 |
| Total | 8,545,560 | | | |

agricultural commodities (2) increasing the production of cash crops and food items being imported and (3) the revitalization of the cocoa industry. Although no target productivity goals were set, the statistics did show some overall gains (see Tables 2 and 3). The problem is that the gains were not enough.

TABLE 2[10]

| | 1968-69 Acres (000) | Tons (000) | 1969-70 Acres (000) | Tons (000) | 1970-71 Acres (000) | Tons (000) |
|---|---|---|---|---|---|---|
| Maize | 671 | 296.3 | 680 | 299.2 | 989 | 435 |
| Cassava | 425 | 1,422.8 | 400 | 1,320 | 476 | 1,570 |
| Yam | 293 | 1,329 | 290 | 1,305 | 337 | 1,616 |
| Plantain | 326 | 754.6 | 350 | 805 | 491 | 1,129 |
| Guinea Corn | 373 | 82 | 370 | 81 | 385 | 84 |
| Millet | 346 | 71 | 432 | 86 | 458 | 91 |

TABLE 3[11]

| | 1968-69 Tons | 1969-70 Tons | 1970-71 Tons |
|---|---|---|---|
| State Fishing Corp | 3,000 | 17,000 | 27,000 |
| Other Fishing Comm | 58,000 | 63,000 | 64,830 |
| Outboard Motors and Canoes | 33,000 | 60,000 | 90,000 |
| Total | 94,000 | 140,000 | 181,830 |

Another major economic problem facing the Busia administration was that of balance of payment. As table 4 indicates, between January and April of 1971, the deficit was to the tune of ¢22,106,000. The 1971 third quarter deficit was about ¢50.1 million. During the last half of 1971, Ghana's monthly import was about ¢30 million. The net effect was the withering away of foreign reserve. Consequently, at the time of the January 13 coup, Ghana's foreign reserve was less than ¢20 million. At the rate of ¢30 million monthly importation this represents about a three week reserve![12]

Table 4
Ghana Import and Export by Principal Countries. January-April, 1971

| Country | Import N¢1000 | Export N¢1000 |
|---|---|---|
| U. K. | 421,101 | 32,653 |
| West Germany | 24,131 | 15,936 |
| Japan | 16,013 | 11,243 |
| Netherlands | 3,971 | 14,747 |
| USA | 25,480 | 30,076 |
| Total for all imports | 118,182 | 96,076 |
| Total deficit for Ghana | | 22,106,000 |

NRC'S PERCEPTION OF GHANAIAN ECONOMIC PROBLEMS

Col. Acheampong tried to deemphasize this problem of balance of payment stating "we are fully aware of the fact that the fundamental problem facing the economy today is not the much-publicized balance of payment crisis, as some experts would make us believe, but rather under-production and under-utilization in all sectors of the economy."[14] Despite this protestation, in my opinion the balance of payment is one of the major problems in Ghana's economy. The record of NRC budgetary policies clearly shows that it considers the restoration of proper balance of payment a major task. In addition, there is the problem of Ghana's external debt. As of January 12, 1972, the principal external debts arising out of medium term suppliers' credits was $294 million. As rescheduled the interest would have caused an additional $77 million. The total in this category amounted to $371 million. A third category of debt included about $286.26 million made up of arrears on import payments, 180 day credits and arrears on service payment. Therefore, Ghana's total indebtedness amounted to $888.26 million[15] Col. Acheampong claimed that a substantial number of the contracts arising from medium-term suppliers credits were:

> inimical to the interest of Ghana. The reports of several commissioners of economy and other investigators clearly establish that some of these contracts are tainted and vitiated by corruption andother forms of illegality. In some cases, there has been a fundamental breach of contract on the part of the contractors. A substantial number of the projects financed by the suppliers' credits were not preceded by any feasibility studies establishing their viability. The price quoted in respect of these projects were inflated and the repayment terms did not admit of the projects generating sufficient resources to amortize the debts. . . . Only 8.6 percent of the project, in value terms could have paid for themselves in the repayment periods granted under the credits.[16]

On January 26, the Ghana Ministry of Finance showed that altogether the financial position of Ghana did not improve under the civilian regimes of Busia. It demonstrated that the external debt left by the twenty-seven month old Busia government was higher than that incurred by the two previous regimes of Nkrumah and NLC. According to the ministry the total debts incurred exclusively during the twenty-seven months of Busia administration were as follows.[17]

1. External debts = $530 million.

2. Short term debts of 180 day credits, import credit service payments $286 million.

3. Long term loans of $130 million.

  Total - $946 million.

## THE NATIONAL REDEMPTION COUNCIL AND ITS STRATEGY

It cannot be argued convincingly, therefore, that Ghana's poor economic woes derive exclusively from the mismanagement of the Nkrumah regime. Nor will it be correct to hold the NLC completely culpable, although there are some who believe that the NLC erred in its failure to repudiate "Nkrumah's debts" tainted with corruption. In any case, the NRC arrived at the following decisions:

1. The principal indebtedness arising out of suppliers' credits contracted during the Nkrumah regime was repudiated.

2. It rejected the accrued moratorium interest arising out of the principal.

3. It declared that it would not honor any indebtedness arising from the remaining contracts unless the contractors can prove that they have satisfied certain conditions.

4. It declared a unilateral ten year moratorium on the payment of any debts arising from any suppliers' credit.

5. It accepted, in principle, its liability with regard to short term debts which arose as a result of goods consumed in Ghana.[18]

What followed from January of 1972, is a clear commitment of the NRC to the concept of economic nationalism at least in principle. As in the case of Nigeria, the NRC declared the principle or doctrine of self-reliance. Clearly understanding its true implications, the chairman declared:

"We are indeed in a critical situation. We cannot expect to be bailed out by some miraculous intervention of the generosity of other countries. What we are declaring to the whole world now is that we have the will power and the human and material resources to be self-reliant."[19] But he added, "with the determination and hard work we will demonstrate to our satisfaction and prove to the world that a small and harrassed country can stand up to the formidable array of forces which have always sapped our national confidence, inhibited our independence and undermined our self-sufficiency."[20] He concluded:

> We cannot as a nation continue to be buffeted by forces which we are powerless to control. We cannot continue to live a life of illusion and self-deception. Once we have fully grasped the implication of the stark realities facing us, we will have to embark on a vigorous program, one of increased productivity in

> all sections of the economy. We will have to distinguish the
> essential from the non-essential. We will have to rearrange
> our order of priorities. Above all we will have to adopt a
> revolutionary attitude to our whole manner of living. In
> short we will have to prove that we are truly independent and
> self-reliant in all respects.[21]

At this point, the Ghana military rulers do not have an elaborate document such as the Second Development Plan of the Nigerian military rulers. Although Col. Acheampong promised to give the country a revolutionary charter, it has not been published.[22] Under the circumstance, the NRC's priorities and program have to be put together from the examination of government budgets and declarations.

Talking with a correspondent of West Africa,[23] Col. Acheampong listed the following items of priority for his new regime:

1. reducing the importation of things that "are not really necessary in order to achieve self-sufficiency;"

2. producing food to feed "our growing population and raw materials for increased industrial production;"

3. providing "adequate low-cost housing for our lower income group;"

4. developing local industries;

5. getting real action on the issue of a West African economic community.

Let me examine the NRC's first budget statement, "the mini-budget."[24] In it, the NRC made initial attempts to cope with the deteriorating economic situation inherited from Busia's administration. As a result of Dr. Busia's devaluation, the recurrent expenditure, capital expenditure, and debt servicing increased to ¢882.8 million. But the total revenue expected from customs and taxes remained at ¢400 million. Acheampong's revaluation of the cedis by forty-two percent obviously improved this picture. However, some additional pruning was necessary in order to maintain a balance. Since seventy percent of the recurrent budget was for wages and salaries, the range of choice was narrow; it was either retrenchment or the maintenance of the status quo. Given Acheampong's promise to Ghanaians, retrenchment was out of the question.

Parenthetically, I should observe that unlike the NLC, the NRC finds retrenchment an unacceptable policy alternative. In the short run then, the best that the NRC can expect is that it will succeed in motivating the workers in the direction of maximum productivity so that each worker would have justified his pay. In addition, some redeployment may become necessary.

The NRC also opted to cut into the capital budget prepared by the ousted regime. It decided that the building of administrative blocks, construction projects "not directly productive: should be stopped. Accordingly, "the constructions of the twelve story ministerial block offices for the Ministry of Foreign Affairs, estimated at ¢2.3 million and another eleven story block of offices . . . estimated at ¢1.3 million...have been stopped." The plan to establish the National Properties Limited to take over the maintenance of Government buildings and bungalows from the Public Works Department was suspended.[25] The total savings from these actions was about ¢14.9 million.

The Progress Party budgeted ¢30.7 million for feeder roads, ¢10 million for trunk roads, ¢19.7 million and ¢11.0 million for bridges. But the NRC regime decided that "all expensive construction of roads and bridges with high import content" should be stopped. However, important bridges like the Bomboi bridge which links the North and South would be built under alternative designs "with low import content."[26] The civilian regime had planned to build 500 feeder-road-miles under Phase IV at a cost of ¢6 million. Col. Acheampong argued that the selection criteria was heavily political. Consequently, he declared that his regime would construct "only those roads which will directly assist food distribution and help combat smuggling."[27] Therefore, all roads which did not meet the criteria were stopped, but roads already constructed under the plan would be maintained. By deviating from the Progress Party Plan, the military government anticipated a savings of ¢10.7 million.[28]

Where does the NRC intend to invest the expected savings? Undoubtedly, agricultural development was the highest priority of the NRC. Col. Acheampong declared: "We hope to produce enough maize, rice, yams, cassava, plantains, cocoyams, vegetables as well as poultry and livestock to feed ourselves and more."[29] The government declared 1972-73-74 as "Agricultural Years" to implement what it calls an "Operation Feed Yourself" program. The first phase of this "operation" covered food production. Every Ghanaian was encouraged to participate in agriculture, in order to reduce the amount of food imported to supplement the Ghanaian diet. The NRC promised that "production of raw materials for our industries will be intensified in the later phase of the program. The first objective of course, is to ensure that we are able to feed ourselves. We should be able to ensure that every Ghanaian is properly fed and has opportunity to build up his energies in order to be able to play his proper role in this grand effort in respect of our national reconstruction."[30]

In pursuance of these goals the NRC set specific targets for the following agencies: State Farm Corporation, Food Production Corporation, Food Distribution Corporation, Settlement Farms, Agricultural Development Corporation and State Fishing Corporation. It assured Ghanaians that the Ministry of Agriculture and the National Investment Bank would be mobilized in "a massive way for Operation Feed Yourself."

The Commissioner of Agriculture, Major General Addo assured Ghanaians that "the Government has declared firmly that agriculture has priority in its scheme of things and that the allocation of financial resources would show unmistakably the bias toward agriculture."[31]

The "mini-budget" allocation for Operation Feed Yourself (OFY) is as follows:[32]

TABLE 5

| Agricultural Development Bank (ADB) | ¢ million |
|---|---|
| Small Loan to Farmers | 5.23 |
| State Farms Corporation | 1.63 |
| Food Production Corporation | 5.10 |
| Settlement Farms | .39 |
| State Fishing Corporation | 1.95 |
| Food Distribution Corporation | 5.89 |
| Total | ¢ 20.19 million |

The banking system was expected to provide this amount and channel it through the ADB. The ADB would work out the repayment terms but interest on all agricultural loans were reduced to six percent p.a. or less. Customs duties on agricultural machinery and spare parts were waived. The Agricultural Development Bank and the National Investment Bank were instructed to complete all agricultural storage facilities started in the regions before the 1966 coup. These projects along with other projects built by the Eastern Socialist countries were stopped by the NLC.

To aid its balance of trade posture, the military regime banned the importation of "luxury cars" and it instructed government departments not to order more cars for the rest of the year. The cars belonging to the banned Progress Party were to be used instead.[33] All manufacturing industries operating in the country were expected to produce their raw agricultural materials locally. It threatened that after August 1972, the Government could deny them the foreign exchange allocation for this item.[34]

The Government thought it wise to assure foreigners that it welcomes any foreign investors who come to Ghana "with open hearts and minds." It will encourage such investors to establish "useful industries" in Ghana. It, however, wants all to understand that the NRC is interested in Ghanaians taking control of the "commanding heights" of the Ghana economy.

In addition to agriculture and industry, housing is a priority area for the NRC. The regime is concerned particularly with providing houses for the "very low income group." In order to keep unit cost of the houses within the ¢1,000 to ¢4,000 cedis range, the service of the Public Works Department, the Tema Development Corporation, the Housing Corporation, the Workers Brigade, the State Construction Corporation and private firms will be used.[35] The apparent Ghanaian priority readjustment also affected government health policies and programs. The NRC declared that its goal was "to bring health facilities to as many people as possible." In the NRC's opinion, "the effective way of doing this would be to build more rural health posts, urban health centers and clinics, rather than gigantic regional hospitals."[36]

To the extent that the fiscal plan was a "mini-budget" i.e., a budget introduced in the middle of the financial year to finish up the rest of the financial year, the decision latitude it offered the NRC was limited. The 1972-73 Budget is more important because it offered the NRC a relatively unencumbered decision latitude to order its own priorities. Nevertheless, it is clear from the mini-budget that agriculture is the area of highest priority. On the whole, the concern is for increased productivity and the nurturing of favorable balance of payment posture of Ghana through an emphasis on maximum utilization of Ghanaian resources.

Now let us consider the 1972-73 Budget. The budget estimates show that twenty-seven percent of current budget allocation goes to the economic sector, forty-two percent of the current budget is reserved for the social sector and thirty-one percent of the current budget is allocated to the administrative sector. About sixty-five percent of the capital budget allocation is for the economic sector, nineteen percent for the social sector, and sixteen percent for the administrative sector.[37]

TABLE 6

|  | Current | | Capital | |
| --- | --- | --- | --- | --- |
|  | ¢ million | % | ¢ million | % |
| Economic Sector | 89.4 | 27 | 63.7 | 65 |
| Social Sector | 139.3 | 42 | 18.3 | 19 |
| Administrative Sector | 100.3 | 31 | 15.8 | 16 |
| Total | 329.00 | 100 | 97.8 | 100 |

This budget allocation shows that:

1. the economic sector will receive a total of ¢153.1 million;

2. the social sector will receive a total of ¢157.6 million; and

3. the administrative sector will receive a total of ¢116.1 million.

If the economic war is the most important thing, then, it might be argued that the current planned expenditure (mini-budget) has not done justice to this priority. The NRC itself is somewhat unhappy with this budget allocation. Acheampong declared:

> There is, however, a clear disparity in the pattern of recurrent expenditure over the sectors, indicating the prominence we give to the social and administrative sectors as against the economic sector, for example in the health sector, the Government will, during the coming year, provide an amount of ¢33.3 million as against expected revenue of only ¢300,000. Pre-university Education receives an amount of ¢80 million as against expected revenue of only ¢250,000 . . . These services are being provided practically free, and with increasing population of the country and greater demand for educational and health facilities, a way must be found to meet the cost of providing these, if Government is to be able to continue to provide these services adequately and also to provide other amenities for the people. At this rate also, how does the Government provide jobs for the school leavers?[38]

It is interesting though that in the 1972-73 budget forty-two percent of budget allocation to the economic sector is going to agriculture. The NRC's goal is to organize agricultural activities into three wings:

1. production for local consumption and export substitution.

2. production of agricultural raw material.

3. production for export.

The Ghana Times of November 8, 1972, reports that the Ghana Export Company has just exported its first consignment of foodstuffs to a firm in the United Kingdom. Under this agreement, Ghana is expected to earn up to ¢3 million in foreign exchange for selling eighty tons of yams, twenty tons of cocayams and ten tons of plantain every week for a period of a year. This announcement indicates the follow up of the NRC goal to organize agricultural activities into the three branches indicated above. Seemingly, Government sagacity is underlined by the fact that "the final tonage of foodstuff to be exported, . . . would depend on the allocation to be approved by the Food Distribution Corporation."[39] Obviously, the first concern of the government is to avoid local shortage of exportable food. The NRC states: "In the years ahead our emphasis will continue to be placed on food production. Our policy will be directed toward increasing the production of our main staple foods such as maize, rice, yams, fruits and vegetables, oils, meat and fish and the production of import substitutes."[40]

The Government plans to speed up the implementation of trunk roads to aid the transportation of agricultural produce. This is more or less a continuation of the goal set in the mini-budget of 1971-72. With regard to the feeder roads, regional organizations will play a greater role, and the monopoly of the Public Works Department is to be discontinued. Now, it has to compete with the Department of Social Welfare.[41] A total of 6.6 million cedis was voted for the construction of pipe borne water, and the digging of 250 wells. A sum of 1.5 million was voted to the Ghana Water Sewerage Corporation to operate a rural water supply system.[42]

In the industrial sector, the problem remains the under-utilization of plants due to dependence on imported raw materials. The government promises to provide scarce material through domestic production and through the limited as well as careful use of the import license system. Discontinued projects would be re-examined and revitalized where economically feasible. The NRC wants direct government participation in mining companies and it will initiate the exploitation of bauxite deposits in Kibi and Nuinahim.[43]

The "duty drawback" will be replaced with an export bonus of thirty percent on timber including sawn timber, cocoa and cocoa products; all minerals and primary metals with the exception of diamonds bought from local miners.[44]

## REVENUE SOURCES

How does the government plan to get revenue to carry out these proposals? As I have pointed out earlier, unless a realistic appraisal of revenue capability is done, self-reliance and economic nationalism can become empty dreams. The actual revenue collected in 1971-72 was ¢499.2 million. In 1972-73, however, the estimated revenue (not actual revenue) is (¢386.4 + ¢84.5) million.[45] The former figure is from the current account while the latter is from the capital account. The important point to note here is that the government expects to collect ¢28.3 million less than it actually collected in 1971-72. It is quite possible that the actual money which will be realized will be less than the projection. In this case, a considerable degree of efficiency, discipline, and dedication becomes imperative. Another point to note is that this budget puts little faith in external financing and relies heavily on domestic sources to raise revenue. This is really a pragmatic policy which makes additional taxation a necessity. The NRC has instituted a road worthiness certificate for motor vehicles. It anticipates a ¢1 million revenue from this source. Secondly, it expects to raise about a million cedis by raising "Retailers Registration Fees" for various categories of traders. Thirdly, it has amended the "Hotel Customers' Tax Law" to include restaurants. Fourthly, it has restructured its import tax system. As a result, finished goods and luxurious materials can be assessed at a higher tax rate. Hopefully, this revision will raise an additional ¢10 million cedis. Fifthly, it has proposed a tax on the electricity corporation as well as the Water and Sewerage Corporation. This will net the government ¢1.3 million. Finally, it will float some premium bonds.[46]

Although the government has not raised personal income tax, some of its taxes will be passed on to the consumers in the long run. It may be suggested that more efficient enforcement of taxation is what is needed. However, in a developing country, the efficiency of the bureaucracy, the executing agents and machinery, cannot be taken for granted. The NRC and the military have worked hard to ensure that as many citizens as possible pay their taxes. Military pressures were exerted on tax defaulters early in the reign of the NRC with success. The regime may have decided that it accomplished the best that could be expected in this regard. Besides, the political costs may have been judged superfluous.

In any case, the option which the NRC seems to have elected is not without its drawbacks. The NRC has imposed new tax burdens on retailers, hoteliers and importers. Undoubtedly, some of these taxes will be passed on to the consumers. But it appears that despite the fact that Ghanaians have been forced to rely on themselves, these additional taxes do not seem to be excessively onerous. Somewhat surprisingly, The Legon Observer has congratulated the NRC for presenting a budget which represents a departure from the past in that it will not generate unemployment, inflation or stagnation. However, given the high personnel emolument component of the revenue allocation, the real danger is that the planned expenditure for the ministries will only go to support unproductive bureaucrats. The paper is particularly concerned about the situation in the Ministry of Agriculture.[47]

## NRC'S APPRAISAL OF ITS OWN ECONOMIC PERFORMANCE

The NRC's own estimation of its achievement from January to June of 1972, is revealed in Col. Acheampong's 1972-73 Budget Speech. It is evident from the speech that on the overall, the NRC has deliberately played down its dependence on external borrowings. Col. Acheampong writes: "We have attempted to cut our cost according to our cloth, and should any aid come, this becomes a bonus to the economy." To some extent, this could be taken as giving substance to the theory of self-reliance. But in another sense it is a testimony to the military regime's reconciliation with and/or understanding of reality.

With regard to the performance of the government's "Operation Feed Yourself" the Colonel has claimed considerable achievement and has promised that this would become more obvious "after the harvesting season which has only just started." On the basis of first returns, he has projected the following:[48]

TABLE 7

| Product | 1971 | 1972 | % increase |
|---------|------|------|------------|
| Maize | 378,000 tons | 485,000 tons | 31 |
| Rice | 136,000 tons | 180,000 tons | 36 |
| Yam | 30,000 acres | 540,000 acres 61% of target already achieved in June 30. | 24 |

The NRC has begun to make claims of success based on actual performance in its 'most important' theater of economic war. The Regional Commissioner of Brong Ahafo claimed that the region cultivated 200,000 acres of corn, 185,000 acres of plantain and 105,000 acres of yams. This indicates that the region has exceeded its quota of the Operation Feed Yourself target by sixty-two percent, seventy percent and two hundred percent respectively.

TABLE 8

| Product | Target | Achievement |
|---------|--------|-------------|
| Yams | 50,000 | 105,000 |
| Plantain | 61,000 | 185,000 |
| Maize | 126,000 | 200,000 |

As a further incentive to farmers the commissioner announced that:

1. ¢300,000 cedis has been provided for irrigated projects in the region.
2. a ¢22,000 fertilizer depot has been completed.
3. 80,000 high yielding oil palm seedling has been produced.
4. Agricultural Development Bank has granted ¢800,000 cedis worth of small loans to farms to produce maize, yams, and ginger.

5. a 700 acre goat and sheep ranch has been established as a nucleus for a modern livestock development in the region.[49]

On November 18, 1972, The Pioneer[50] reported that the Volta Region Commissioner announced that his region has exceeded its cassava and yam acreage target by 37,000 and 2,000 acres respectively. He further stated that the schools and colleges in the region have planted over 3,000 acres of various crops, and that the private sector has grown over 120,000 acres of maize and 16,000 acres of rice.

Lt. Col. E. A. Baidoo, addressing a "Regional Agricultural Show" in Kumasi on November 24, 1972, said, "I am very pleased to report that in this region (Ashanti) our farmers did exceedingly well and we were therefore able to exceed our targets for the production of maize and vegetables and we also realized significant increases in the production of cocoa, yams, cassava and plantain."[51]

Even in cosmopolitan Accra, the Regional Commissioner of Greater Accra was reported by the Daily Graphic[52] to have indicated that his region had exceeded its target by acreage as well as by tonnage in its production of maize, cassava and vegetables.

To further motivate the farmers, the government has established guaranteed minimum prices for maize, millet and other products.

TABLE 9

| | | |
|---|---|---|
| Maize | = | ¢10.00 per bag of 220 lbs. |
| Millet | = | 10.00 per bag of 240 lbs. |
| Guinea Corn | = | 9.00 per bag of 240 lbs. |
| Yam | = | 12.00 per 100 tubers of 500 lbs. |
| Plantain | = | 1 1/2 per lb. |
| Cassava | = | 2.25 per bag of 200 lbs. |
| Groundnut | = | 13.00 per bag of 180 lbs. |
| Onions | = | 11.00 per bag of 169 lbs. |

In addition, the Government claims that it is increasing its storage facilities. The Grain Development Board is now equipped with mobile shelters to help farmers with storage facilities for maize and a sum of ¢764,000 has been made available

for the building of silos. If these figures are validated, they will represent a
significant achievement for the NRC and Ghana. Another indication of the success
of "Operation Feed Yourself" is the performance of the Mankoadze Fisheries which,
according to the NRC, exceeded its target by forty-eight percent. As of the ending
of June 1972, sixty-one percent of national target of fish had been achieved while
the State Fishing Corporation had reached eighty percent of its target.[54] In the
past, Ghana imported N¢8.5 million (1969) and N¢14.9 million (1970) worth of
sugar despite its sugar factories in Komenda and Astsuare. This was because the
two factories operated at minimum capacity. In 1960-70 it produced only 5,349
tons of sugar or about one-seventh of its capacity. "The situation is now different,"
according to the Chairman. Unfortunately he advanced no statistics to support this
claim.

The NRC also has granted a cost of living allowance of 33.3% for minimum wage
and additional proportionate increases to government employees coming up to
¢1,000 p.a.

In the area of balance of payments the provisional figures for January through
June, 1972, indicates an average monthly surplus of ¢18.8 million visible trade.[55]
This amount is encouraging when one compares it to the monthly deficit of ¢4.1
million for the same period in the previous year. Of course, this has been
possible because of the abolition of the Open General License, improvement in the
world price of cocoa as well as an increase in the quality of cocoa export. However, the government remains understandably unhappy as long as a majority of its
export comes from the mono crop. (Sixty percent of its exports in 1971-72 came
from cocoa.) The government recognizes the need to diversify its exports, and
the 1972-73 budget statement reveals this concern and a plan of action.[56]

## STRUCTURAL AND INSTITUTIONAL CHANGES BY THE NRC

The 1972-73 development strategy of the NRC manifests some institutional reconstruction. For example, it calls for the expansion of the rural areas to give

prospective investors and farmers in the rural areas easy access. Moreover, it advocates the modification of old <u>institutions</u> and demands fundamental institutional rearrangements. The National Investment Bank, the Agricultural Development Bank, the Bank for Housing and Construction are cases in point. The Bank for Housing is a new institution to deal with real estate development, a house ownership scheme, a workers' housing scheme, a low-cost housing scheme "and joint venture projects relating to building and construction."[57] Another new organization is the Regional Development Corporation which is to invest directly in agricultural, commercial or industrial projects. These are all devices to help make economic nationalism a reality, particularly in the absence of adequate Ghanaian capital. The Regional Planning Committees under the direction of regional commissioners are to "play more positive roles in resource allocation and the strengthening of physical infrastructural bases of the region."[58]

There is a departure from the reliance on direct government borrowing from the bank and from the assumption that people save only to get interest. The NRC has promised that "the banking system will be called upon to take certain specific development projects and to finance them through surplus funds in the system."[59] Although it agrees that prudent banking procedures and an appropriate interest rate structure will not be ignored, it is resolved not to leave the credit and financial institutions without guidelines. In fact, the government will set guidelines on the kind of credit that financial institutions should advance, the amount of such credit, the structure of interest rates and the priorities. Finally, although the government will continue to rely on the interest rate to get people to save, it will encourage savings to acquire "houses and real assets."[60]

The NRC is committed to avoiding a credibility gap. Consequently, the government has created what it calls a special action unit. In doing so, it acknowledges the structural weakness of government machinery in terms of following up government promises with government action. Similarly, it accepts the need for feedback devices for official policy pronouncements and programs if maximum cooperation and success are to be attained.

Following the theme of decentralization and local involvement of its 1972-73 budget, the NRC has announced that regional units of the Special Action Units will be set up "to liaise with national headquarters of the Special Action Unit and work closely with Regional Planning Committee."[61]

In a further effort to ensure bureaucratic responsibility, the NRC has decided to pass a "decree making it an offense to exceed a department's budgetary allocation, vary a contract price, or take overdraft from a banking institution without prior authority from the Commissioner for Finance and Economic Planning."[62] To some extent, this should be welcomed by the bureaucracy particularly since it will insulate it from the regional pressures exercised by a few regional commissioners in the early period of the NRC.

The attempt to make people change their tastes for foreign products may not have been as successful as the NRC would have wished. It is true that the university students now advocate the use of local food products in their cafeteria. It is also true that the state hotels have been ordered to serve more local foods. Nevertheless, the fact remains that there is still a preference for imported cube sugar, as opposed to local sugar.[63] However, this is an area of attitudenal change which, like customs, tends to die hard. In the defense of the NRC, one must take this into account.

## OBJECTIVE ASSESSMENT OF ECONOMIC PERFORMANCE CLAIMS

One of the first acts of the NRC was the subsidization of seven commodities which it declared as "essential goods." The declared goal was to ensure that the price of these goods would be such as to make it possible for the average Ghanaian to buy them. This subsidy cost the government as estimated ¢23 million.[64] Despite this act, the consumer did not experience a relief from exorbitant prices.

The government agencies then took over direct responsibility for the importation and distribution of these commodities. In turn, the agencies were given direct government subsidies. It was felt that this would eliminate the problem of middlemen who, the government claimed, hoarded goods in order to sabotage government efforts. In addition, the takeover of the importation and distribution of these commodities was expected to ensure adequate supply and proper distribution of these goods. It was also designed to make the government price control policy work. In this area, government expectations were not realized. Consequently, direct military participation in the enforcement process became inevitable. This direct participation frightened traders. The sporadic check by soldiers disrupted the traditional Ghanaian market environment and the indiscriminate execution of the policy of "no hoarding" made it difficult for retailers to maintain adequate commodities in storage. As a result, traders who bought auctioned commodities hoarded them and resold them at higher prices. Quite often, it was difficult to determine the real cause of high prices; genuine shortages or hoarding. The NRC was quite nervous on this score since it realized the close relationship between a widening credibility gap and the erosion of legitimacy.

Another problem related to the price control policy is the problem of smuggling. In its anti-smuggling as well as anti-hoarding efforts, government scored below par. A Ghanaian scholar has observed:

> The government is spending over twenty million cedis to subsidize prices of foreign foods and commodities, yet few Ghanaians get these commodities. They are either smuggled out to neighboring countries or hoarded by unscrupulous traders and sold at fantastic prices. There is no longer any economic justification to keep on subsidizing these commodities. The army personnel who now guard our border have not made any impact either on the volume or the rate of smuggling despite the amount of resources poured into combating it; the constant checks in the markets for hoarded goods have not in any way reduced traders' propensity to hoard; the only solution to these malpractices is to remove the subsidy.[65]

Of course, such an action, while economically sensible, may be politically suicidal. The government has slowly edged away from its original position by referring to these subsidized commodities no longer as "essential commodities" but as "foreign foods and commodities." It probably has calculated that in the not too distant future, Ghanaian economic nationalism would be sufficiently entrenched to the point where the Ghanaian would find it unpatriotic to put high premiums on these commodities.

To those who are impatient, it is reasonable to stop the subsidy at once. They counsel that, simultaneously, the government should declare that this ¢23 million be used on some specific projects or be given to the National Trust Fund for use in productive ventures. In their opinion, this is not an unacceptable political risk in the present circumstances.

Government attempts to have a favorable balance of payment posture has been successful. Here, the government has succeeded in imposing strict administrative control on imports. One must, however, recognize that the ¢133.6 million trade surplus for January-September of 1972 owes a lot to a favorable world price of cocoa. One also needs to know more about the effect of this achievement on domestic industrial productivity.

It is difficult to measure how much the NRC restoration of the privileges taken away from the higher civil servants and army officers has affected their economic performance. There is no doubt that it is of immense political value. In the long run, it is necessary for these members of the elite to recognize the need to increase their economic contribution because the military rulers are very conscious of this fact.

In a different context, the _Legon Observer_ observed the same problem. Commenting on the 1972-73 budget, it noted that although ¢39.3 million was allocated to agriculture, it "is not significantly above the approved allocation for last year when the government was not operating the present guaranteed minimum price for scheduled commodities, nor should one forget that the personal emolument component of the allocation is rather high."[66] The real danger as the _Legon_

Observer sees it is that the planned expenditure for the ministry will only go to support unproductive bureaucrats.

> As we have said before, the National Redemption Council prefers gradual measures in solving our economic and social problems to the shock of sharp and drastic methods. Our strategy is to control and correct short-term problems while at the same time priority the long term structural changes which the economy requires particularly, in the fields of agriculture, imports, exports, prices, income and productivity.[67]

The declared policy, therefore, is that of gradualism. In the area of labor, the government is opposed to retrenchment. The government strategy with regard to labor is "to reduce the size of the government establishment as much as possible by allowing those department and government agencies that can stand on their feet to be hived off as independent bodies. Some of these departments and agencies do provide valuable economic goods and services, and we believe the time has come to stop treating such economic activities as social services."[68] In this case then, the strategy for modernization appears to be a de-emphasis of socialistic method. The Post and Telegraph Department has become economically independent. The Cocoa Marketing Board has inherited part of the government's agricultural structures such as the Produce Inspection Unit, and the Cocoa Division. The NRC's goal is that, "In the coming budget year,--encouragement will be given to such departments toward becoming independent and efficient organizations with their own budgets outside the main central government budget. These organizations will be required to contribute toward the development effort of the government. If they fail to achieve their targets, Government will take drastic action against them."[69]

Is this a government attempt to shift responsibility? This does not appear to be the case because the P & T which is being given its "independence" has performed well economically. The Cocoa Marketing Board which is being enlarged as a result of the amalgamation of the bodies outlined above has performed well, and the divisions added to it logically belong to it. But lest we interpret this as pro-Western orientation and the blind adoption of capitalism, we should note that the government plans to turn the engineering and architectural branches of the Public Workers Department into a "public self-financing consultancy company" which will be allowed to compete with the private companies, take up jobs from the private sector, and charge fees.

The question I posed cannot be conclusively disposed of until we know which "certain Government Departments" will be encouraged to become independent organizations. In any case, this is a clear indication that the government is only interested in pragmatic economics within the frame of economic nationalism. Abstract ideological commitment to socialism and capitalism is not the preoccupation. Another index of the rejection of ideology in economic affairs is the adoption of the proposal for the Bank of Housing and Construction in which the Government, the Bank of Ghana, the Commercial Banks and the State Insurance Corporation will hold equity shares.

One of the weaknesses of developing countries like Ghana is the absence of capital. Therefore, if one is serious about Ghanaians "controlling the commanding heights" of the Ghana economy, the government must find a way to help people buy the shares in foreign owned enterprises and newly created ones.

A further index of economic pragmatism is seen in this Government statement regarding the construction of feeder roads.

> The present cost of ¢13,000 per mile is considered too high. The National Redemption Council have accordingly decided that regional organization should, with immediate effect, take over the responsibility for construction of feeder roads. In this regard, the regional organization may commission either the PWD or the Department of Social Welfare in the construction of particular feeder roads and bridges. The Department of Social Welfare may also advise the Regional Organization on the construction of feeder roads in areas where local fervour for commercial labour has been demonstrated or will be forthcoming.[70]

A final indication of the absence of irrelevant ideological consideration in the economic policy is the decision of the NRC to reactivate some of the projects started before but abandoned after the 1966 change of government. These include:

a. Temma Fish complex

b. Pencil Factory Project

c. Gold Refinery

d. Tannery Project

e. Prefab concrete panel[71]

In short, the 1972-73 budget indicates a new approach to rural development. The new approach is that of decentralization where regional administration forms a regional development corporation. The regional corporation will depend on the banking system for its operation and regional planning units under the direction of the regional commissioners are to play a more positive role. Of course, the old age dangers of duplication, and waste may become real. Secondly, the new budget intends to trim government approaches and wean off department producing marketable goods and services into autonomous commercial institutions.[72] Thirdly, it provides a serious signal of the government's intention to make it possible for Ghanaians to control "the commanding heights" of the economy. The current effort to secure for Ghana majority shares of mining concerns is one of the cases in point.

A clear distinction between the economic policy of the NLC and the NRC is evident by comparing the Lonrho and Abbott agreements of the NLC with the NRC negotiations and agreements with various concerns now operating in Ghana. In effect, the NRC has now nationalized the mining and timber companies in Ghana (through the acquisition of majority shareholding). Under the present arrangement, the Ghana state is to acquire fifty-five percent of participation. In addition, it is to have a majority on the board of directors of the individual companies involved. Compensation is to be paid out of profit earned in the next eight years. This is a departure from the Lonrho and Abbott type agreements of the NLC. Yet both the NLC and the NRC have had a predominant percentage of their members trained in England and the West. In fact in a few cases the personnel were the same! The companies involved are the Ashanti Gold Fields, Consolidated African

Selection Trust, African Timber and Plywood, Glicksteu (West Africa), Takoradi Veneer and Lumber, R. T. Brisco-Timber Division.[73]

Col. Acheampong has given a number of assurances with regard to the acquisition of controlling interest in these foreign owned companies. The foreign companies involved have been assured of full and fair compensation, and the expatriate and Ghanaian employees of the companies have been promised that their conditions of service would not be allowed to deteriorate.

The rationale for the government's action was that it found unacceptable the system by which vital Ghanaian resources were controlled by governing bodies based outside Ghana and "virtually immune from the laws of Ghana."[74] Under the present NRC system of local incorporation, Ghanaian authorities would have full access to the books, records, and all operations of the mining companies. The government was careful to state that foreign private capital and expertise would still be welcomed in the effort to harness the country's natural resources as well as in other areas of economic activity. But it can only hope that "with the clarification of its policy in respect of this vital sector of the economy, a firm basis has been established for a meaningful and viable partnership between the state and foreign private capital."[75]

The Government's initial uneasiness about the takeovers is betrayed by two events. First, is the fact that Col. Acheampong found it necessary to explain the action to the officers and men of the First Battalion, Reconnaissance Regiment and Base workshops. The action was justified as an effort to gain Ghanaian control of the economy. In fact he asked them to deal "drastically with anyone caught rumour-mongering."[76] Secondly, the Commissioner for Labour, Major Asante, exhorted the Ashanti Gold Fields Corporation staff to work harder to increase their productivity and to act as "watch dogs" against sabotage.[77] These moves could be interpreted as motivated by initial genuine fears of foreign "agents." Or, it could be seen as an appreciation of possible disincentive which their action could engender on the part of foreign technicians and workers. Such disincentives could lead to lower expatriate staff productivity or mass expatriate exodus. In that case, it would be absolutely essential to have increased productivity and determination on the part of the Ghanaian workers in the corporation. Of course, it is quite probable that this is a demonstration of political skill involving masterful exploitation of anti-imperialistic sentiment to engender support for the NRC regime; unity in the face of the "foreign enemy."

Indeed this seemed to have followed. All the three daily newspapers welcomed the government decision. The <u>Daily Graphic</u> suggested the extension of this policy to other foreign owned major companies. The students at the University of Ghana showing their approval in a public demonstration, called for "total nationalization now," "100 percent or nothing."[78] They wanted the NRC to take over all foreign-owned banks, oil companies, timber concessions and rubber plantations. They further urged that foreign companies should be seen, not as individual firms, but as "neo-colonialist operating for their mutual benefit." "An attack on one sector of the foreign companies without an accompanying attack on the rest of them leaves the rest free to engage in acts of sabotage as protest against government decision to participate."[79] They wanted Ghanaians to be aware that the imperialists are going to engage in "economic blackmail by cutting off supply of commodities with the express aim of bringing us to our knees."[80]

## SUMMARY

The evidence in this chapter suggests that the National Redemption Council has embarked upon the policy of economic nationalism. By way of recapitulation, it has taken majority shares in the timber and mining industries which had been owned and controlled by foreign concerns. It has insisted on the national incorporation as well as Ghanaian majority control of the boards of directors of these concerns. Moreover, it is seeking to diversify its export market. As of now, there are no statistics available to measure its success or failure in this effort. All we can do is point out the vigorous attempt to reestablish trade relations with the socialist states. It will be recalled that the trade and foreign aid ties with the socialist states were discontinued following the coup againstthe Nkrumah regime. It should also be noted that the NRC is vigorously seeking the establishment of a West African Economic Community.

On the overall, the NRC has de-emphasized foreign aid. The examination of the budget statement clearly points out this. The regime is making strong attempts to raise capital internally by retuning the banking system. The regime is prepared to advocate structural rearrangements which may make it possible for Ghanaians to rise to the commanding heights of the economy."

Obviously, the NRC did not attain total success in the pursuance of its policies of self-reliance and of Ghanaian control of the economy. However, it is very clear, at this point, that the NRC policies are not pro-West as the reference group theory advocates would have us believe. Nor can the policy be described as "capitalistic." Furthermore, it will be incorrect to label it as "socialistic" because the NRC has made it abundantly clear that state power is used only in the absence of sufficient Ghanaian private capital and because of the total resolve to capture the "commanding heights of the economy" for Ghana and Ghanaians.

Certainly, the final judgment can only be made after all the scores are in and tabulated. As of January, 1973, the following tentative conclusions could be made with regards to our propositions.

The first economic proposition of the reference group theory that military governments of an ex-colonial army would behave in non-nationalistic fashion and would often give high priority to their identification with reference groups connected with another political community was not borne out in the case of the NRC. There was no "absence of economic nationalism." Similarly, the second proposition was not borne out. The second proposition states: military rules will not necessarily introduce rationality and pragmatism with economic policy making. Military officers trained in the "West" will behave in irrational ways toward the "Eastern bloc" economic interest just as many left-leaning nationalistic leaders are alleged to behave toward Western economic interests.

Finally, the third economic proposition was also negated. It states: when military officers have governmental control, they will be unconcerned with the realization of economic change and reform. Moreover, when there are certain organizations or groups pressing for such economic changes, these military officers will oppose them.

In short, we found that in the NRC regime:

1. the military officers were concerned with the realization of economic changes and reform and that there is no evidence to suggest that they were opposed to civilian groups advocating such reforms;

2. although the military rulers in power were trained in the West, they were not irrational either to the West or the East as far as their general economic policy was concerned;

3. although the Ghana military was an ex-colonial army, the NLC did not behave in non-nationalistic fashion. They practiced economic nationalism.

According to Berg,[81] the Ghanaian economy performed poorly under Nkrumah because of poor coordination between state enterprises, inadequate supervision of operation and mismanagement. In addition, disproportionate amounts of money was spent on state farms at the expense of private farms.

The agricultural performance of the NRC seems to suggest various attempts to avoid the pitfalls. Although there is still the problem of excessive bureaucratization, the government has now taken steps to minimize the frustration of the farmer by decentralizing the Ministry of Agriculture and by giving the regions greater autonomy. One change introduced involves the creation of an Assistant

Director of Agriculture to be located in each region. In turn, he is to be directly responsible to his regional commissioner. This change should strengthen the hands of agricultural experts in the Ministry and make agricultural officers more available for consultation in the field. In addition, the regional commissioner can carry out the job of integration of governmental institutions and functions without excessive national centralization.

The "OFY" has been criticized as depending largely on spontaneity. In the years ahead, if the spontaneous efforts continue to reap bountiful rewards, both tangible and intangible, the efforts would be sustained and perhaps institutionalized into the Ghanaian system. Undoubtedly, this will be the ultimate test of the success of the government's economic development effort.

Although the state of knowledge about Ghana economy is still insufficient, we now know much more about the economy than we did when Nkrumah made his plan. There is still the problem of inadequate technical competence, but the problem of administrative incompetence and organizational inability has been minimized by the apparent government's determination to disperse its manpower resources throughout the country. Nevertheless they have not been eliminated completely.[82] There are those who may still feel that the state is trying to do too much. In this connection, it is important to remember that the government is determined and anxious to stop treating economic activities as social activities. As I have pointed out, up to this point the NRC has avoided the weakness of depending on external financing of development. Parenthetically, I should note that there are other economists who do not agree that the failure of Nkrumah economy was due to structural transformation, but to fall in world cocoa prices after 1958 in a country in which cocoa has always produced about sixty percent of its foreign exchange. These economists also adduce other reasons for failure.[83]

## FOOTNOTES

1. <u>Ghana Economic Review</u> 1971-72, Accra: Editorial and Publishing Service, p. 13.

2. <u>Ibid</u>.

3. Col. I. K. Acheampong, Budget Statement for March to June 1972, p. 3. Accra: Ministry of Finance and Economic Planning, 20th February 1972, <u>Ghana Economic Review</u>, 1971072, p. 13.

4. Economic Review, <u>Ibid</u>.

5. <u>Economic Review</u>, 1971/72, p. 13.

6. Economic Review, <u>Ibid</u>., p. 13.

7. <u>Ibid</u>., p. 19.

8. <u>Ibid</u>., p. 19.

9. <u>Ibid</u>.

10. From <u>Ibid</u>., p. 22.

11. From <u>Ibid</u>., p. 23.

12. <u>The Legon Observer</u>, February 11, 1972, p. 48.

13. Extracted from <u>Ghana Economic Review</u> 1971-72, p. 48.

14. <u>West Africa</u>, 8 September 1972, p. 1202.

15. <u>Op. cit</u>., <u>Economic Review</u> 1971072, p. 336.

16. Reproduced in <u>The Legon Observer</u>, 11 February 1972, p. 62.

17. <u>Ibid</u>., p. 66.

18. In accordance with well-settled principles of laws governing suppliers' credit contracts, and in consonance with our declared policy of eradicating all forms of improper conduct or moral turpitude from public life, the National Redemption Council unequivocally repudiates all contracts which are vitiated by corruption, fraud or other illegality.

    All debts and other obligations arising under such contracts are cancelled with effect from today. The National Redemption Council also owes a duty to the people of Ghana to repudiate all debts and other obligations arising from contracts where there has been a fundamental breach of such contracts on the part of the contractors. These ground were relied upon by the previous government in cancelling the Drevici contracts in January, 1970. The National Redemption Council is satisfied that on the same grounds the available evidence is sufficient to sustain the cancellation of contracts of the total value of <u>$94.4</u> million entered into with the following companies: <u>Parkinson Howard Group</u> of Companies, Seawork Limited, <u>Newport Shipbuilding</u> and Engineering Company and Swan Hunter and Richardson. All indebtedness arising under these contracts is accordingly cancelled with immediate effect.

The government of Ghana will repudiate other contracts on such grounds without any hesitation if appropriate evidence becomes available at a later stage. In this regard the National Redemption Council wishes to make it clear that all suppliers' credits entered into before February 24, 1966, will be subjected to a thorough and rigorous review. The National Redemption Council considers that the repudiation, or cancellation of contracts and debt obligations on the foregoing grounds is perfectly legitimate under any civilized legal system. The government of Ghana would be prepared to go to arbitration in respect of all disputes arising from our action, and for this purpose we would be willing to submit to the jurisdiction of the International Center of Investment Disputes at Washington, D. C., U.S.A.

With regard to other debts arising from suppliers' credits, the National Redemption Council does not propose to adhere to the policy of accepting them unconditionally as valid without any review. Such debts would only be accepted as valid and binding on the National Redemption Council government if the following preconditions are complied with:

First, the contractors concerned must establish to the National Redemption Council that such debts arose of valid contractors;

Second, it must be further established that the contracts are not otherwise vitiated by fraud, corruption or other illegality; and

Third, the National Redemption Council must be satisfied that the said contracts were in respect of technically and economically viable, as well as productive, projects.

The National Redemption Council government would in principle be prepared to accept and pay all debts arising from suppliers' credits which are duly established as valid and binding in accordance with the criteria which have just been stipulated.

TERMS OF PAYMENT

However, having regard to our critical economic condition and balance of payments position the National Redemption Council wishes to declare in emphatic terms that the government of Ghana cannot honour such debt obligations on any terms other than those currently applicable to credits granted by the International Development Association.

In effect such debts would be paid over a fifty year period, including ten years of grace. Then percent of the remaining ninety percent over the following thirty years.

Since we have rejected the debt settlements entered into by previous governments, the capital amounts to be considered under this formula would be exclusive of all accumulated moratorium interest.

With respect to debts arising from suppliers' credits contracted after February 24, 1966, the National Redemption Council government will accept them as valid and binding without further examination.

However, on economic and balance of payments grounds, the government has no alternative but to pay such debts on the terms applicable to credits granted by the International Development Association.

The National Redemption Council wishes to make it clear that the cumulative effect of these policy announcements on our indebtedness arising from the suppliers' credits contracted during the Nkrumah regime is as follows:

First, a third of the principal amount of the debt arising from these suppliers' credits is repudiated outright.

Second, the accrued moratorium interest of U.S. $72 million on this principal amount is emphatically rejected.

Third, no debt obligation arising from the remaining contracts will be accepted by the National Redemption Council government unless the contractors concerned have satisfied the conditions that have been laid down, and

Fourth, there will be no payment of any debt arising from any suppliers' credit for the next ten years.

In the case of short-term debts, defined as the total of arrears on import credits, 180-day credits and liabilities of service payments, the National Redemption Council will in principle, accept liability to pay these debts. These obligations arise in respect of goods which have in fact been consumed in Ghana and there would be no basis for denying liability. Nevertheless, our economic situation makes it impossible to settle these debts on the original terms. In the circumstances, the National Redemption Council has instructed the Bank of Ghana to make a steady, if even a small, reduction in our short-term indebtedness as the nation's resources will permit.

DETERMINATION

As to long-term debts which arise principally out of long-term loans and credits granted by the World Bank, International Development Association, the governments of other donor-countries, the National Redemption Council considers that the relevant loan and credit agreements are not open to the objections raised to suppliers' credits, and it is accordingly the intention of the National Redemption Council to honour them in accordance with the terms already agreed. Ibid., pp. 63-64.

19. Ibid., p. 64.

20. Ibid., p. 64.

21. Ibid., p. 64.

22. The Revolutionary Charter with "Unity and Self Reliance" as its motto was released on January 10, 1973.

The Revolutionary Charter
Motto: Unity and Self-reliance

Chapters:
One nation, one people, one destiny;
Total manpower Development;
Revolutionary Discipline
Self-reliance.
Service to the People
Patriotism and International Brotherhood
Mobilization of Spiritual, Intellectual and will power.

23. West Africa, May 11, 1972.

24. Op. cit., I. K. Acheampong Budget Statement for March to June 1972.

25. Ibid., p. 1.

26. Ibid., p. 2.

27. Ibid.

28. Ibid.

29. Ibid., p. 3.

30. Ibid.

31. Press Conference of Major General Addo, February 17, 1972.

32. Op. cit., Budget Statement, March-June 1972, p. 11.

33. Ibid., p. 3.

34. Ibid., p. 11.

35. It is estimated that at an average constructional cost of ¢3,000 per house, consisting of two bedrooms, a total of 2,300 housing units can be provided by the end of the current financial year. The infrastructure in the housing estates will be provided by the Public Works Department in full cooperation with the Water and Sewerage and the Electricity Corporations and the Local Authorities wherever necessary. In some cases the infrastructure will be provided and prospective house owners will be given plots to build their own low-cost houses according to approved plans. The type of houses should provide a minimum of accomodation, comprising one or two rooms with sanitary facilities, kitchen and compound and with provision for further expansion to two rooms or three rooms. Improvement and expansion can be undertaken later by the occupant whenever he finds himself in a position to do so. In all cases, full consideration will have to be given to using materials available or manufactured locally (e.g., sandcrete blocks, bricks, timber, wood-wool slabs, aluminum, asbestos, locally made sanitary fittings, timber shutters, or louvres in lieu of glazing, etc.) The basic local materials that can be used for low-cost housing will of course have to be identified first and steps also taken to ensure that taxes and duties on imported ones are meanwhile appreciably reduced to bring the cost of construction within the reach of as many of our people as possible in the low income group. Ibid., p. 12.

36. Mini-budget, p. 2.

37. I. K. Acheampong, Budget Statement 1972-73, quoted in The Legon Observer, 22nd September 1972, p. 459.

38. Ibid., p. 459.

39. Ghana Times, November 8, 1972.

40. Acheampong, Budget Statement, 1972-73 in Legon Observer, 22 September, 1972, p. 461.

41. Ibid., p. 462.

42. Ibid.

43. Ibid.

44. The Legon Observer, October 20 - November 2, 1972, p. 508.

45. Acheampong, Budget Statement 1972-73 in The Legon Observer, op.cit., October 20, 1972, p. 510.

46. Ibid., pp. 510-511.

47. See Legon Observer, 12 January 1973, p. 2.

48. Acheampong, Budget Statement 1972-73 op. cit., The Legon Observer, September 22, 1972, p. 460.

49. Pioneer, November 18, 1972.

50. Pioneer, November 18, 1972.

51. Pioneer, November 25, 1972.

52. Daily Graphic, November 4, 1972, p. 8.

53. Daily Graphic, November 25, 1972, p. 9.

54. Acheampong, Budget Statement, 1972-73 in The Legon Observer, September 22, 1972, p. 460.

55. The Legon Observer, October 20, 1972, p. 508.

56. Ibid.

57. The Legon Observer, September 22, 1972, p. 461.

58. Ibid.

59. The Legon Observer, October 20, 1972, p. 510.

60. Ibid.

61. The Legon Observer, November 3, 1972, p. 535.

62. Ibid.

63. The NRC announced that its import bill of foreign food was 125 percent of that of the Busia regime. The Legon Observer, February 9, 1973, p. 55.

64. Ibid., p. 71.

65. Kwabena Manu, The Legon Observer, 12 January 1973, p. 6.

66. The Legon Observer, 22 September 1972, p. 437.

67. The Legon Observer, Ibid., p. 459.

68. Ibid., p. 460.

69. Ibid., p. 462.

70. Ibid., p. 438.

71. Ibid., p. 462.

72. West Africa, p. 1705, December 18, 1972.

73. Ibid., A New company, the Ashanti Gold Fields (Ghana) Corporation LTD. and the Ghana Consolidated Diamonds LTD. would take over the Ashanti Gold Fields Corporation and Consolidated Africa Selection Trust respectively.

74. Ibid.

75. Quoted in Ibid.

76. Ibid.

77. Ibid.

78. Ibid.

79. Ibid.

80. Ibid.

81. See Berg in "Structural Transformation versus Gradualism Recent Economic Development in Ghana and the Ivory Coast," pp. 187-230 in Phillip Foster and Aristide Zolberg (ed.) Ghana and The Ivory Coast (Chicago: University of Chicago Press).

82. The Legon Observer, February 6, 1974. See the Editorial.

83. See E. Ashag and J. Richard "A Comparison of Economic Development in Ghana and The Ivory Coast since 1960." Bulletin of the Oxford University Institute of Statistics (December 1967), pp. 353-371. Also, see R. H. Green, "Ghana and The Ivory Coast, 1957-1967: Reflections on Economic Strategy, Structure, Implementation and Necessity," paper presented at the African Studies Association, 1967.

# PART III

## LEGITIMACY ENGINEERING

# CHAPTER V

## INTRODUCTION

In Chapter I, I proposed that the military regime's legitimacy strategy is partly dependent on the circumstance of military take-over, and the ambition and goal of the military regime. Furthermore, I argued that the military regime's legitimacy strategies are not necessarily static. Rather, they are subject to changes depending upon:

(a) how established the military regime feels;

(b) its clear minded perception of its mission(s) and its resolve to pursue them;

(c) the degree of unity within the military organization;

(d) the relative political strength of competing groups and sectors in the society; and

(e) the coincidence of the military regime's societal goals with those of the various groups in the society.

Finally, I suggested that the coalition dictated by the strategy of legitimacy will tend to affect the policy outputs of the military regime. Let us examine the military regimes to see how well these propositions hold up. The next two chapters address themselves to aspects of these propositions.

## THE IRONSI REGIME*

It is not unusual for man to find himself in less than ideal situations. Admittedly, this is not an enviable position in which to find oneself. In public affairs, the worth of a political regime and that of its political leadership is greatly enhanced if, having found a country in a political nadir, its political leadership succeeds in lifting it from the doldrums. Most political leaders aim for such dramatic successes but only a few accomplish them.

The circumstances leading to the first Nigerian military take-over have been discussed in Chapter II. When, on January 15, 1966, the civilian Federal Executive Council somewhat involuntarily abrogated its authority and handed over power to General Ironsi, the latter found himself in less than an ideal situation. First, the coup d'etat which took place was essentially an imcomplete coup d'etat. The majors who carried out the coup d'etat had only partial control of the country. Second, and most notably, the immediate casualties of the coup were overwhelmingly members of the Northern establishment and their Western Nigerian political allies. Third, it appeared that within the officer class, Northern and Western, not Ibo, officers were killed. There was bitter resentment among the Northern officers about this fact. There was even greater resentment among the Northerners who constituted the majority of the rank and file of the army. Thus, in essence, General Ironsi headed a military regime divided against itself. The apparent disunity was centered along primordial lines of regionalism and ethnicity. (For the feelings of other Nigerians see O'Connell, "Political Integration: The Nigerian Case in Hazlewood, African Integration and Disintegration, Oxford University Press, 1967.)

---

*The factual data presented in "From Military Coup to Civil War" Nigerian Politics and Military Rule: Prelude to the Civil War, S. K. Panter-Brick, ed., is essentially correct. However my interpretations of the data is somewhat different. By the way, I was in Nigeria as researcher during this crucial period.

At this point, it is necessary to recall Chapter II where, among other things, I discussed the problems confronting the Nigerian political system. These were:

1. the problem of differing political cultures among the various ethnic groupings in the country as well as the inability of those in authority to reconcile differing norms with one another;

2. the problem of differing impact of colonialism which manifests itself in uneven educational opportunities which in turn results in sharp differences in the rate of growth among various parts of the country;

3. the problem of ethnic based political parties which, for the selfish interest of maintaining themselves in power, accentuate sectional feelings and intensify primordial attachments;

4. the loss of idealism, the reckless pursuit of personal wealth by the fortunate few, and the widening of the gap between the haves and the have nots;

5. a sense of frustration by citizens regarding their future and fortune in the political order, (the issue of rigged elections and the absence of freedom to pursue economic activity anywhere in the Federation);

6. the politics of cultural sub-nationalism and the politics of regional security;

7. the apparent unwillingness to attack Nigerian problems at their foundation, (i.e., the preference for patchwork has led the country to develop a vicious cycle of crises);

8. the problem of making national institutions behave in truly national fashion.

On the part of the man in the street, I found that the immediate reaction was that of relief. As soon as the picture of the coup emerged in detail and as soon as the disaffected interpreted the seeming partiality of the coup, the coup leaders conjured up differing images in the perceptions of various Nigerian groupings. They remained as national heroes to some ethnic groups; appeared as national villians to others; and were perceived as opportunists by the rest. The most unfortunate fact is not the divergent perceptions, but the fact that the perceptions again followed along ethnic lines. In short, the politics of cultural subnationalism were heightened by the military take-over which was supposed to diffuse the ethnic animosities which had built up over the years.

The Nigerian governmental bureaucracy has been discussed by me elsewhere.* Therefore, I should not repeat myself. The study which was done up to the time of the coup showed that the Nigerian bureaucracy suffered from the same malaise which afflicted the entire society. It is not surprising, therefore, to see them, bureaucrats, share the same sentiments as the civilians possessing the same primordial backgrounds. Indeed, the situation in the North was such that some bureaucrats openly demonstrated against the military regime.[1] The point is that the circumstances under which General Ironsi usurped or accepted power required a most carefully thought-out and properly executed legitimacy engineering. In part, this is the message that Henry Bienen conveys below:

> In this regard, the type of take-over which transforms the army into a military oligarchy is crucial. Whether the army acts in a premeditated way or reacts to a breakdown of civilian rule affects its legitimacy as a ruler. And whether an army coup calls into question the rules of a particular leader, a government or the legitimacy of a state system determines in part the new pattern which will emerge.[2]

Be that as it may, the fact is that for General Ironsi, the use of violence as an effective tool for compliance was not a very viable option, given the nature and the circumstances of the coup.

How did General Ironsi go about his legitimacy engineering? General Ironsi sought to please all, but he ended up pleasing none. One of his first actions in the military was to promote military officers. He attempted to placate the

---

*Olorunsola, "The Relationship Between Bureaucratic and Political Leadership," Journal of Developing Areas, October 1968.

Northern soldiers by promoting the lower rank Northern officers. At the same time, some Ibo officers due for promotions were promoted. However, there was considerable resentment among some army officers regarding this action. In hindsight, even many Northern non-commissioned officers regarded the exercise as a payoff to Ibo officers.

Moreover, there was the question of what to do with the coup leaders. If they are officers who mutinied, then they must be court-martialed in accordance with the military code of justice. Northern soldiers, bureaucrats and other members of the Northern political establishment demanded it. However, Southern radical intellectuals saw the coup leaders as heroes and so did the Ibos. Within the army and in the Supreme Military Council, these leaders had sympathizers. Finally, there was a dilemma; how could Ironsi court-martial his benefactors? These put General Ironsi into a situation of indecision. He compromised by imprisoning the coup leaders despite his purported promise not to punish them. Again, this action did not generate support for his regime.

It would not be accurate to suggest that General Ironsi fondly surrounded himself only with Ibo higher civil servants. Somewhat discounting the dangers of primordial sentiments, he invited Federal permanent secretaries to join the Federal cabinet as full members. His offer was rejected.[3] Several reasons can be deduced for the rejection of this offer by the higher civil servants. The first of these is that this is contrary to the normative definition of the role of British and Nigerian higher civil servants and that nothing has happened to shock the Nigerian higher civil servants into a flagrant and open rejection of their professional code. Another plausible explanation is that Federal higher civil servants of Northern origin would have found it inconsistent to play such a role given the dearth of good will for that military regime. A third reason is the feeling that the regime will not last and it is therefore desirable to insulate oneself from possible future recriminations. Consequently, Ironsi had to avail himself of the advice of a few individual civil servants who agreed to help. It is important to note that not all Ibo permanent secretaries were willing to play this role. Some obliged, however.

General Ironsi did not attempt to include politicians--discredited or non-discredited--in his council of advisers. The first President of the country, Dr. Azikwe, was ignored. He would only consider him a private citizen. Chiefs Awolowo and Enahoro remained in detention. The talent of J. S. Tarka remained untapped and unused even after he had more or less volunteered himself for service.[4] In this case Professor Shils' contention of military distrust for politicians seems validated (see Chapter I). Perhaps Ironsi was of the opinion that no politician could be an asset to his regime so soon after the dismal performance of politicians. Whatever the reason, Ironsi apparently lived in awe of the unfavorable circumstances under which he took over power. This paralyzed him for quite a while.

Even during the May, 1966, riots, he was afraid to use the army to restore order. Thus, we had the ironic situation in which a military regime appeared to be incapable of maintaining law and order. In a sense, this was one of the major weaknesses of the deposed civilian regime.

By the time Ironsi's regime had made up its mind to rule, it had lost the initiative by giving the image of indecision and incompetence.[5] The General had tried to please all the factions, including the Northern traditional rulers, but he had failed. He ought to engineer a coalition without consensus. Decree 39, in my judgment, was an attempt to please all. He made a pronouncement which would restore the confidence of the Ibo and a few radical constituencies which were becoming frustrated with his regime. At the same time, he refused to back it up with a force of action beyond the possible rotation of the topmost administrators. Unfortunately, the deliberate vagueness which could have given him the latitude he desired was once again a weakness. His adversaries interpreted Decree 39 in a way which threatened the job security of all Northern higher civil servants.

The point is not that of the doctrine of the inevitable fall of a military regime. Rather, it is that the legitimacy strategy available was restricted because of the circumstances of the take-over. Despite the circumstances, one could suggest that, given a different type of military leader, the legitimacy engineering would have succeeded. Indeed, Professor O'Connell has suggested this.

> Much of the failure to sustain the enthusiasm of January or to build a new legitimacy must be traced to the character of Aquiyi-Ironsi. His position of command called for one who would play an executive-presidential role. But in spite of having the best intentions and being a man of personal integrity, the army commander was an indecisive leader. He never made up his mind whether he was carrying on the legitimacy of the previous government or whether he was carrying through the 'revolt of the majors.'"[6]

Ironsi's short military rule is seemingly characterized by functionally schizoid pronouncements and actions. On the one hand, he probed the assets and actions of the old politicians to expose corruptions and malfeasance, but he did so rather grudgingly, desultorily and in a biased fashion.[7] This angered a substantial section of the country who wanted a radical cleanup, but it was not operationally palliative enough for the Northern establishment. He announced Decree 39 only after the Northern regional establishment had had time to organize against it. He paid respect and homage to Northern traditional rulers--witness the 'royal' treatment he accorded the Sultan of Sokoto's visit to Lagos--but maintained Ibo advisers who later disclosed to this writer that "he did not follow their crucial advise."[8]

A conventional position is that the political weakness of the Ironsi's military regime was accentuated--at least in its early stages--by his failure to recruit the talents and organization of other groups, except civil service, to help it either in policymaking or in developing political support.
In my opinion, however, it is more appropriate to argue that the failure of Ironsi to develop legitimacy (a very important political weakness) is due to the

circumstances of the take-over, the political environment, and the political tradition. It is by no means certain that in the circumstances, he could have effectively recruited the talents and organizations of groups who would have made the difference.

The only source of legitimacy which would have saved Ironsi's regime was that based upon performance. If, for example, the regime had managed to achieve and/or display noticeable economic attainment, that would have provided it with the crucial period of grace, at least. Unfortunately, six months proved to be too short a time for such a task in the circumstances.

## NIGERIA: LEGITIMACY ENGINEERING--GOWON REGIME

On the overall, General Gowon was presented with better opportunities for the legitimation of his regime. However it is a testimony to his political skill and perceptiveness that he took advantage of these opportunities.

The leaders of the second coup were not politically organized. They seemed to have detested the Ironsi regime so much that all they were initially interested in was the right of the North to secede. They had not undertaken a serious political and economic calculus of Northern secession.[9] A number of crucial questions were not asked. For example: Is the North a viable economic entity? Can the North achieve unity among its heterogenous components without the benefit of a common enemy? Is it in the interest of the majority of Northern soldiers to have an independent North? In any case, this lack of clear definition of goals and interests by Northern soldiers and officers in the early days of the second coup may have made things tolerable for the East and, perhaps, for the West, both of whom were alarmingly fearful of the possibility of the return of Northern domination. Right from the beginning the Midwest region found secession unacceptable because the disintegration of the Federation was not in their interest.[10] At first sight, then, the engineering of legitimacy under these circumstances would seem to be herculean and less likely to be productive than the situation in January of 1966.

Since most of the Eastern officers were killed and the Eastern soldiers and the remaining officers had escaped, power in the army tilted to the Northerners. As I have pointed out in Chapter II, a majority of the rank and file soldiers came from the North. The Majority of the Northern soldiers came from the area of the Middle Belt. General Gowon, himself a Middle Belter, was therefore acceptable as a leader to these men, given the primordial nature of things.

Although a sense of Northern solidarity was temporarily engendered among the Middle Belt soldiers and officers and their Northern counterparts as a result of the killings and coup d'etat of January 15, 1966, historically, the Middle Belt has felt oppressed by the Northern establishment.[11] Therefore, it was not difficult to persuade the Middle Belt soldiers that in the long run their interest did not reside in secession with the North. Nor was it too tedious to convince the remaining Northern soldiers about the inadvisability of Northern secession. Moreover in addition, the higher civil servants and lecturers from the Midwest, West Lagos and the Middle Belt realized that their own personal interests did not repose in a dismantled Nigeria Federation. Unlike the situation under General Ironsi, where they refused to be politically helpful, the permanent secretaries "volunteered to go over to Ikeja barracks."[12] It is the opinion of Mr. Ayida that this intervention had a decisive effect on the political events in Nigeria.

In addition to the salutary predispositions discussed thus far, I must add the credentials which made General Gowon acceptable to significant segments of the society. For the Northern establishment, they saw him as a Northern representative who was not likely to decidedly undermine their interest in the Nigeria Federation.[13] (The tradition of sending Middle Belters to the Federation to fill Northern quotas in the Federation bureaucracy and government corporations had been established under Sir Ahmadu Bello.) While Gowon was not the most desirable choice for the Northern establishment, it was the best they could do, given North-South hostility and the reality of power within the military. As a Middle Belter, Gowon had a firm support base within the military given the disarray among the liquidation of Eastern soldiers. His command was the one least likely to be questioned. Third, since he came from a small tribe the major tribes did not see him as a major threat or a powerful traditional enemy. For the southerners who were afraid of Northern Islamic domination, Gowon's Christian background was an asset indeed.[14] Among his colleagues he had a reputation of being a personable human being and a good officer.

Following the decision to reject the Aburi agreements because of their effect on the Nigeria Federation, Gowon promulgated the decree which created twelve states. (Incidentally the opposition to the Aburi agreement came largely from the Federal bureaucrats, not from the military whom Professor Shils claims are opposed to politics of negotiation.) This decree more than any other action before the end of the civil war was very instrumental in the Gowon legitimacy engineering. It was a successful attempt to restructure power so that it could be more amenable to the Federal regime. Since the military power was held by the Middle Belters, they were quite enthusiastic about the decree which represents the fulfillment of the desire of the people of the area. In addition, the southerners who had been very afraid of what they regarded as the North's domineering posture, were happy because it meant the reduction of Northern influence. The Hausa-Fulani establishments were generally not enthusiastic but they felt it was necessary in the circumstance of national emergency and in order to allay southern fears. It might be added that the people of Kano were not at all unhappy since it gave them their own state. The fact that the East was divided into three had a soothing effect on the North. The decision to divide the East obviously represents a decision that nonviolent confrontation between Nigeria and the East was no longer avoidable.

By freeing Chiefs Awolowo and Enahoro and eventually associating these men with him, Gowon was able to get the support of very substantial numbers of Western and Midwesterners. Again this move negates Professor Shils' contention with regard to politicians and the military rulers. Gowon further broadened his political base by appointing certain civilian advisers. As it will be obvious later, General Gowon carefully balanced the composition of the Federal Government by having his advisers and leaders in the government from a variety of ethnic, regional and religious backgrounds. Furthermore, the fact that not all the advisers were military men gave credibility to the promise of eventual return to civilian rule. The table below is instructive.

## THE FEDERAL EXECUTIVE COUNCIL*

| Party | Name | Portfolio | Nationality | Religion | Region |
|---|---|---|---|---|---|
|  | Major-General Yakubu Gowon | Head of State, Chairman of Executive Council Cabinet Office and Defense | Angas | Christian | Benue Plateau |
| A.G. | Chief Obafemi Awolowo | Vice-Chairman of Executive Council, Finance | Yoruba | Christian | West |
| A.G. | Dr. Okoi Arikpo | External Affairs | Ekoi | Christian | South-East |
| AG/UMBC | Mr. Joseph Tarka | Transport | Tiv | Christian | Benue Plateau |
| NEPU/ NCNC | Alhaji Aminu Kano | Communications | Fulani | Islam | Kano |
|  | Dr. J. E. Adetoro | Health | Yoruba | Christian | Kwara |
|  | Attorney-Gen., Dr. T. O. Elias | Justice | Yoruba | Islam | Lagos |
| NPC | Alhaji Yahaya Gusau | Economic Development and Reconstruction, Agriculture and Natural Resources | Hausa | Islam | North-West |
|  | Rear Admiral J. E. A. Wey | Establishments | Yoruba | Christian | Rivers |
| A.G. | Chief Anthony Enahoro | Information and Labour | Ishan Edo | Christian | Midwest |
|  | Inspector-General of Police, Alhaji Kam Selem | Internal Affairs | Kanuri | Islam | North-East |

| Party | Name | Portfolio | Nationality | Religion | Region |
|---|---|---|---|---|---|
| A.G. | Mr. Wenike Briggs | Education | Ijaw | Christian | Rivers |
|  | Mr. Femi Okunnu | Works and Housing | Yoroba | Islam | Lagos |
| Founder NPC | Dr. A. R. B. Dikko | Mines and Power | Fulani | Christian | North-Central |
| NPC | Alhaji Shettima Ali Monguno | Trade and Industry | Kanuri | Islam | North-East |

*Source: Adapted from Olav Stokke, Nigeria: An Introduction to the Politics, Economy and Social Setting of Modern Nigeria, (1970), p. 137. (Modified by this author)

Although political parties were banned, ex-politicians were used at the federal and state levels. More specifically, civilian politicians were brought into the Federal Executive Council with ministerial responsibilities as Commissioners. Of the fifteen Commissioners of the Federal Executive Council, three were from the military and the police--Gowon, Wey and Alhaji Kam Selem. Of the rest, only one-- the Commissioner of Health, Dr. Adetoro--had not been committed to one or more of the old political parties. Four Commissioners belonged to the Action Group: Awolowo, who was leader of the Action Group from the beginning; Enahoro, who was second Vice President of the Action Group; Arikpo, who was an AG leader in the Eastern House of Assembly; and Briggs, who was an AG member of the House of Representatives.

The ethnic composition of the Federal Executive Council was also diverse: five Yoruba, two Fulani, two Kanuri, one Hausa, one Tiv, one Angas, one Ijaw, one Ishan Edo and one Ekoi. This implies that eight of the fifteen Commissioners came from three of the four major tribes--Hausa, Fulani and Yoruba--and none from the fourth, Ibo.[15] Many minority groups were also represented.

| Region | Majority groups | Minority groups | Total |
|---|---|---|---|
| Northern | 3 (2 Fulani, 1 Hausa) | 5 (2 Kanuri, 1 Yoruba 1 Tiv 1 Angas) | 8 |
| Western | 1 (Yoruba) | 0 | 1 |
| Eastern | 0 | 3 (1 Ijaw, 1 Ekoi 1 Yoruba) | 3 |
| Midwestern | 0 | 0 | 0 |
| Lagos | 2 (Yoruba) | 0 | 2 |
| Total | 6 | 8 | 14 |

\*\*\*Source: Olav Stokke, Nigeria: An Introduction to the Politics, Economy and Social Setting of Modern Nigeria (Uppsala, The Scandinavian Institute of African Studies, 1970), p. 140. (Modified by this author)

All in all, the attempt of Gowon to balance the leadership of the Council was an indication to many Nigerians that he was committed to national unity without domination by any particular ethnic group or region.

As a result of earlier disturbances the Ibos had left the territory where the Federal Government had de jure authority. This meant that, for the most part, there were no Ibos in the Federal establishments such as the Federal bureaucracy, corporations, etc. (Midwest Ibos remained in some cases.) Thus the most dissatisfied elements of the Federal bureaucracy had left it. It also meant that there were vacancies to be filled. Conceivably, this created an incentive for hard work on the part of non-Ibos. Furthermore, the operation and maintenance of government operations became a matter of personal pride, given the Biafra propaganda that the Ibos were indispensable because of their technical skills.[16] The important point is that these views were there and clearly exploited by General Gowon's military regime. It is therefore not surprising that an essentially impotent bureaucracy, relative to integrative capability, started to play a crucial role in this respect.

The war created the need to expand the army and the Yorubas insisted on the quota system in military recruitment.[17] Gowon accomodated this wish and military leaders of the West as well as other Nigerian states openly recruited to meet the quota. In short, whenever possible, Gowon exercised compromise, provided such compromises made the maintenance of Nigerian unity more of a reality.

The military leadership presumed that religious leaders, just as traditional leaders, had considerable influence in local communities. Consequently, it thought it desirable to try to work through them in spreading its messages and proclamations. One cannot categorically state that the military regime regarded this as a two-way communication. The military leadership seemed to have recognized this as a two-edged sword. Consequently, it tried to avoid the impression of favoring one religious group over the others. The government's caution is evident not only in the representativeness of various religious groups in the government decision instrumentalities, but also in the care with which the Head of State or his appropriate surrogates send messages of congratulations to various religious groups upon important and appropriate religious occasions.

During the civil war the government appointed religious leaders to travel around the world and explain the Federal Military Government's position. For example, fifteen prominent Nigerian church leaders went to Europe and the United States "to explain the situation to Christians abroad," denying that the civil war was a religious war and asserting that most members of the Federal Military Government were Christian.[18] The churches were important organs used by the Federal Government to remind the population of its moral obligation to maintain stability. Through sermons and speeches, religious leaders told Nigerians what was expected of them by the Church and the State. Gowon and other military leaders participated in religious observances. Often, they were asked at religious services to deliver the sermon or to read passages from the scripture.

At a service in Lagos, the Anglican Bishop called on Nigerians to make spiritual sacrifices as they entered the twelfth year of independence in order "to save the country from degradation and spiritual death." Gowon then read the only lesson of the service. Bishop Kale warned that "though we have got political freedom we should not allow rivalry and inordinate ambition to push us back into the bondage of selfishness and greed as was the case in some African countries where united leaders in the pre-Independence days fall . . . because of rivalry and inordinate ambition." In other words, Nigerians must not fight among themselves and must support the Federal Government in its efforts to unite Nigeria."[19] Religious leaders and military leaders considered it an honor to be photographed together on religious occasions. Many such pictures of General Gowon and religious leaders have found their way to the front pages of the newspapers. If one considers the number of newspaper pictures of Gowon and his wife praying, one is not surprised at the image of Gowon as a "man of God." All in all, the instrumental use of religion has resulted in greater exposure and increased support for the Gowon regime during the civil war.

Other symbolic outputs used by the military regime included the affirmation of traditional values by the Gowon regime. Indeed, one of the foremost traditional leader's son was the Chief of Staff of the Army. At the beginning of his rule General Gowon often sent representatives or letters of congratulations to newly installed important traditional rulers. He also congratulated them on their birthdays. These served to reassure the traditional leaders that the Federal Government had not forgotten them and also served as a legitimation mechanism. Not insignificantly, the end of the civil war has witnessed a diminuation of such activities. In the West and Northern states, the local military regimes have moved to formally limit the power of traditional rulers. In the Midwest they are operationally impotent in terms of political power vis a vis the military government.

The successful termination of the civil war increased the prestige of the Nigerian military leader. Except insofar as the military has emerged as a powerful economic group, it cannot be argued, however, that Nigerians hold them in high moral esteem. The point is that the successful completion of the war gave credibility to the ability of the military leadership in one area. Since the military regime extended its concern to the economic development arena, the population was willing to acquiesce and give them an opportunity to prove themselves.

The argument here is that Gowon took over the government under a more fortuitous environment than was the case with the Ironsi take-over. I submit that Gowon's legitimacy strategy has demonstrated a judicious exploitation of the circumstances of the military take-over. The ultimate low political profile approach to modernization, the distrust of labor,[20] the creation of new states, the prosecution of the war until the revocation of secession reflect policies which the coalitions dictated.

Now that the Gowon regime is more securely established, the university constituency, the old politicians of Awolowo's persuasion and, to a certain extent, some sections of the traditional establishment have fallen out of grace.

The strike by the Association of University Teachers and the strong military's response to the strike, the students' opposition to the National Youth Service Corps, the resignation of Chief Awolowo, the dissatisfactions expressed by most politicians associated with the military regime as civilian advisors, and the increasing local authority reforms attest to this point. I will elaborate upon many of these later. For now, however, it is sufficient to stipulate these points and to point out that new coalitions are probably in the process of emergence. Judging by Mr. Ayida's bold assertions and those of other young bureaucrats, one may suspect a phase of the coalition between Federal bureaucrats and the military rulers.

## THE DYNAMICS OF COALITION AND REALITY OF POWER

Bienen has aptly observed that "to rule, the army must form alliances with civilian groups."[21] However, these alliances need not necessarily be formalized. Nor do they need to resemble a cut, dried and baked cake.

Feit sees a national alliance between the military men and the bureaucrats.

> It does not take much imagination to understand why the top and middle ranks of military and civilian hierarchies are drawn to each other. Not only do they operate in a similar organizational milieu, but since both are involved in administration, they also tend to see the world in a somewhat similar way. The world, as they perceive it, is essentially plagued by poor organization and it is organization that can provide the means by which problems can be overcome. Organization is the key. The solution of problems is merely a matter of finding the right key for the particular lock. Conflicting factions and structures of bureaucracy tend to center on the "right" organizational form and the "right" persons to control the reorganizations."[22]

In my judgment, these alliances need to be neither static nor formalized. To his credit, Feit recognized that bureaucracies are not monoliths and that the only time bureaucrats act in unity, if they do at all, is "when the expedient interests of the whole are equally threatened"[23] (p. 12). Such coalitions in the face of a common enemy may be short-term, for the duration of the crisis.

The Nigerian coalition involves the military, the bureaucracy and the civilian commissioners. Before we can talk about this supposed center of power, we must examine the traditional relationship between the higher civil servant and the political masters, the civilians, prior to the military intervention in the political arena of Nigeria. In 1965 and up to the time of the first _coup d'etat_, I carried out an investigation regarding the relationship between the higher civil servants and their ministers, the political masters at the time. Here, I shall only outline the findings pertinent to this discussion.[24]

By way of recapitulation, I found that during the civilian rule ethnicity, regionalism, and political identification were crucial determinants of informal communication not only among higher civil servants but also between higher civil servants and political leaders. Moreover, all indications pointed to the fact that "when the chips were down," the higher civil servant's loyalty was to his tribe or region and not to the nation. The high primordial attachments of higher civil servants and the existence of regionalism and ethnicity in the civil service attested to the degree of fragmentation prevalent in the bureaucracy. Moreover, the negative correlations between similar educational background and informal communication underscored the point that professional identification and group solidarity in the federal bureaucracy was very low.

The positive correlation between a higher civil servant's bureaucratic attainment and similar regional and ethnic backgrounds with members of the political leadership demonstrated the strength and importance of these sectional groups in Nigeria. Furthermore, it showed the weakness of the bureaucratic group, and manifested the bureaucrats' extreme dependence.

Given the lack of single group identification in the Nigerian bureaucracy, it was unable to constitute itself into an independent effective group. It seems to me that a bureaucracy which suffers severely from all these sectional fetters as well as low morale and absence of professional solidarity can hardly demonstrate integrative capability. To do this, it must first rid itself of these weaknesses.

There can be little doubt that the executors of the first coup d'etat did choose a most opportune time for the execution of the plan. Nigerian public opinion seemed to be rebelling at the political excesses of the politicians. The British press and, later, influential opinion in Nigeria had subscribed to the hypothesis that the January coup d'etat was an Ibo coup d'etat carried out in conspiracy with Ibo civilians. If this is found to be true, it can be postulated that the January event was a desperate gamble by Easterners who increasingly felt denied meaningful access to points in the Nigerian polity.

Given the heavy frustration of Eastern higher civil servants and the possible implications of this for the aggregation of Eastern Nigerians' interests, it can be argued that, in desperation, they sought to destroy the system through revolutionary means. Similarly, the disturbances in the West between 1965 and January 1966, can be viewed as a resort to a series of anomic political acts, i.e., violence, arson, as instruments through which the Ijebu-Ekiti Yorubas[25] could effect a restoration of the influence they had under the Awolowo regime. An interesting phenomenon during the Western regional crisis was the declining influence of Ijebu-Ekiti higher civil servants and the ascendency of Oyo Yoruba civil servants into powerful positions in the civil service of the West.

A common feature of the first and second coup d'etats was the fact that in each case, the political change was accompanied by changes in the assignments of the higher civil servants. Since the Nigerian bureaucracy is a career bureaucracy, neither appointive nor electoral, administrators, as long as they are of "good conduct," cannot be dismissed. They can, however, be relegated to unimportant offices.

Following the January event, the North began to lose its political influence. Northern higher civil servants were transferred into less powerful positions and less influential ministries. Efforts were made to centralize the political decision-making machinery, as well as the entire civil services. Many civil servants, following the coup d'etat, expressed grave fears about their future. Personal secretaries to the ministers lost their positions. Those of them who had good qualifications were given positions commensurate with their academic and professional qualifications. Since the Northern Nigerians ranked lowest in the possession of high qualifications, many Northern personal secretaries were demoted to junior service positions. To the extent that they were not able to readjust to this low status and style of life, many of them went back to their villages and towns in the North. This fact, in addition to the waning influence of the Northern region and Northern higher civil servants, made the remaining Northern higher civil servants unkindly disposed to the Ironsi regime.[26] Distrust and sectional solidarity were intensified within the bureaucracy.

At this point in time we have not been able to fathom precisely and completely what role the Northern higher civil servants played in negotiations which resulted in a Northerner leading the Federal Government after the second coup d'etat. However, the fact that Northern permanent secretaries reportedly took active part in these political negotiations should not go unnoticed.[27] Initially its leaders were bent on declaring the secession of the North. "Only a persuasive stand by Northern civil servants at the center and other Nigerian minded civil servants convinced the Northern army officers that secession would bring social and economic disaster upon the North and involve insuperable problems for the army."[28] Indeed, it has been speculated that conditions after the first coup d'etat were such that many Northern higher civil servants would have welcomed a counter coup, or even advocated one.[29]

Eastern Nigerian higher civil servants, following the second coup d'etat, suffered reverses similar to those experienced by Northern higher civil servants. Although I was not in Nigeria at the time of the second coup d'etat, it is reasonable to assume that many Eastern Nigerians were unhappy about the event.

As a result of several events which stemmed from the second coup d'etat, and its aftermath, Nigerian civil servants of Eastern origin were transferred to their region. The effect of this was to remove Eastern higher civil servants, formerly residents in Lagos, away from the geographical center of decision-making. One may argue that their presence would have had a moderating effect on the Nigerian crisis; this is by no means indisputable. What is indisputable is that their presence in their region of origin made it easier for the East to achieve a higher solidarity and carry out their threat to secede. On the other hand, and more important for this discussion, their removal from the bureaucratic seat in Lagos, and the eventual seizure, by the Ojukwu regime,[30] of Federal bureaucratic institutions located in the East had the effect of eliminating from the Federal Executive Council of the Federal Military Government, meant that heavy reliance had to be placed on the bureaucracy. This gave the remaining bureaucrats a sense of importance.

The military coup d'etats, by default, seem to have accomplished three things. First, they ultimately tended to increase the power of the central government. Second, the ensuing civil war seems to have made the remaining civil servants aware of their stake in the existence of a united Nigeria. Third, the civil war seemed to have generated some solidarity in the country; it then became the "Nigerians" against the "rebels."

Prior to the first coup d'etat, one found that in the Nigerian social system, ethnic and regional groups were very powerful, that attachments to these groups were more profound than national attachments, that such attachments increased the dependence of a bureaucrat upon them, and that the consequent high sectional and primordial attachments tended to fragment the existence and operations of governmental bureaucratic groups. But, by the time of the declaration of the civil war, the higher civil servants had gained in morale and stature.

Seemingly, at the beginning of the war an apparent troika was being formed. The troika included the military, the civil servants and the civilian commissioners. Now let us examine the relationship between the civilian commissioners and the bureaucracy.

Prior to the inclusion of civilians in the governing structure of the country, the Gowon regime, like its predecessor, had only two formalistic structures, the Supreme Military Council and the Federal Executive Council. The Supreme Military Council under the Gowon regime consisted of General Gowon, Commanders in the navy, air force and Army Chief of Staff, eleven military governors, one civilian administrator of East-Central State and two ranking police officials. The permanent secretaries represented the ministries.

It was not until the establishment of the Federal Executive Council, (FEC) that the civilians were brought into the regime. The Supreme Military Council

(SMC) delegated some of its functions to the FEC. Almost all the functions of the SMC under the Constitution Suspension and Modification Decree of 1967 (No. 8) were delegated to FEC. The exceptions were:

1. matters of defense and security;
2. constitution and political matters;
3. appointment of judges of the Supreme Court and the High Court of Lagos;
4. appointment of ambassadors and officers of group six and above in the Federal Public Service;
5. higher education institutions.

In theory then, with only minor exceptions, the civilian commissioners in the military government regarded themselves as having the power of the old ministers. Indeed, all of the thirty regional and Federal commissioners interviewed indicated that this was their understanding of their status and power at the time of their appointment. In this respect, most of the civilian commissioners have been very disappointed. Many said that they found some of their permanent secretaries to be too arrogant. Some have claimed that civil servants run the country and are too powerful. Others have gone so far as to say that the civilian commissioners are figure heads.

Most civilian commissioners were not bashful about the reason for their political impotence. One said:

> In the colonial days the business of government was the responsibility of senior officials whose main job was to please the Colonial Office. It seems to me today that the impression is gaining ground that we are experiencing something similar to what used to obtain during the colonial days. The senior officials, we are told, are not so much concerned about their responsibilities to their respective commissioners in certain governments but to the military rulers direct whom they have always tried to impress: in most cases they have direct access to the Heads of Government and are said to have more influence on them than the Commissioner.[31]

In my judgment the reason for this increased influence over the military derived from the early post second coup days when the military officers found themselves in the position of political governance without prior training. In the absence of civilian advisers, the permanent secretary filled the vacuum and they played a direct and important role as policy adviser and executants. The military officers, the new political masters, have therefore developed a working relationship of considerable trust with these civil servants. Psychologically then, the new political masters have ingratiated themselves to the higher civil servants. The higher civil servants have been suddenly thrust into positions of greater efficacy and higher status but the new civilian advisers, contrary to their expectations, are now experiencing a revolution of rising frustration. A commissioner explained the predicament of the civilian commissioners this way:

> Conscious of their position, and sometimes out of fear for what they might have done which they do not want exposed or lack of principle, the Civil Commissioners have accepted their position as "fait accompli." They therefore do not have the courage to challenge certain actions of their Permanent Secretaries nor do they dare say or do anything contrary to the wishes of their "overlords." The most annoying thing is that they keep grumbling as do most other people, but the courage to voice out is lacking. This is the unhealthy situation in which the present Administration has found itself, and any honest and impartial observer cannot fail to see this naked fact. Whether this is true or not there seems to be a lack of coordination and/or cooperation as a result of this lack of confidence, jealousy, envy, rivalry and suspicion.
>
> In fairness to the Civil Service one must admit that the experience they had with the "Politician" ministers during the Civilian Regime has made them suspicious of their new "masters," and therefore made them adopt this attitude. Also, the Military Rulers, it should be realized, did, and they could not do otherwise, have to rely on the Civil Servants who have been continuously running the Administration more than on these mere "public relations consultants."[32]

A minister in the civilian administration was an elected official with a political base. He could speak with authority, disagree and offer advice. The worst that could happen to him is that he would no longer be a minister; he would still be a member of the House. He was not likely to be detained. In other words, the civilian commissioner on the one hand saw his role as that of a political minister, but he was cognizant of the fact that unlike the political minister, he had no sound basis of power. He could be dismissed summarily by the military governor or the Chairman of the SMC. He felt that the military officers, as well as his permanent secretaries, recognized his achilles heels too easily.

Another reason for the feeling of impotence on the part of the commissioners had to do with their perception of their relationship with the military Governor as opposed to their relationship with his civilian counterpart, "the Premier." "A Prime Minister in an elected government fears his colleagues and party members, for they are all elected and even if he dismissed a minister or has the Party Whip withdrawn from him in Parliament, he cannot dismiss him from Parliament so that he and his ministers must treat each other as colleagues and with respect, of course. This is not the case in a military regime."[33]

Civilian commissioners indicated that they were not consulted before the decision of the military to stay in power until 1976. In fact, they did not have prior knowledge of this information until it was publicly announced. Similarly, there were no prior consultations on portfolio changes of commissioners. One commissioner joked that it was as if the power-that-be was afraid to keep the commissioners in a ministry long enough to acquire the good knowledge and expertise necessary for one to do the job of a commissioner.

The fact is that many, not all, of the commissioners are former politicians. Therefore, their advice is sometimes viewed with suspicion out of fear that they might be paving the way for their return to power.

Many Federal civilian commissioners indicated that the higher civil servant was no longer the "power behind the scene" but the "power on the scene." Obviously, this represents a reversal of power relationship.

A prominent civil servant has advanced a different perception of the power and the role of the civilian commissioners. Admittedly, not all higher civil servants have boldly espoused this point of view but many have acted in ways which suggest their acceptance of Ayida's definition. The permanent secretary, Federal Ministry of Finance, state, "Civilian commissioners were appointed to help run the government not as political masters but as servants of the military, who are the new political masters." He regarded permanent secretaries and commissioners as "fellow advisers to the power-that-be." He felt that, "If the commissioners had exercised less powers than former ministers, it was not because their function has been 'usurped by civil servants' but because authority now resides in the military."[34]

In the quotes that follow, one sees a sample of the attempts of higher civil servants to legitimize their new role.

> It is my belief that the bureaucracy, depending of course on its leadership, is unlikely ever again to be the silent onlooker in vital national issues to the same extent as before our crisis. The tendency of those elected into office to say that they were answerable to the people and therefore entitled to set aside rules and regulations which were designed to achieve equity is not likely to be mutely accepted in the future . . . When trouble comes it is not only the elected that suffers. The electors suffer even more . . . The bureaucratic elite, if properly integrated can, I hope, play the role of the impartial abiter between the political underdog and the political top dog in the future. (p. 24)
>
> The bureaucracy is now in a situation where it has, with great brilliance, defined set objectives for the nation and thereby raised high hopes. The people who, as I said early, provide the environment in which the bureaucrat operates now demand implementation of policies aimed at attaining these objectives "with maximum equity and minimum error."[35]
>
> In like manner national objectives which could be called the will of the nation are not drawn up by the people. Ours were produced by bureaucrats on behalf of the people, with the people providing the environment from within which support is obtained and demands received which help to define the bonds within which bureaucrats try to define the nation's interests."

It is interesting to note that it is not only the civilian commissioners who bemoaned the new power of the Federal bureaucrats. Brigadier Esuene, a military governor, complained publicly to the press when he claimed that the "Federal Ministry of Mines and Power is frustrating his states' development by placing obstacles in their way for rural electrification."[36] What is important here is not the substance *per se*. Rather, it is the fact that a member of the Supreme Military Council, one of those with whom "authority now resides" felt the need to resort to public pressure rather than pressure within the authoritative structure of the SMC. (Of course, the example here falls within the state-federal relationship which shall receive further explication later in the discourse.)

The business community has started to grumble at the apparent ubiquitous civil servant. The President of the Lagos Chamber of Commerce has criticized the appointment of permanent secretaries to multiple jobs. He feels these will lead to inefficiency and untimely death.[37]

Of course there remains a few higher civil servants who hold on to the old school in terms of the relationship between the bureaucratic elite and the political class. This school is represented by Peter Odumosu, the head of Service of the Western Civil Service. He argues that:

> A civil servant must not allow himself to play the role of a politician. His job is to assemble facts, analyze them objectively and suggest alternative courses of action, leaving it to politicians to decide on a course of action after passing political judgment on the matter. Politicization of the Civil Service can only lead to sycompany.
>
> Politicization is therefore not the answer. Nor is it in the public interest.[37]

On the whole, I have found that the civilian commissioners who have expressed relatively few dissatisfactions with their jobs were those who have informal and personal access to their military governors, a sound knowledge of their ministry, a strong political base and an assertive personality. The most important single variable relates to the relationship between the commissioner and the military governor. Where the relationship was excellent, the commissioner was most likely to be successful.

In Kwara, South-East, Midwest and West there have been incidents which clearly demonstrated that all was not well between the Chief Executive and the bureaucracy. In the Midwest there was a celebrated "confidential" feud between the military governor and the regional head of the civil service which led to the dismissal of the latter. The substance of the feud, which cannot be discussed here, is perceived by many as indicative of problems involved in active personalistic style of political leadership when the bureaucracy is headed by men who adhere to a more orthodox definition of their role. The South-Eastern State as well as Rivers State have had forced resignations. Kwara State military governor has demonstrated his lack of trust in the bureaucratic leadership by ordering the search of the homes of his higher civil servants.[39] Indicative of the danger of personalistic political leadership is the reported feud between Major General Adebayo and his attorney general regarding matters of bureaucratic rules and norms. Generally, most military governors and certainly General Gowon have placed great confidence in the bureaucracy. General Gowon, time and again, has publicly acknowledged his own indebtedness to the higher civil servants whom he holds in the highest esteem.

In Nigeria, unlike Ghana under NLC, disagreements between military governors and civil servants have not led to the demise of military governors. In Ghana, for example, two regional commissioners were posted back to the military following interference in administrative process. (See Pinkney, pp. 111-112) General Adebayo's posting was a consequence of political unrest and extremely heavy and persistent demand from the West.

FOOTNOTES

1. See Olorunsola, <u>The Politics of Cultural Subnationalism in Africa</u>, Chapter 1. Garden City: Doubleday and Company, Inc., 1972.

2. See Henry Bienen. <u>The Military Intervenes: Case Studies in Political Development</u>. (New York: Russell Sage Foundation, 1968)

3. See Mr. A. Ayida, paper presented to the Nigerian Association of Economic and Social Research in Enugu on June 22, 1973.

4. Interview with Mr. J. S. Tarka, Lagos, October, 1972.

5. O'Connell in <u>African Integration</u>. Arthur Hazelwood (ed.) Oxford University Press, 1967, p. 176.

6. <u>Ibid</u>.

7. In the North, therefore, there were no Commissions of Inquiry during the Ironsi regime.

8. Interview with some advisers of Ironsi, Freetown, Sierra Leone, 1972. Also see <u>Nigerian Opinion</u>, December 1966, p. 1, Vol. 2, No. 12.

9. See <u>Nigerian Opinion</u>, December 1966, p. 1, Vol. w, No. 12.

10. General Gowon's statement on the occasion of his first visit to the Midwest. "The Midwest has always been in the forefront in the struggle to keep Nigeria as one country. I have always insisted that if the Midwest people did not consistently advocate the principle of One Nigeria in the darkest days of 1966, there would be no Nigeria today."

11. Consider the efforts for a Middle Belt state particularly the Minorities Commission created by the British Colonial government prior to the granting of self government. See Cmnd 505, 1958.

12. Ayida, <u>op cit</u>.

13. The tradition of sending Middle Belters to the Federation to fill Northern quotas in the Federal bureaucracy and governmental corporation had seen established under Sir. Ahmadu Bello and Sir Tafawa Balewa.

14. Parenthetically Gowon did not encourage the use of his name "Jack" or "Jacob" in the North.

15. An Ibo has been added to the Federal Executive Council.

16. Certainly the Nigerian civil servants and intellectuals who visited this country took pride in asserting that no one is indispensable. The Nigerian consulate publications stressed how other Nigerians proudly fill the vacuum created.

17. On November 19, twenty-five Western State leaders led by Chief Awolow were presented a memorandum to Gowon. It called for the withdrawal of Northern troops from the West and their replacement with Western troops. <u>Africa Report</u>, January 1967, p. 39.

18. West Africa, June 15, 1968, p. 706.

19. West Africa, April 1, 1972, p. 405.

20. This will be discussed in Part IV.

21. Brewer, op. cit., pp. xvii.

22. Feit, The Armed Bureaucrats, Boston (Houghton Mifflin Company, 1973), p. 11.

23. Ibid., p. 12.

24. A comprehensive explicative is available in Journal of Developing Areas, October, 1968.

25. See Olorunsola, Chapter 1, Politics of Cultural Subnationalism in Africa, op. cit.

26. General Ironsi took over the Federal Government following the coup d'etat in January 1966.

27. See West Africa, August 13, 1966.

28. O'Connell in Hazlewood, op. cit., p. 176.

29. Father O'Connell's article in Africa Report of February 1966 testifies to deep sectional bureaucratic involvement.

30. Col. Ojukwu led Eastern Nigerians into secession.

31. Alhaji Maitama Sule

32. Ibid.

33. Ibid., pp. 5-6. (Alhaji Aminu Kano is in complete agreement with this position).

34. Reported in West Africa, May 7, 1973, p. 615.

35. Quoted here and there from S. B. Awoniyi "Integration Within the Bureaucratic Elite."

36. Mimeo, October 11, 1971, pp 17 and 24, West Africa, April 16, 1973.

37. West Africa, May 7, 1973, p. 616.

38. Peter Odumosu, "The Civil Service and the Political Class," Mimeo., October 14, 1971, p. 12.

39. Even the East Central State Administrator, exercising his power as the equivalent of a military governor, detained a permanent secretary and six other government higher civil servants, under the Public Land and State Security Order, without prefering charges. See West Africa, May 7, 1973, p. 616.

CHAPTER VI

LEGITIMACY ENGINEERING OF NLC

From February, 1966, to June, 1969, the NLC was a government centered around a coalition of the army, police and higher civil servants.[1] Around the periphery were a number of advisory committees without executive authority. With the exception of the economic and administrative committees, the former opposition politicians, together with the academicians attempted to use these committees to proffer advice and exercise influence on the policy of the NLC. Two pressure centers vied for control--the former opposition politicians vied with academicians on the one hand and the bureaucrats on the other. Seemingly the bureaucracy had the upper hand in this battle for influence. In any case, the military was anxious to retain its excellent relationship with both groups as they represented the key to the success of its legitimacy efforts. The National Advisory Council was supposed to consolidate the works of the committees and help to broaden the support base of the NLC. Its membership therefore included opposition politicians, academicians, trade unionists, traditional rulers and businessmen. The unsuccessful countercoup provided the signal, the opportunity, and the impetus for the broadening of NLC political base.

When the army overthrew the Nkrumah regime on February 29, 1966, it established the National Liberation Council (NLC). This council was composed of an equal number of police and army personnel. The first problem which faced the new regime was that of legitimacy. Although the CPP regime had had its legitimacy eroded as a result of poor economic performance, poor party organization and the excessive use of coercion, the leaders of the coup were unsure of the durability of the deposed regime. Consequently, the NLC took judicious precautions to garner support and sustain its power.

The new regime sought to ascertain its support by including major ethnic groups in the NLC and by establishing a joint military-police regime. Thus its membership included four army officers:

        General Ankrah      a Ga;
        General Kotoka      an Ewe;
        General Ocran      a Fanti;
        General Afrifa      an Ashanti;

and the four police officers:

        Mr. Nunoo      a Ga;
        Mr. Deku      an Ewe;
        Mr. Yakubu      a Gushigu-;
        Mr. Harlley      an Ewe.

Military or police officers were appointed as "Regional Commissioners" to govern the regions.

One of NLC's initial tasks was to break Nkrumah's symbolic instruments of legitimacy. Thus, the statues of Nkrumah were damaged and/or removed; streets were renamed,      (Black Square became Independence Square), and Nkrumah's picture was removed from Ghanaian money. The CPP, the only legal political party, was banned in Ghana. Moreover, through the Ministry of Labor and Social Welfare, an organized campaign was carried out in 700 towns and villages. The purpose of the campaign was to discredit the deposed regime and explain the reasons why the coup was necessary. In addition, durbars of chiefs and traditional peoples were held in various parts of the country. At these durbars the members of the NLC or their representatives, regional commissioners, were presented with addresses of welcome by the traditional leaders and their people and the government took the opportunities to stress the failures of the deposed regime and justify the action of the military leaders. In short, the NLC projected the image of liberators, restorers of the rule of law, patriots who risked their lives for Ghana,    haters of corruption, dictatorship, nepotism and inefficiency.

The NLC members attempted to calm the fears of civil libertarians by making the relatively early preparation for return to "representative democracy," and portrayed themselves as the true lovers of African unity because of their belief in noninterference in the domestic affairs of other African states. They presented themselves as Ghanaians tired of Nkrumah's duplicity. Furthermore, in their legitimacy engineering, they: (1) carefully cultivated and favorably responded to the friendly overtures of the West; (2) thoroughly dismantled Ghana's ties with the East; (3) pictured themselves as true believers in the United Nations; (4) froze the assets of prominent CPP members and CPP officials; (5) introduced the disqualification decree to ensure that the survival of the CPP would never be a reality; (6) appointed about forty judicial commissioners of inquiry; (7) decided to eradicate what they regarded as Nkrumah's successful propaganda efforts in Ghana. Seemingly the NLC agreed to fight fire with fire. The NLC portrayed Nkrumah as a "socialist crook," "architect of waste" and it used the various commissions of inquiry to discredit the person and the administration of Nkrumah; (8) rounded up the leaders of the CPP and those suspected of strong alliances with Nkrumah and put them in protective custody. Some of them were kept in protective custody until about the end of 1968. By that time, however, all of these people had been cleared. As a counterpoise, those who had been imprisoned under the Preventive Detention Act (PDA) of Nkrumah were released. For the most part, these were either opposition members or former party colleagues of Nkrumah who had dared to express disagreement with the deposed President. Quite understandably there was no love lost between these people and the deposed President. The released victims of the PDA were grateful to their liberators. Consequently, they worked eagerly to support the new regime. The CPP leaders who were detained and later released by the NLC seemed eager to desert a sinking ship. Therefore, they felt the need to support the new regime and they demonstrated their loyalty beyond any reasonable doubt. This helped the new regime in its legitimacy engineering efforts.

In the broadcast (radio broadcast, D. G., 25 February, 1966) announcing the military take-over, the military justified its action in terms of:

1. dislike for the concentration of power in the hands of Nkrumah and the capricious use of that power;

2. the abuse of independence, rights and liberties of Ghanaians;

3. chaotic economic conditions.[2]

These were the reasons publicly adduced.

The NLC set up a Political Committee in June, 1966. This committee offered invaluable assistance to the NLC with regard to the engineering of its legitimacy. It sent very detailed memoranda to the NLC regarding what it should do to promote its legitimacy. The details regarding the political image of the NLC were completely put into effect by the NLC. The memoranda advised the NLC regarding pacification. The committee submitted plans on the projected use of the news media as an instrument of legitimacy, and warned about the danger of increasing unemployment. It provided the NLC with lists of persons to be considered for appointments to the commissions of inquiry and other commissions.

The Political Committee's greatest difficulty with the NLC arose out of the NLC's tendency to ignore the political implications of economic policies. The Political Committee did not believe that politics and economy were unrelated. Consequently, they demanded to be informed regarding economic proposals so they could have an input. It is in this field that the Political Committee suffered frustration.[3]

Perhaps the most plausible explanation for the lack of receptivity to the efforts and desires of the Political Committee to have an input in economic policy formulations is the NLC belief that Ghana found itself in the predicament because Nkrumah "eliminated completely from the decision-making process and policy formulation, technical and professional officers at all levels of administration, thus depriving the nation of the best available use of technical and professional expertise."[4] This should not be seen as a disdain for the politics of negotiation. Rather, it should be viewed for what it is; an effort to separate the economic from the political considerations.

The analysis of the membership of the civilian commissioners with ministerial responsibility is revealing. About fifty percent of these commissioners were technocrats or experts in the fields to which they were appointed. Consider the following: the commissioner of agriculture was an agriculturalist, the commissioner of economic development was a former government statistician, the commissioner of education was an academician, the commissioner of health was a doctor, the commissioner for justice was a lawyer, the commissioner for labor was a former International Labor Organization official, the local government commissioner was a town clerk and the trade commissioner was a permanent secretary. About twenty-five percent of the commissioners were ex-civil servants.

These facts gave rise to the same problem as was discussed with regard to Nigeria; namely, the role and power of the civil servant in a military regime. Before the civilian commissioners were appointed, NLC committees (administrative, economic, foreign affairs) were composed almost exclusively of civil servants who wielded effective power. Since most of the military men were unfamiliar with civilian administration and because of the importance that the NLC attached to the restoration of the economy, they had to depend initially on the bureaucrat.[5]

In terms of other professional representations, it is pertinent to observe that the lawyers held ten of the thirty-one memberships on the National Advisory Committee, and that seven of the twenty-three member Political Committee were lawyers. There were nine academicians on the National Advisory Committee and six on the Political Committee. Only one former politician was appointed as a commissioner, but five lawyers and two accountants were chosen.[6]

The civil servants were accused of proffering short-run economic policies and charged with being incapable of perceiving the ramifications of economic policies. They were seen as consciously trying to preserve their newly found power at the expense of national interests.[7] Significantly, the United Party members were approved as diplomat, public board member, and newspaper editorships. Fourteen of the twenty-three members of the Political Committee were active anti-CPP politicians, ten of them were in fact United Party members. Interestingly the former Chairman and Vice Chairman of the Political Committee became the President and Prime Minister of Ghana, succeeding the NLC regime. Although there was no serious attempt at ethnic balancing of the Political Committee membership, there was regional balancing. The Attorney General was a former United Party politician.[8]

Right from the beginning the military regime wanted Ghanaians to recognize it as a corrective regime. Therefore, in September of 1966, Constitutional Commissioners were appointed. They were charged with making proposals regarding the future constitution of the country. This was designed to prevent any anxiety which the liberal section of the population may have had about military rule.

Relative to the strength of the original committee; it is generally believed that the Economic Advisory Committee was the most powerful. Part of the alleged power of this committee reflected the desire of the military to get away from what it regarded as the politization of the economy. In any case, the academicians and other Ghanaian libertarians deeply resented this fact because they felt that the civil servants increased their power by isolating the NLC from public opinion. The unpopular decisions taken by the NLC were put on the doorsteps of the civil servants who were sometimes accused of misleading the NLC in order to weaken the government. The NLC was being pressured to rely less on the civil servants. Functionally, then, it seems that the civil servant became a scapegoat for poor government performance and the NLC remained pure for the time being. For its part, the bureaucracy did in fact attain greater power and higher status. The constraints they porportedly suffered at the hands of party functionaries of the CPP disappeared. All in all, the civil service morale was high.

It is an interesting indication of the change in the status of the bureaucracy in Ghana that it responded directly and publicly to these charges. Seemingly, the days when civil servants were to be seen and not heard were gone. Mr. Boaten, the principal secretary in the ministry of external affairs, responded to the charges in the Legon Observer, 22 July 1966.[9] Other civil servants addressed themselves to aspects of the public charges.

Part of the criticisms against the civil servants included the charge that they prevented the implementation of NLC plan to eradicate the Administrative Committee. Furthermore, the Ghana economic policy was said to be myopic because of its control by civil servants who are said to be short-sighted.[10]

Robert Pinkney[11] reported that civil servants did admit that in some areas they did have free hand. The Administrative Committee reduced the ministries from thirty-two to eighteen. The Economic Committee, made up of mostly civil servants, could decide for themselves how to deal with budgetary problems, inflation, deficits and foreign debts. Within ministries it was possible to reverse policies the civil servants disliked. Consequently, the officials were able to get rid of many state farms which they did not like. Similarly, the Ministry of Labor ended compulsory trade union membership, which they were never enthusiastic about. My own informal interviews confirmed these observations.

The significance of these is that in terms of reference group theory, many of the actions which seemingly show the NLC as pro-England or pro-West sometimes represent the acquiescence of the ruling military-police regime in the advice of the pro-West governmental bureaucracy.

After the abortive coup in 1969, NLC decree 183 of 30 June 1969 was promulgated. This decree established the institution of civilian commissioners with ministerial powers. Fourteen civilian commissioners were appointed. These new civilian commissioners, together with the members of the NLC who survived the abortive countercoup, constituted the National Executive Council, charged with the general direction and control of the government. The new civilian commissioners were included in a new body, the National Advisory Council. The National Advisory Council displaced the political, legal, foreign affairs and publicity committees. Nine members of the defunct political committees were included in the new council. Eight other members representing various groups were added to the council.[12]

In establishing its legitimacy the NLC regime used the traditional institutions, the bureaucracy, the intellectuals, and members of the opposition. In all cases only those institutions which were dissatisfied with the deposed CPP regime were used as instruments of legitimacy. By coincidence, those institutions, and particularly their members, upon whom the NLC relied, were of a more conservative bent. Nkrumah's theory of socialism and anti-capitalism had to be discredited if the coup was in fact undertaken to bring about fundamental changes. Therefore, if NLC policies were pro-Western it may be just because the military officers were pro- the country where they had their military training. It is more plausible, in my opinion, to argue that the NLC was pro-West because it was the pragmatic thing to do, given their goals and the circumstances under which they took over the government of Ghana. In any case, it is well to remember that the economic policies which suggest a pro-Western orientation of the NLC in fact came from civilian technocrats of the Economic Committee.

## NRC. LEGITIMACY ENGINEERING

In Chapter IV, I observed the poor economic condition in which Ghana continued to find itself during the Busia regime. While some of these economic problems were clearly inherited from the previous regime, others had their roots in the policies of the Busia government. Apparently, the straw that broke the camel's back was the drastic devaluation of the cedis (Ghanaian currency).

Unlike the first military regime of Ghana, the second military regime was not very favorably regarded by the academicians. This will be obvious in the chapter dealing with Ghanaian academicians. Whatever good-will the Busia regime might have had among the rural dwellers quickly evaporated with the drastic devaluation and its attendant high prices. The bureaucracy was not very happy with some policies of Busia. For example, they did not approve of the withdrawal of privileges and allowances from the senior civil servants. Nor were some of them very happy about the unilateral termination of 500 civil servants without due process. Generally, the Busia regime had little support from the military. First, the devaluation of the cedi gave the military a feeling of _deja vue_ which they detested very much. In addition, like the senior civil servants, their privileges had been withdrawn and there were rumors of more to come.[13] The Ewe military officers were still a factor to reckon with in the Ghana army because of their number. Many of them had not been happy with the later days of NLC and the disqualification of Gbedema. Consequently, they were not eager to defend the Busia regime. Labor perhaps felt most disaffected with the Busia regime. The TUC was disbanded, devaluation had hit them hard and there was an equation of the Busia regime with anti-labor sentiments.[14] The students and their leaders had been publicly disgraced in parliament for daring to request the government partly to declare their assets in accordance with the law. In addition, there was a general feeling that the Busia regime was too pro-British and that it had deliberately become anti-nationalistic and anti-African unity.

This was the environment under which Col. Acheampong took over the reigns of power with his coup. If my legitimacy proposition that the strategy of legitimacy adopted by a military regime is dependent partly on the circumstances under which it took over control is correct and to the extent that the NRC ousted the government of the Progress Party led by Dr. Busia one can expect the following strategy of legitimacy in Ghana under NRC:

1. the detention of Progress Party political functionaries and leaders;

2. the banning of political parties and activities;

3. the freezing of the assets of the Progress Party and those of political functionaries to deny them the financial sources for resistance;

4. the regard of academicians with benign neglect or hostility;

5. the use of media resources to discredit the Busia regime; this should include changes of newspaper editors and editorial policies, as well as the use of television and radio; and

6. the negation of policies regarded as unpopular and obnoxious in the eyes of most Ghanaians or specific groups whose support may be regarded as crucial.

Subsequent discussion in this book shows that these actions were taken by the NRC. In addition, the discussion in Chapter IV documents the pursuance of legitimacy through performance strategy. There was:

1. the subsidization of essential commodities;

2. the restoration of civil servant allowances and those of the armed forces;

3. the restoration of the TUC and several policies designed to entice labor support (labor has been alienated by the Busia government);

4. the repudiation of certain categories of debts;

5. the assertion of economic nationalism;

6. the revaluation of the cedis; and

7. the "Operation Feed Yourself" program.

To underscore the point, the university students did not give their support to the NRC until after the speech repudiating the debts of Ghana and asserting economic nationalism. The _Legon Observer_, the organ of the Ghanaian academicians, did not have any supportive statements until after the repudiation of certain categories of debts.

Of course, the second military regime had an advantage over the first one; it learned from the NLC experience. For example, the basic structure of government was followed--national commissioners, regional commissioners. It refrained until now from the inclusion of civilians as commissioners (with the exception of the Attorney General). This was a surprise since Col. Acheampong promised to do that in his second broadcast to the nation. There were suggestions that the inclusion of only one civilian in the ruling council indicated hesitanc or unwillingness on the part of prominent civilians to getinvolved with the military. However, the fact that the National Advisory Council made up of civilians agreed to serve would tend to negate this suggestion. (The advisory had to be disbanded because Ghanaians reacted unfavorably to its members.) Since then, it appears that the notion of a standing advisory council has been discarded.

All in all, the NRC used essentially identical legitimacy strategies as the NLC; e.g., regional commissioners visiting durbars, personal visits and speeches by national and regional commissioners, news media appeals. Some members of the former opposition party during the Busia government became unofficial advisers of NRC. The image of Busia government was elitist. Here is one significant difference between the NLC and the NRC; the image which the NRC sought to convey was that of service-oriented soldiers who were unaffected by high status. They drove small cars, no motorcycle escorts, no pomp and majesty, no change in military ranks of the members of the council. Col. Acheampong succeeded in conveying this image of "the man of the people." Ghana's image of pro-West was being transformed into one of nationalism. This transformation accorded Ghana symbolic support on the part of most black African countries with the possible exception of Ivory Coast. Unlike the previous military regime, the present one has involved more military men in the administration and governance of the country.

## FOOTNOTES

1. For a more detailed study of NLC, see Robert Pinkney. *Ghana Under Military Rule*, 1966-69, London: Methuen and Company, Ltd., 1972.

2. *Daily Graphic*, February 25, 1966.

3. Informal discussions with two members of the Political Committee, May 1972.

4. "A New Era in Ghana." Ministry of Information, 1966, p. 20. State Publishing Corp., 1966, p. 20.

5. BDG Folson, Legon Observer, July 8, 1966.

6. See Robert Pinkney, *Ghana Under Military Rule, 1966-1969*. London: Methuen & Co. Ltd., 1972.

7. See *Daily Graphic* January 30, 1968, and June 24, 1967, *Legon Observer*, May 12, 1967.

8. See Jon Krause in *Politics of Coup d'etat*, op.cit., pp. 120-123.

9. Other civil servants addressed themselves to aspects of the public charges. See *Daily Graphic* of January 16, 1967 and January 19, 1967.

10. See *Daily Graphics*, January 30, 1968, June 24, 1967.

11. Robert Pinkney, op. cit., p. 64.

12. *Ibid.*, 75.

13. Not insignificantly Col. Acheampong's first broadcast after his seizure of power flatly expressed the military's anger on this score.

14. For more details see the section dealing with the military regime's relationship with various segments of their societies.

PART IV

THE MILITARY REGIMES' RELATIONSHIP WITH CRUCIAL SEGMENTS
OF THEIR POLITICAL COMMUNITIES

## CHAPTER VII
## NIGERIAN ACADEMICIANS

### A. LECTURERS

During the civilian period the Nigerian lecturers could not exercise meaningful influence because, like their counterparts in the bureaucracy and in active political life, they suffered from sectionalism and primordial sentiments. Consider the following facts in support of these contentions. Professor Njoku, an Ibo, had been the first Vice Chancellor of the University of Lagos. Factionalism surfaced between the Ibo lecturers and Yoruba lecturers at the university. As a result, two candidates, one Ibo, one Yoruba, were put up for the position. There were very intense demonstrations of support for the Ibo candidate by the Ibos. This controversy eventually spread to the students, leading to mass resignations by Ibos when their candidate was defeated. Moreover, at Ibadan where an Ibo was the Vice-Chancellor, the Yoruba lecturers claimed that the Vice-Chancellor practiced favoritism towards his tribesmen. Prior to the beginning of the civil war, therefore, there was considerable sentiment for his replacement. Generally, the lecturers who participated as active politicians in the old regime were perceived to have performed less than honorably with regard to the issue of Nigerian unity and public service.

When the second coup d'etat broke out, the Yoruba intellectuals were ambivalent. On the one hand, some found their sensitivities offended by what they regarded as the unnecessary brutality and bloodshed by the leaders of the coup. Indeed, most of them were afraid of the implications of the new power structure which they perceived, then, as conservative. For many, there were problems of personal, job and regional security. But as the days progressed and concessions were made to guarantee their regional security and as the East became intransigent, the dominant sentiment among them became the preservation of Nigeria as an entity because there lies the job security of most of the lecturers of two of the three Nigerian national universities. Ahmadu Bello University was a regionally owned university and employed largely expatriate lecturers. The University of Ife was owned by the Western government. The lecturers then joined together to support the war effort. The "hawks" among them wrote letters in support of the war effort. For example, there was a spirited public discussion in the Daily Times by two colleagues at Ahmadu Bello University, one of them advocating the right of the FMG to ignore the principle in international law in the conduct of war. Some lecturers were sent abroad to solicit support and sympathy for the Federal government's position. These were some of the many symbolic supports which the lecturers gave to the FMG. In addition, some of them were appointed as commissioners in the regions and in the Federal government. There were also a series of newspaper articles written by the lecturers in 1968 and 1968 regarding what the future structure and policies of the Nigerian political system should be after the war had been successfully terminated. Most of these were lofty and idealistic suggestions, at least they were perceived as such by many power Federal bureaucrats.

Upon the conclusion of the war the committee of ten lecturers issued a broadsheet calling for a longer period of military rule. The committee felt that three more years would be sufficient.

> The immediate objective should be: consolidation of the military victory; rehabilitation of displaced persons throughout the Federation; and reconstruction of essential services. A specified time limit of three years should be set as a target for their achievement . . . The government will need to move closer to the people, understand their aspirations and genuinely plan to alleviate economic hardships imposed by the war conditions; ruthlessly wipe out corruption in all classes and at all levels of society . . . not excluding high government officials and military personnel; . . . look in to the state structure of the Federation with a view to satisfying the genuine aspirations of some dissatisfied parts of the country . . . and crack down sharply on all manifestations of sectional strife and distrust.[1]

This passage clearly demonstrates that the appraisal of the academicians regarding the political performance of the military at this point in time, was not overwhelmingly positive. At the same time, it shows that some lecturers were optimistic about the potential of the military. In general, the lecturers were unhappy with the manner in which low level soldiers went about their security duties with maximum arrogance and what they regarded as disrespect for their status and disrespect for the citizens. However, these were tolerated as necessary compromises in periods of war.

As soon as the war was over, however, there was more openness regarding the views of the military establishment concerning the Nigerian academicians and vice-versa. Consider this general assessment of the military regime by *Nigerian Opinion*, a publication of the Nigerian Current Affairs Society and compare this with the attitude of the paper in the early period of military rule. (See Chapter 9, Footnote 4.)

> Psychologists call it *deja vu*, that sensation which one has of having been in some place even though one had in fact never been there before. This is what is so disturbing--perhaps the right word is frightening--about the present. It seems we have been here before, and we can tell what it (is) on the next turning. 'Strikes' of technicians at the Airway, of workers at the textile mills in Kaduna; doctors and nurses on a 'go slow' and the two main teaching hospitals, university workers on a "work to rule' in Lagos and Ibadan; threats of strikes in the Midwest and the West; students protesting. The list can be extended almost indefinitely. It seems there are few places without some form of unrest or the other. It is also so reminiscent of 1964-65 and we know what came after that; or March/April 1966 and we also know what followed not very long after. The frightening thing is the feeling that we seem to be back to those times and can almost tell what next to expect. Everything seems so predictable.
>
> It seems predictable that in the face of social unrest, the reaction of the authorities will be to pretend there is nothing wrong. This capacity for self-deception is now so ingrained in us that it has become a national characteristic and there are of course those who are only too prepared to play on it. What visitor, which departing diplomat, has not told us that we have a great future if we are not so great? . . . . Another facet of our capacity for self-deception is the inability or perhaps unwillingness, to see the expressions behind the mask, a propensity for taking most things at their face value. How else could we explain the fact that after his tour of the states, General Gowon could tell us all was well with the country when only a few months before he had said we have never had it so bad! And yet not much had changed between the time the first statement was made and the second. If anything, what changes there had been was certainly not for the better. There are, of course, times when those in authority have had to recognize the

fact of unrest and, not untypically, the reaction follows a predictable high handedness as in the closure of Sketch publishing for one day by the Military Governor of the West and the threat to close Asaba textile mills by the Governor of the Midwest. Typically rather than examine the basis of the unrest, both men sought to wish the problem away. You can coerce people for some of the time but not for all of the time. This was a lesson the politicians proved incapable of learning. By all indications, it seems to be one that the present rulers are also unable to appreciate.

There seems to be a pattern to the present social unrest . . . . The basis of this is not difficult to see. The affluence of a small section of the population contrast too sharply with the poverty of the general mass whose plight has not been improved by rising prices. In the towns, paying for living spaces is proving to be an impossible burden on the meagre incomes of the large section of the urban population who cannot even look to the four year development plan for some hope of relief. And the Price Control Board has turned out to be worse than useless-- its inception was perhaps misconceived in the first place. Moreover, while one appreciates the noble intentions which spurred the creation of the Adebo Commission, it was open to question whether the commission would not end up creating more problems than it was intended to solve. The main problem of course lies in the choice of priorities. A Wage Review Commission is not likely to solve the problems of rising prices. Instead it is more likely to raise aspirations, which if not met can only lead to rising frustration. And in the context of rising prices, one wonders why it should still be thought expedient and desirable to retain the more or less blanket import restriction demanded and imposed by the Federal Ministry of Finance. That policy like many others, is only creating more difficulties for the government beside encouraging some very obvious evil in the society . . . .

A rethinking of priorities is urgently required if the present growing social unrest is to be arrested. To close our eyes to the existence of social dissatisfaction, and to the rising alienation of the population is nothing short of asking for trouble which the government may be incapable of controlling. In this respect, while we appreciate General Gowon's concern for African unity, we wonder whether this end would not be better if he paid rather close attention to pressing domestic issues that he seems to have found time for recently.[2]

Addressing itself to the implications of the riots at the University of Ibadan, the <u>Nigerian Opinion</u> wrote:

Few people will refuse accession to positions of authority; but in Nigeria only very few people in authority are inclined to accept and emphasize the duties, responsibilities and sacrifices of leadership. Rather, their preoccupation is with the gains and privileges which authority confers. Few people in authority in this country ever want to relinquish their positions when time comes; rather a sizable portion of their energies are directed to perpetuating themselves in office. In this country, few people in authority are willing to accept that they would be wrong, that they are not the source of absolute truth, that there would be others who could be more correct than they are. The result is that they are usually impatient of criticism, they view every criticism as a threat to their positions and advancement. They either surround themselves with sycophatic advisers or their advisers perforce become sycophatic in order to enjoy the favour and patronage of these top men."[3]

There seemed to be a considerable degree of frustration among the Nigerian lecturers. The two-thousand members of the Association of Nigerian University Teachers made the following demands from the Federal Military Government:

1. abolition of five percent contribution by members to the superannuation fund;

2. increasing the university contribution to this superannuation fund from ten percent to twenty percent;

3. raising basic car allowance from ₦ twenty six to ₦ fifty a month;

4. increasing children allowance from ₦ one hundred to ₦ two hundred per year up to three children;

5. increasing holiday allowance from ₦ two hundred to ₦ three hundred a year;

6. the establishment of a special salary review panel along the lines of those set up for the judiciary, policy and armed forces to bring university staff salary up to date; and

7. restoring the autonomy given to university countil to determine conditions of service of university staff.[4]

The Federal Commissioner of Education announced:

1. the increase in university contribution to superannuation salaries from ten percent to fifteen percent;

2. in increase in basic car allowance from ₦ twenty six to ₦ forty a month; and

3. the increase in milage rate from five to eight kobo a mile.[5]

The association rejected these government offers stating that the lecturers "could no longer tolerate living in penury on the grounds of patriotism."[6] The association threatened to resort to industrial action. The lecturers made good on their threat. Since this was the first time that the university lecturers, who viewed themselves and were viewed as part of the system, have resorted to industrial action, a number of conclusions can be proffered. First, by stating that they "cannot continue to live in penury on the grounds of patriotism," they were suggesting that either the other members of the elite, i.e., soldiers, have not been asked or forced to make financial sacrifices. Second, the resort to industrial action suggested a loss of confidence in the efficacy of dialogue as a negotiation instrument and the ability of the new political masters to empathize with the lecturers. Finally, it may well have been that for various reasons, including the civil war, the lecturers had become radicalized. A <u>Daily Times</u> editorial depicted the paradox succinctly when it wrote:

> . . . the nasty side of its crops is when trained minds--of a very high order for that matter--resort to flexing their muscles when they should be using their minds. And they are in battle dress not for more salaries which they deserve . . . but for fringe benefits (privileges) which they consider inadequate[7]

General Gowon was furious. He made an emergency broadcast in which he ordered an end to the "illegal act in five days." Those who did not abide by this ultimatum would face dismissal. He announced that the University of Lagos and the University of Ibadan would remain closed. He said he had always had:

> . . . great confidence in the good sense of the staff of our universities and I have always felt that they could be relied upon under any given circumstances to know what is in the best interest of their students, their academic institution and, above all, of this nation.[8]

> . . . Considering what has happened in our universities in the past three months, I now wonder whether the trust I have in our university teachers and students is not misplaced.[9]

It is indeed debatable whether, in fact, the soldiers have had much confidence in the universities.

> . . . . As for the universities they too have tended in this country to be sited on the outskirt of big towns. In my undergraduate days at Ibadan I had a feeling that the indigenous academician who at that time was still a fairly rare being, enjoyed the siolation of his campus. Admittedly, he emerged from time to time to pontificate on some national issue mostly political, if not wholly partisan. But I stand to be corrected when I say that it was only within the last few years that contact on anything that could be described as continuing basis between the university elite and their Civil Service or Armed Forces counterparts gradually developed. Outside academic circles only a handful of top Civil Servants who had to "scrounge" for ways of providing funds for the universities had any ideas about what the universities were doing. Ignorance about the universities and what services they could render was, I am sure, true within the elite of the Police and Armed Forces as well. By and large, the universities had a free hand in determining what courses to introduce and the nation referred to them as the best judges of what courses were best for the future leaders of this country.[10]

Awoniyi's view was supported by a Brigadier who is probably the most senior military officer ympathetic to the intellectuals.

> The academicians have been aptly described as seen by the other groups of the bureaucratic elite and the general public by Mr. Awoniyi in his paper and I have nothing to add except that if nothing drastically is done by the society and/or by the academicians themselves, it would be tragic that they will continue to perpetrate themselves and their type in the present form as their proteges who are more idealistic and less realistic will not be seen in any different form tomorrow. I have deliberately generalised, it is not that there are no exceptions to the rule.[11]

Reflecting on the posture of the educated elite in Nigeria, Professor Aluko registered a minority dissent.

> I really feel that the educated elite in Nigeria have to make up their minds whether they want to join the bandwagon of exploiters or if they want to constitute a new cadre for justice and equity in our land.[12]

Let me return to the dispute between the FMG and the university teachers. Like the Nigerian Union of Teachers, the Association of Nigerian University Teachers respected General Gowon's ultimatum. Whether this affair has increased or decreased the esteem which a few members of the military establishment may have had for the academicians is not a difficult proposition to answer; it has. However, it is questionable whether at this point in time, as a group, the lecturers are interested in good public relations with the new political masters. It is equally debatable whether the military is particularly desirous of the same. The military, for example, has been extremely cautious about recruiting university graduates into the military.[13] The following general comments by Nigerian university lecturers are instructive of the state of affairs.

>--People feel envious of lecturers; it seems as though there is a calculated effort to suppress us.

>--Our role as advisors "appears to be mere academic exercise. The suggestions aren't implemented."

On their impression of the military:

>--The civilian is a bargainer. The military man is not and is less receptive to new ideas. With the military you can't tell it like it is.

>--They aren't united on goals, so you don't know what they're doing. The military behaves like fighting politicians instead of a unified force.

>--Less people feel pleasant about what the government is doing. Lecturers are a bit jealous of the high benefits of soldiers.

>--Shorten their reign and give government back to the civilians. The longer they stay, the more corrupt they become.

>--They should "get out before their luck runs out."

By and large the academicians have been relegated to a more specialized, less central role by the military and it would not be long before they, along with the students, would be demanding increased status. The pity of it all is that they need each other.

There are increasing indications that on matters which they considered of primary and common interest to the students, Nigerian students are putting aside primordial sentiments and advancing united fronts. One suspects that government approach to student grievances has fostered greater unity among the students. However one cannot go so far as to say that primordial sentiments are now irrelevant among students. Nor can one predict what would happen after relatively idealistic university life is ended.

We do know, however, that despite attempts at unity, the lecturers' posture and power is broken down because of primordial sentiments and the inability to form a united front. For example, following the Gowon ultimatum against the strike of university teachers, three alternatives were considered: (1) ignore the ultimatum; (2) respond to the ultimatum; (3) respond to the ultimatum and form a united front of non-cooperation with the FMG. The third alternative was opted for and a "Disengagement Committee" was formed. Ironically some members of the disengagement committee remain chief advisers to the military.

In many societies, the relationship between both groups is seemingly characterized by tension and ambivalence. Because of the tendency of the military to resort to force in order to obtain goals, the academicians have regarded them as an anathema probably because of the latter's preference for reason. But out of frustration, even university dons have sometimes had to relegate reason to the background. The truth of the matter is that both groups have specialized roles to play in development and nation building. Now the tension and the ambivalence that seems to characterize the relationship between both are not merely due to the role specialization. The competition between academicians and group in power has been aptly depicted as a derivative of their interdependent nature. Political authority, in this case military authority, needs legitimation provided by the academicians. For their part, the academicians and their organizations need the protections and assistance of the political authority. The root of the conflict is the attempts of each group to maintain maximum autonomy and control over the other. As a group, the academicians participated in the Nigerian military regime, but it cannot be argued unequivocally that they identified with it. Rather, one gets the distinct impression that the academicians no longer identify with the military government. There seems to be a situation of mutual disillusionment that the one group does not appreciate the invaluable contribution of the other. Quite frankly, the contribution of the academicians to the legitimacy of the military falls below that of governmental bureaucrats.

## B. NIGERIAN STUDENTS

Prior to the civil war the involvement of Nigerian students in Nigerian politics was a rarity. One notable exception was their demonstration against the Anglo-Nigerian Defense Pact which, in the opinion of the students, compromised Nigerian independence and foreign policy principles of "neutrality." Otherwise, the students' demonstrational activities were centered around occasional complaints about catering or housing; in short, they were directed toward matters immediately affecting their own welfare. One of the reasons for the infrequency of even this type of protest is that in the earlier period, the numbers of Nigerian universities as well as students were small, and the university students did not suffer from deprivation. In fact, the Nigerian university student was pampered. After independence, some of these variables changed somewhat. The university student did not immediately become politicized. As I have mentioned there was only one incident which could be regarded as a political protest. Generally, the students were happy to await the time when they would be abosorbed into the establishment which was not top heavy until about 1962. It should also be noted that the university suffered from the same malaise of overwhelming primordialism which afflicted the other institutions of society. I shall return to these points later.

It is interesting to note that the first successful political protest of the students was in the area of foreign relations. Given the absence of internal cohesion as a result of primordial attachments, this is not a coincidence. During the civil war, demonstrations were held by university students in Ahmadu Bello University, University of Ibadan and University of Lagos to protest against foreign governments such as France, Tanzania, Ivory Coast and the United States of America, who were seen as supporting or encouraging Biafra. In 1968, during one of these demonstrations, the students called for the immediate drafting of students into the army. Significantly, these demonstrations which were pro-government were seldom met with violent reactions by the military, the only notable exception being that of a Lagos University demonstration against Britain's Rhodesion policy.

All in all, until the middle of the Nigerian civil war, it would appear that the Nigerian students looked at education from a personalistic and instrumental point of view. Judged by the performance of its graduates, the impression given is that the diploma is necessary not for service, but as an instrument of social mobility. Overwhelmingly, the graduates were eager and anxious to get cars, and to join the senior service without questioning societal values. Enough of the general remarks.

What does the military regime expect from the universities?

General Gowon, at a "Foundation" ceremony at the University of Ibadan, discussed his opinion of the role of the universities. He asserted that in the past there had been a lack of student interest or involvement in societal affairs; the university was only concerned with acquiring knowledge. He went on:

> The modern society expects a great deal more from a university and rightly so. A university is now regarded as a public institution on which a substantial proportion of the nation's financial resources are to be expended . . . The people are no longer interested in any institution which isolates itself from society or is unable to contribute more directly to the growth and development of that society. One of the challenges of the future is the extent to which our universities can meet the needs and aspirations of the society which they are established to serve, without in any way compromising the autonomy that is so essential for a healthy academic atmosphere . . .[14]

But General Gowon praised the students for not becoming "too" involved:

> The biggest change which has occurred in the university firmament in the last few years has been in student attitudes. It would appear that the students in most parts of the world have been attempting to take over control of the university government. This might be because of the apparent inability of university authorities to put their own houses in order . . . However, I would like to congratulate the students of our universities for the comparatively high sense of responsibility which they have shown in the midst of the formidable exhibition of student discontent and unrest in the university world . . . It will be an abuse of privilege to visit upon the university, grievances which may well be against the shortcomings of society

as a whole, or to pitch a destructive battle in a university which is run with the monies from taxpayers and with assistance from abroad. Our students have been sensible enough not to be misguided by many of their counterparts elsewhere. We cannot afford that luxury in a developing country like ours.[15]

Gowon directed the final parts of his speech to graduating seniors, many of whom would soon be serving the government, hopefully, in one form or another;

> . . . you are now required, in return for the opportunities which you have had in this great institution to dedicate your talents and your life to the service of your fellow citizens and the development of your country. Live not for yourself alone, but also for others. Above all remember your country. Nigeria offers you a challenge--now and in the future, to meet that challenge, you will need an unflinching faith, loyalty and a sense of dedication to the course of your country--Nigeria. We must not fail.[16]

Although student unrest had not become rampant in Nigeria at this time, the government had begun to betray a gingerly attitude by stressing the importance of order in its speeches. Occasionally, newspaper editorials supported the military government's admonitions.

Consider this passage from a Nigerian newspaper:

> . . . a good national identity can be fostered by the students . . . We had a bit too much of student riots and squabbles arising from personality clashes, parochialism, selfishness and allegations of corruption and mismanagement of funds. Whereas the conditions elsewhere in the world might be such that justify student involvement and thuggery, our economic and political conditions are such that make such things adverse to the national goal and objectives. More than any group of persons, the FMG needs the services, knowledge, skill and dynamism of the students to be able to reach the laudable goals . . .[17]

Believing that the student unrest could ignite the rest of the country, the government had to approach youth suspiciously. Another appeal by Gowon emphasized why youth should "stay in line".

> The future of our great country depends on you the youth, to cultivate a sense of belonging, of understanding and tolerance and a readiness to be guided by the noblest of ideals in all your endeavours . . . The nation expects you and it behooves you to be responsible and sober. I urge every youth of this nation to resolve to lead honest and dedicated lives and to place the interest of the nation above all else. The nation looks to you for its future stability and greatness and you must not fail us . . .[18]

The end of the civil war probably removed student restraints against the deomestic policies of the military regime. Although the students had become politicized during the war, the politicization was an acceptable one because it was generally supportive of the government's war effort and uncompromising in its vilification of outside powers perceived as imperialists. But the civil war had also caused the students financial hardship. Moreover, as a result of the war, there was a change in the power structure so that less educated men in military uniforms who had suddenly become the new political masters were viewed critically by the students. Following the successful termination of the war the new President of NUNS (National Union of Nigerian Students), Olu Adegboro, asked that the State of Emergency be lifted. This call, he said, was made "with utmost recognition of our responsibility to the fatherland." He argued that the State of Emergency had been justly declared but it should have ended with the end of the civil war. Because military rule was to end by 1976--it was necessary to begin frank discussion at all levels for political education of the masses. Mr. Adegboro declared that the Nigerian students had reiterated their solidarity with the Nigerian press in its crusade to cure the nation's ills. The new leadership of NUNS was mandated by the Nigerian students to forge a new identity for students in "our struggle for academic freedom, social justice and the building of a truly great Nigeria."[19]

The students saw themselves as patriots of the new Nigeria while the Federal Military Government saw student discontent as disruptive to their plans for the development of Nigeria. It was necessary not to alienate students, though, because they were a highly visible and vocal part of the population. The students often looked down upon the Nigerian military officers because most of them barely had a secondary education and partly because most of them were perceived as corrupt and dishonest.

There were indications suggestive of a development of a new sense of unity among students at different universities. This bears out Lewis Coser's analysis of functional utility of conflict for integration. For example, students at Ibadan University sealed off the university, locked the offices and cut telephone lines in response to the closing of ABU (Ahmadu Bello University) one month earlier. They burned an effigy of the Vice-Chancellor of ABU, Dr. Audu.[20] The signs of a cohesive student movement seemed to be developing. An incident at Ibadan University in the winter of 1971 helped to increase this developing sense of unity. The university was closed down following the death of a student during a police-student clash in which the police opened fire on approximately 3,000 students demonstrating against catering deficiencies in a residence hall. The students then staged a march to Government House in Ibadan to protest against the shooting. The student organization, NUNS, called for the resignation of the Vice-Chancellor, Lambo, and demanded the withdrawal of police and army units from the campus.[21] They also released a statement calling on the FMG to see that nothing less than death sentences were given to all connected with the death of the student. A resolution of a congregation of students at the university demanded that:

1. police should be removed from the campus;

2. a broadly-based public inquiry into the events of the past two days be held immediately;

3. the detained students should be released at once;

4. the halls should be opened. (The university had been temporarily closed.)[22]

The Federal Executive Council sent personal letters of condolences to parents of the dead student and promised to investigate the allegations and grievances of the students. Later in the week, 4,000 students battled with police over the death of the student at Ibadan. The Students' Union led a delegation of students to General Gowon and Inspector General of Police to present their demands which included the release of the arrested students and a court hearing on the matter.[23]

University students at Lagos University rioted over the death of the student at the University of Ibadan. The confrontation between the Lagos police and Lagos University students was almost deadly. The police barricaded roads into Lagos after several hours of rioting by students during which two police posts were burned down and at least two policemen were injured. Police used tear gas to stop the march and demonstrators retaliated with bottles, stones and other objects that came to hand. Allegedly, male students threw petrol over a police post and set it on fire while women students supplied added fuel to keep the fire burning. Students set up barricades in several main approach roads to the business areas and caused many traffic jams. Policemen were chased wherever they were seen; students even boarded buses to attack policemen who were passengers.[24] Soon thereafter, the Vice-Chancellor of the University of Lagos suspended the Constitution of the Students' Union and declared that all offices of the Union would be closed until further notice, saying that it was necessary in the face of crisis.[25] Increasing hostility of the youth to the military regime was becoming more and more manifest as their demonstrations became more and more political.

The Government soon announced that an inquiry into the conditions that caused the Ibadan riots would be opened. Justice Kazeem was appointed to head the inquiry and was given until April 1971 to complete the report. Ibadan University reopened and students returned, but many abandoned their lectures and dressed in black to demonstrate their mourning. Students were very dissatisfied that General Gowon would not meet personally with them (they had met with General Ekpo) and said that they would boycott classes until all of the following demands were met:

1. that Vice-Chancellor Lambo be dismissed; and

2. that a residence hall be named after the dead student, Kunle Adepeju.

The discontent spread beyond the student population. In Ibadan, thousands of market women protested against the police action and demanded that action be taken against the police officers involved. They were addressed by the Military Governor of the West who assured them that such an incident would not occur again.

General Gowon appointed a commission of inquiry, the Kazeem Commission, to look into the indicent. The Kazeem Inquiry ended in May after hearing thirty six witnesses in fifty two days. Although Gowon received the Kazeem Report in June 1971, it was not until January 1972 that the government finally publicly released the report along with a White Paper. The Kazeem Report saw the riots as part of the general picture of student unrest attributed to several remote causes such as inadequate hostel accomodations and catering services; strained relations between domestic staff and students; the use of law enforcing agencies by the university authorities and the lack of adequate staff and communication. It criticized Vice-Chancellor Lambo's actions and the use of rifles by police.

What was the Federal Military Government's response to this report? The government White Paper asserted that, ". . . it was totally wrong for students generally to turn what began as a peaceful demonstration into a violent one at the mere sight of police on the campus" and that ". . . students could not be regarded as peace-loving citizens when they failed to disperse after tear gas was thrown at them by police; but instead they continued to throw stones at the police . . ."[26] Although the Kazeem Report condemned the use of rifles, the White Paper pointed out ". . . that the police have the duty to be on the campus as elsewhere in order to maintain law and order by whatever appropriate but lawful means they may have at their disposal.[27]

> Riot in any form, committed whether by students or by any other group of citizens, deserves to be quelled by law enforcement agencies in a manner and to the extent necessary to restore law and order. Government expects and believes that all men of good will must deprecate student indiscipline and rowdyism, especially when accompanied, as in the instant case, by resort to violence and to wanton destruction of and damage to public or private properties.[28]

Thus the FMG rejected the notion of the university as a pseudo-private estate where the police have no jurisdiction. Similarly, the military government came down on the side of "law and order."

What was the students' reaction to the FMG White Paper? The report by the Kazeem Commission and the government White Paper did not satisfy the students. At Ibadan, student leaders burned 300 copies of the White Paper. They described it as: "damnable, fascistic and militaristic, unjust, inequitable and inconsistent with the pretended spirit with which the inquiry was set up."[29] They rejected the findings, in particular they castigated the government's position that each of the 4,000 students must pay N£1 each for damages. They accepted the Report's findings concerning police actions which the government had rejected.

Another incident demonstrating that unity was beginning to develop among the students at the various universities against the Government occurred at ABU in November, 1971. Thirty students, including six young women, were arrested after a demonstration involving several hundred students against a recently announced agreement between Britain and Rhodesia. During the demonstration, anti-riot police physically clashed with angry student demonstrators. The students were subdued when the police exploded tear gas bombs. Many students were arrested and the Students' Union declared it would not return to the university until the detained students were released.[30]

University of Ibadan students also called for the immediate release of the thirty arrested students. A formal student statement said that police action was "unwarranted, mean and inhuman." In an appeal to Gowon, the students said that "the latest attack on the progressive student movement in Nigeria is related in the catalogue of premeditated acts of repression and injustice by the Nigerian police on the students." They called for immediate interdiction of the Police Commissioner of the North Central State because of "anti-national, anti-aspirational, and colonialist rule in Kaduna." Police were warned to steer clear of actions of the student movement. A telegram was also sent to the ABU Students' Union expressing solidarity with them and condemning the "fascist, brutal and suppressive action" of the police.[31]

The years 1970-1972 saw a great increase in the number and intensity of student unrest in Nigeria. University unrests could no longer be characterized as localized because an unrest at a university in the North--once it met with unfavorable reaction of some sort--was often carried to another Nigerian university. This was a reflection of general student dissatisfaction with the military regime.

Government appeals, made to quell student unrests, often did not touch on the grievances of the students. Some government appeals called on religious and family institutions to do their jobs better. For example, the Western State Commissioner for Education, Mr. Olaniwun Ajayi, suggested that in order to contain the incessant rioting of students[32]--both parents and teachers should do their best to ensure that food, tuition and good accomodations were not denied the children. He then called on various religious organizations to redouble their efforts to preach against rioting. He felt that only teachers with good moral standards should be employed and he regretted that many of the students were reflections of their parents and came from broken homes. There is an irony that a regime made up of young men should have such paternalistic attitudes toward students.

Another case study which sheds some light on the relationship between the students and the military regime involves the National Youth Service Corps (NYSC). The Federal government had budgeted six million naira for the creation and running of the National Youth Service Corporation. The corps was scheduled to commence in June 1973 and it was aimed at providing skilled manpower, especially for the less desirable areas of the country, e. g., the rural areas.[33] According to the Federal government sources, its purpose is to "bring our young men and women together with the primary objectives of inculcating in them a sense of discipline, dedication, national pride and consciousness, through employment in nationally directed productive activities.[34]

> The proposed youth corps will be a potent instrument for national unity, cutting across political, social, state and religious and ethnic loyalties--General Gowon told a delegation of the National

Youth Council of Nigeria. He said that the corps was designed
to afford Nigerian youth the chance for rendering selfless and
honest service to the nation.[35]

At the federal level, this may well be the only cogent example of the FMG's serious attempts at a high profile approach to political integration. Other less serious attempts at high political profile for political integration included the attempt of the Federal Public Service Commission to encourage and guarantee job security for Nigerians whose services are needed in places other than their regions of origin. The increase in the number of Federal secondary schools attended by students from all regions of the country, the attempt of the Federal government to take over the financing of the universities, the East Central State's take-over of the private schools, the interstate visits among the military governors and the voluntary bilateral exchange of secondary school students have been seen by pro-government forces a high profile approaches to political integration.

In candor it must be stated that the states are not bound to accept civil servants who are not from their states, and that the announced Federal take-over of the universities is now being considered optional from the point of view of Ahmadu Bello University and the University of Ife. The point is that while the Federal government has encouraged and suggested, it has seldom compelled, in the interest of political integration. To date, it has not used the military organization in a way to suggest high political profile of integration. The war is a notable exemption. Although a Midwesterner had been appointed as the Vice-Chancellor of the University of Ibadan, the move is not as high profile as it may appear at first sight. It would have been more interesting had an Ibo been appointed the Vice-Chancellor of Ahmadu Bello University and a Hausa appointed the Vice-Chancellor of the University of Ibadan. This is why the ultimate outcome and intention of the NYSC is important in terms of the strategy of Modernization Performance proposition. Up to this point, with the exception of the civil war, the Federal government's approach to political integration is rhetorically mobilizational but operationally <u>laissez faire</u>.

There was no attempt by the government to change labor laws in such a way as to discourage the proliferation of unions and encourage the propensity for integration of the unions. Moreover, with the notable exception of North Central State, all military governors rule over their states of origin. The point is not that high political profile is more desirable than low political profile. Indeed, it is a testimony to the political competence of the Federal Military Government that it refrained from forcing its wishes over the states in the matters to which a state may have strong opposition.

To return to the NYSC, the originally proposed term of the NYSC called for a two-year term of compulsory service for college graduates up to the age of thirty. The members of the corps would be provided with free accommodation and with stipends of 100 naira a month. Graduates would not be allowed to take on permanent employment until the completion of their service.

Members of the NYSC would build roads, bridges, schools and clinics. They would work on farms, and help in other ways to push rural development. They were to reside in rural 300 acre camps across the country in groups of 500. Each camp would be expected to be partially self-sufficient in food and, under professional guidance, they would build their own living quarters.[36]

There were student demonstrations in four of the six Nigerian universities against the projects. The students' objections rested on a number of points. First, they were unhappy about the absence of details on the project. The government did not elaborate beyond the bare outline provided in several addresses by General Gowon.[37]

The Federal Public Service Commission together with the universities were required to offer advice on the scheme. In accordance with this instruction, an inter-university workshop was held on the scheme, under the sponsorship of the Vice-Chancellors of the universities.[38] This Ibadan workshop which was held on February 23, 1973, was attended by representatives of the National Union of Nigerian

Students. The signal of a crisis was given when the student representation walked out of the meeting because, according to him, ". . . the FMG and Committee of Vice-Chancellors have taken vital decisions affecting students without bringing students into decision-making."[39] The students also asserted that they had been kept in the dark with regard to the terms of service and that the FMG was required to discuss matters with them.

Although it is true the Nigerian government now subsidizes university education to the tune of eighty to ninety percent.[40] Only about fifty percent of the university students receive state and Federal scholarships. In the opinion of NUNS the fifty percent of the students who have to pay their own fees believe it is unfair to impose compulsory NYSC on all. The students have therefore demanded that free university education be a prerequisite. They demanded the initiation of free university education in September, 1973, and the conscription of first graduates into NYSC in June of 1974. As an alternative, the government should make university education at all levels free immediately.

The students, most of whom were from the southern states, understood the implication of the NYSC conscription in terms of its effect on their own preference for employment in urban areas and southern states.

The students, as I have argued, have increasingly become dissatisfied with the new ruling class. They carried placards which read, "Top Men Enjoying Oil Boom, Young Ones Suffer," "Service Corps or Suffering Corps?," "Enlist Prominent Men Also," and "Gowon: Beware of Advisors."[41] These placards speak for the students' lack of faith in the selflessness of the present Nigerian political leadership.

At first it seemed that the students would win their fight for a postponement because the states' public service commissions were recruiting graduates for employment next year despite the NYSC issue. Many 1973 graduates have, in fact, secured employment. Also, one would have thought that given the nature of extended families in Nigeria and the role the members tend to play in the financing of education for the non-scholarship students, parents of these students were not likely to be passive about such a "semi-philanthropic" organization. The president of NUNS declared, "The promulgation of any decree on NYSC without prior discussions with us as promised and without the acceptance of our recommendations shall not be binding on us."[42]

The students demanded the following:
1. introduction of free university education;
2. direct consultation with the FMG;
3. NYSC should be voluntary, not compulsory.

In the end, the only concession granted to students by the FMG was the reduction of the length of service from two years to one year. The intransigence of the Federal government in this matter indicates the significance attached to it by the FMG.

The students' opposition to NYSC was violent and unequivocal. At the University of Lagos, students wrecked a number of cars, smashed windows and stripped General Gowon's name from the university library name plate. At other universities, students boycotted classes and demonstrated against government policy. Despite all of these, 2,600 students were drafted by the FMG into the NYSC in June, 1973. The students lost the fight once again.

Whether the NYSC will perform in the way its advocates expected, in the face of widespread dissaffection by the draftees, remains to be seen. However, there is no doubt that Gowon views the NYSC as a high political profile instrument to political integration and modernization.

## FOOTNOTES

1. West Africa, April 18, 1970, pp. 430-431.
2. Nigerian Opinion. Vol. 7, 2, February 28, 1971.
3. Ibid.
4. West Africa. April, 1973, p. 507.
5. West Africa. May 7, 1973, p. 591.
6. West Africa, Ibid.
7. West Africa. April, 1973, p. 547.
8. West Africa. May 7, 1973, p. 591.
9. Ibid.
10. S. B. Awoniyi. "Integration within the Bureaucratic Elite." at the Conference on Public Service Reform, Institution of Administration, Ahmadu Bello University, Zaria , October 11, 1971.
11. Brigadier Obasanjo, discussion of Mr. Awoniyi's paper.
12. West Africa. May 7, 1973, p. 591.
13. See Robin Luckham. Officers and Gentlemen: The Nigerian Military. London: Cambridge University Press, 1971.
14. Yakubu Gowon, "An Address by the Visitor, His Excellency Major General Yakuba Gowon at the 21st Foundation Day Ceremony of the University of Ibadan," November 17, 1969.
15. Ibid.
16. Ibid.
17. Daily Sketch, December 21, 1970, p. 5.
18. New Nigeria. October 5, 1971, p. 10.
19. Daily Times. May 28, 1969, pp. 1 and 3.
20. West Africa. February 7, 1970, p. 178.
21. West Africa. February 12, 1971, p. 177.
22. Daily Express. February 3, 1971, p. 1.
23. Morning Post. February 8, 1971, p. 1.
24. West Africa. February 19, 1971, p. 205.

25. West Africa. April 16, 1971, p. 433.

26. West Africa. January 7, 1972, p. 5.

27. Reported in Ibid.

28. Ibid.

29. West Africa. January 7, 1972, pp. 5 and 25.

30. Daily Sketch. November 29, 1971, p. 1

31. Daily Sketch. December 2, 1971, p. 12.

32. Morning Post. October 6, 1971, p. 1.

33. West Africa. April 9, 1973, p. 482.

34. West Africa. April 9, 1973, p. 482.

35. West Africa. October 16, 1972, p. 1404.

36. Christian Science Monitor. July 13, 1973.

37. Yakubu Gowon, Convocation Address, Ahmadu Bello University, Zaria, December 2, 1972.

38. West Africa. February 23, 1973.

39. Ibid.

40. West Africa. April 9, 1973, p. 482.

41. West Africa. April 2, 1973, p. 441.

42. West Africa. April 30, 1973, p. 581.

CHAPTER IIX

GHANA: THE RELATIONSHIP BETWEEN THE ACADEMICIANS AND THE
NATIONAL REDEMPTION COUNCIL

Unlike the relationship between the students and the National Redemption Council, the relationship between the university lecturers and the NRC has not been very cordial. As it will become evident, part of the problem is the extreme reluctance or unwillingness of most lecturers to accept the legitimacy of a regime which by threat of force outsted what they regarded as a duly elected democratic government. Another difficulty may well be a disapproval of what they perceived as the military regime's style, strategy, and ideology. In any case, there is a situation of mutual distrust and dissatisfaction between both groups.

Let me start by examining the role which the NRC expects the Ghanaian universities and academicians to play. In a speech Col. Acheampong pointedly asserted: "In my judgment the concept of university education with which we have grown should be due now for some well-deserved refinement."[1] He went on: "The universities cannot, therefore, fully discharge their duties by operating in isolation, and out of touch with the people." In his judgment, "it is . . . imperative that their activities and attitudes should relate to the needs of the nation . . . . The urgent social challenges around them, demand and compels a greater participation in the activities of their society than ever before."[2] With specific reference to the university lecturers of Ghana, he declared: "There is . . . a certain lackadaisical attitude which is inhibiting achievements in our universities. The creative spirit which is the prime motivation of university dons elsewhere has been absent for too long in our university communities."[3] He asked rhetorically: "How many of our students have been able to say with pride 'I am the product of Professor Akasi Mensah?' At least I have not heard of one. Where are the works of art and learning created by our people?" He regretted that most of the works on Ghana were done by young foreign scholars.[4] Obviously, this is a blatant indictment of the creativity and productivity of the Ghanaian academicians.

The NRC is quite aware of its lack of popularity among the Ghanaian academicians. Quite frankly, it is very suspicious of them. Continuing his important speech at the University of Cape Coast, Col. Acheampong said: "Ladies and gentlemen, I hope that this university would not be used as a seat for subversion. The NRC will encourage you in all respect to air your grievances and will welcome constructive criticisms, and suggestions from your academic community."[5] He went on: "We believe in the principle of academic freedom, but we equally believe that this freedom must be used realistically and responsibly . . . . The successful observance of this concept requires good will, understanding, continuous re-interpretation and dialogue. A measure of tact on the part of all concerned is also essential."[6]

For its part, the academic community seemed decidely set against the regime right from the beginning. A prominent Ghanaian professor asserted: "I am positively of the opinion that a constitutionally elected government should not be overthrown by the gun when it has served only two of its five-year term of office and even more firmly still that the military should intervene only as a last resort, that is, only when all the other possible means of intervention by civilians mentioned above have proved abortive."[7] He agreed that to the extent that the armed forces constituted a group, they are part of the body politic like other Ghanaian groups. "They therefore share the right of sovereignty with the sovereign people. What this means, however, is that they should ordinarily exercise the right of changing government as part of the sovereign people of Ghana."[8] He wondered if the failure of the parliamentary system could "not be attributed as much to the blunders of our politicians as to the impatience, the ambition and the selfish considerations on the part of other groups in the society not excluding the military?"[9]

The sketpicism or hostility of some intellectuals is articulated again by Kontopiaat, a fictional character. Notice the negativistic tone of the passage.

It was decided at this meeting that instead of wasting time on
what went wrong, or telling the N.C.R.--pardon N.R.C.--what is
going wrong, we should rather concentrate on what will go wrong
or what the N.R.C. will not do. After about twelve solid hours
of deliberations and the consumption of a corresponding number
of large posts of palm wine, we decided on the following "what-
will-go-wrong" for transmission to the N.R.C.-

1. The N.R.C. have declared to us already their policy of one
man one bread but they have not told us and we are not sure
they ever will tell us the size of that bread!

2. The N.R.C. will not set up an Economic Committee to run the
economy of the country consisting of one Makola woman, one
fisherman from Biriwa or Axim, one Kwahu trader, one big cattle
dealer, one cocoa farmer, and one onion planter from Keta, under
the chairmanship of the Kwahu man, of course, and with the
Kontopiaatkrom economists as the consultant. They will rather
rely on the same governors on whom both the N.L.C. and the Busia
government relied.

3. The N.R.C. will not invite the wives and/or girlfriends or
concubines of Mao-tse Tung, Chou en Lai, Herr Ubricht, Podgorny,
Kosygin, Brezhnev and for good measure the King/Queen of Denmark
to visit Ghana!

4. They will not pack all the Mercedes Benz cars owned by the
Black Star Line (or rather the White Star Line since the word
Black is anathema to the members of the N.R.C.) ships and send
them to either Nigeria or Kuwait or one of the other oil-rich
kingdoms for sale. They will rather not only keep them but
ride in them too. Indeed, information has already reached us
that at least one of the Colonel Regional Commissioners is
already using one of Benzes with Number GV 40! If this is so
then to borrow a friend's phrase, did we go or did we come?

5. The N.R.C will not put a ban on the use of foreign experts,
on visits to this country by people from the IMF and on the
attending of conferences and courses by Ghanaian officials and
officers. Is it true incidentally that the recently appointed
Commander of the Ghana Army has in fact already left for the
U.K. to do a year's course?

6. The N.R.C. will not turn the soldiers into farmers, road
builders, builders of damn in the Accra plains, etc., etc., or
station them at arms length from each other along the borders
of Ghana to stop smuggling so that they can give the taxpayers
something for all the money we pay to keep them. These soldiers
will rather be left alone doing their own thing in their barracks
and at least we in Kontopiaatkrom will never hear of them again
until the next coup!

7. The N.R.C. will never, we are sure, abolish the wearing of
suits and gowns in this tropical climate of ours, or stop or at
least impose a tax on funerals and memorial services.

8. The N.R.C. will not change the existing rule of driving on the left. With the shift to the right by Nigeria in April of this year, Ghana will be the only West African country that will continue to drive on the left. This of course will make us a true relic of the colonial past and therefore a big attraction to tourists!

9. The N.R.C. will not abolish the payment of tolls on the motor-way even though, thanks to their guns, we do not even have to pay for the building of that road any more.

10. The N.R.C. will not stop official cocktails nor will our favourites, palm wine, VC 10, Bramsco, Pito, Lai Momo Vermouth and the other local concoctions ever be served there. White Horse (mind you not Black Horse), Johnnie Walker (born 1820 but still walking) and Professor Gordon's Gin, etc., will continue to be served.

11. The N.R.C. will not make False Start in Africa by Rene Dumont compulsory reading for all civil servants including Principal Secretaries, all members of the N.R.C., all Regional Commissioners, all traditional rulers, and all Managing Directors and Executive Chairmen of all Corporations in the country nor will they compel every Ghanaian to read the article entitled, "The Ghanaian who is he?" by Mrs. J. Maud Kordylas, a Ghanaian housewife, which appeared in the Graphic of Friday, February 11, 1972. Indeed that lady should be made a member of the National Advisory Committee, but of course this will not be done since she is not only a woman but she is not above fifty either.

12. The N.R.C. will not convert Tema into a free port to attract foreign companies, industrialists, smugglers, etc., to set up industries here.

13. The last but by no means the least, the N.R.C. will not even freeze the liabilities of Kwadwo Kontopiaat so that he will have an excellent excuse for his creditors when they do show up, nor will they freeze the remaining external debts of the country. If they can freeze and have indeed frozen the assets which may jolly well include the debts of many Ghanaians, we don't see why they cannot freeze all the remaining external debts.

In an editorial captioned "Dons Must Sit Up," the editor of the Daily Graphic accused the faculty and staff of the universities of being insincere, overindulged, parasitic and overly concerned with minor problems of academic freedom. He warned that "If past coups have spared academics, they must remember that they will not be always spared. The anger of a hungry people may surpass the zeal of soldiers with guns and anybody who feels he should live off the state just because he has collected a string of letters after his name may find himself swinging from the nearest tree on the campus."[11]

For its part, the academic community was becoming impatient. The depth of the animosity was being manifested increasingly in the battle of words. On July 14, 1972, the Legon Society for National Affairs declared:

> It has long been a favourite pastime of certain people, when they so feel to mount unprovoked attacks on Legon, accusing this community of intellectualism, unpatriotism, and other vague sins. From Legon, the characteristic response has been silence. But increasingly, in recent times, the sport has been extended to its vicious extremes. The Legon Observer, the prime target, is being castigated with charges of frivolity, corruption and conspiracy, while the citizens of Legon are being hysterically recommended for hangman's noose, come the next coup. Still the response remains either silence or at best very polite if mildly sharp replies. Legon's attitude may well be explained in terms of the low level at which the attackers customarily operate; it has variously been interpreted as the silence of disdain, indifference, and impotence. Be that as it may, for the Legon Observer, this is a luxury that we can no longer afford. Our traducers are operating on the gullibility of the uncritical and impressionable average Ghanaian, and on the assumption that, being academics, we darenot come down to their level and show them up for the pretentious fudge that they really are. It would be a mistake to refuse to prove them wrong; nor, in so doing is it necessary to even go close to the gutter where they are."[12]

It went on:

> But the Legon Observer will not flinch from the truth. It is our duty to scrutinize public affairs, since we are Ghanaians. Let anyone who does not like this stay away from public office. Or if they have nothing to hide, let them come out into the open and stop hiding behind women and using feeble-minded characters and dotards as their media."[13]

In a column of the Legon Observer, a lecturer commented, "I write to comment on a rather curious incident which occurred on the T.V. program, "Talking Point" on Sunday, 30th January. About eight minutes after the discussion dealing with the debt allegedly left by the ousted Busia government, the programme went off, and an announcer appeared to repeat the usual excuse that the programme could not be continued due to a technical fault. I speak of the debt allegedly left by the Busia government."[14] But after a few minutes, the technical difficulties were announced overcome. The writer declared: "What I do not understand is why the authorities decided to forget about the unfinished discussion programme altogether and to go ahead with other programmes like the "Break for Music and Sunday Service which being tansmitted live presumably require the same type of machine as for Talking Point. . . . " He asked: "Whom do the broadcasting people think they are kidding?"[15]

This passage reflects the suspicion of the academicians regarding the legitimate use of the news media as a legitimacy engineering instrument. By and large, the Ghanaian academic community, in its relationship with the NRC military regime behaves as if the Ghanaian society were in a stage of constitutional liberalism. It would seem that the academicians have not been able to make the transition between a colonial stage and the stage of indigenous political leadership. Strategies of direct confrontation may be functional at a constitutional liberalist stage or even in a colonial regime where the assumption of the solidarity of the intellectual bourgeoisie is accepted as axiomatic by the colonialists and leaders of the colonized. In an independent country with a tendency for ubiquitous government run by an indigenous elite uncommitted to the sanctity of academic and press freedom, a new strategy or a modified strategy is desirable. Perhaps, the problem is that the Ghanaian academician feels that Nkrumah's alleged misgovernment was due, in part, to their failure to assert themselves politically and vocally. If this is so, the elaborate self-examination and self-criticisms in the debates about "what went wrong" support this position, then the academicians are motivated by a desire to atone for past inaction.

In addition, as I have mentioned earlier, there is a resentment against an overthrow of a duly elected democratic government by a threat or use of force. The sentiments of many academicians about the NRC intervention is reflected in "Kwadwo Kontopiaat's" fictional writing.[16]

If the people of Kontopiaatkrom are terrified of armed soldiers, I, Kwadwo Kontopiaat, am terrified of guns of any sort, and it certainly took me a long time to take in what was really happening. Having regained consciousness, I asked whether he was telling us that we had got another Redeemer: "No, No, you ass," he answered, "We have not got a Redeemer, but we have got a Redemption Council." "Yes Sir," I shouted as I stood at attention and saluted. Strangely enough, he saluted back.

Somebody then asked him why the N.R.C. had decided to become our next redeemers. The answer was swift and angry: "Mainly because of the murder of Mr. N. Cedi." "But did you try the murderers first before you decided to depose and imprison them?", asked the editor of the Kontopiaatkrom Gossiper. "Try whom? Nonsense, don't you remember the 'No Court!', 'NO COURT!' speech? And if there is no court, how could we try them?"

The editor hit back rather courageously, much to the surprise of most of us there? "But if there are no courts, then we thought the people should have been asked to express their views in an election or plebiscite as to whether they approve of the murder of Mr. N. Cedi or not. After all, when the murder took place, the murderers did have the mandate of the people. Moreover, is a single blunder enough justification for the overthrow of a government?" The soldier yelled back that nobody had got time for that nonsense of elections and plebicites, that these people had committed many other blunders and, in any case, that if somebody had committed such cold-blooded murder, he must be summarily dealt with and that was all.

Kwadwo Cow, alian Kwadwo Nantwi, cut in: "They have indeed committed many other blunders. Do you know the price of kako, rice, milk, sugar, 'konbeef', and even cutlasses now? Do you know that a tin of Wolfaltin costs nearly two cedis, yes, two new cedis? Do you know these people were riding in big cars instead of using donkeys or 'Ag-One-One', as we here do." But Kofi Ananse intervened: "You Cow, when was the last time you saw, let alone bought, a tin of milk?" Nonsense, I bought one recently and this was when the first attempt was made on Mr. Cedi's like," replied Mr. Cow. "Oh that is five years ago, why all this fuss then? Would you have good water to drink and electric lights rather than milk or sugar or konbeef. Kofi Spider replied, "All right," admitted Kwadwo Cow, "but what about kako? Indeed, I am going to call this Kuup the Kako Kuup."

Somebody then asked whether Mr. IMF and his team had also been arrested. The soldier replied that since they were foreigners, they could not be arrested, and that in any case Mr. IMF and his men had quietly slipped out of the country immediately after the take-over. This was news that really stunned everybody and brought Kontopiaat to a perfect standstill.

The silence was only broken by some noise from the other end of the village. This was a massive demonstration in support of the soldiers. The leader was of course the only victim of Apollo

568 and the others were his four children and three 'unbis' people. The ex-civil servant's wife had died a month earlier and so she could not join them. All of them were clad in white and were of course carrying placards.

One of these read "Down with Hypocrisy," the other "P. P. Sacked," the other "Defreeze their assets," and the last "Try IMF and foreign advisers." One of the workers' placards read "Busia who born you by mistake," and the second read "Kafo didi too much," and the third, carried by the fattest of the three, read "Perishing citizens of Ghana . . . ." The people around the box who had just been joined by virtually the whole population of the village with one or two who had run away from the lorry park, which was also under the occupation of another single, armed soldier, looked on in silence as this massive demonstration passed by.

The mood of the people of Kontopiaatkrom was aptly summed up by Kofi Sabesabe:

"One king go, one king come; one soldier go, one soldier come; we of Kontopiaatkrom, we dey!"

By contrast, the relationship between the NRC and the university students can only be described as warm and very cordial. Consider this statement by Col. Acheampong: "Since the National Redemption Council took over the reins of government, the students of this country have given eloquent demonstrations of their willingness to serve the nation. And they have done so not by making pious declarations of intention, but by concrete actions spontaneously initiated by themselves. My government has already expressed its appreciation to the student body for their encouraging gesture, and I can assure them that their patriotic gesture of voluntary service and self-help will never be forgotten."[17]

On another occasion, the chairman said: "We need your power working with farmers, the industrial and office worker, to promote a new national consciousness which will inspire us to the victorious tomorrow." He expressed his gratitude to the university student for the encouragement and inspiration they have given to the NRC revolution. Operation Feed Yourself campaign owed no small credit to the spark which students ignited at Asutsuare and Komenda."[18]

Not surprisingly therefore, the NRC has been very receptive to the student interests. One government policy that the Ghanaian university students have been vehemently opposed to is the Student Loan Scheme which was introduced by the Busia government. Despite the possible financial constraints which its abandonment would inflict on Ghanaian financial resources, Col. Acheampong went along with students. He expressed the view that each Ghanaian had a right to free education and unfettered development of historical and cultural well being. But he added: "If this goal is to be reached, genuine efforts must be made to cut down the costs of university education in areas which border on luxury."[19] He invited the students to draft proposals on cost cuts which will make free university education financially possible. The students accepted the challenge, and in less than a month they presented a memorandum to the University Financial Inquiry Committee on ways to reduce the high cost of university education so that free university education could be restored.

As reported in the Daily Graphic,

> The memorandum presented by the Loans Scheme Committee of the university said: "Viewing with great concern the high cost of university education in Ghana and being aware of the country's economic situation whereby the importance of the committee set up by the N.R.C. to investigate certain non-academic aspects of our university will be recognised, we hereby stipulate certain glaring evidence of waste in our university with the hope that they will be accordingly investigated and necessary action taken."
>
> The memorandum listed the following areas which should either be abolished or reorganised to avoid the unnecessary waste: Tutors' tutorial masters' and hall masters' allowances, sweeping of halls by the university workers, maintenance of the central cafeteria sabbatical leave, scholarship awards for post graduate courses, official entertainment funds, the University Primary School and the numerous university workers, the university bookshop and books, employment of external examiners and over employment.
>
> The memorandum said allowances paid to tutors, senior tutors and hall masters were unnecessary because the presence of these academic staff were not felt by the students.
>
> The sweepers, it said, should be retrenched as the students were willing to sweep their halls as their colleagues at the Kumasi University of Science and Technology have been doing.[20]

While one cannot be sure of what will become of all the specific proposals advocated above by the students, it is now a fact that the loan scheme introduced by the Busia government has now been abolished by the NRC in accordance with the wishes of the students.

It should be interesting to see what happens when the military regime experiences intense cross pressures from two social groups it regards with favor. In that vein, we should observe what happens to the NRC decision to sell 200 government bungalows to the civil servants occupying them because the student organization, The National Union of Ghana Students, has expressed its opposition to it. The organization has also called for the probe of the administration of the NLC, Ghana's first military regime.[21]

Instead of setting up an organization like the NYSC as Nigeria did, the NRC has proposed the introduction of compulsory basic military training in Ghanaian universities in order "to bridge a natural gap in university life (in the country) created by the absence of conscious training programmes in the fields of discipline, leadership, man management, motivation, sensitivity and so on in the universities."[22] Col. Acheampong went on: "Having been given the assurance that our university students want to contribute positively and constructively to our national development, the National Redemption Council wants to give them the opportunity to do so."[23]

If this proposal is carried out, it would mean a fundamental change in the structure and content of the university. Unquestionably, the military regime recognizes the importance of the university as a socialization agent. In addition, one may argue that if the regime is interested in mobilization approach to modernization, such a change in education is imperative.

I suspect that as long as the university students continue to support the NRC as enthusiastically as they have done, the military will continue to regard the academicians with benign neglect. However, there is no question that the military will resort to desperate actions against the university if and when it judges this to be necessary. The arrest of some university lecturers in connection with an alleged plot to overthrow the regime is a pointer.

## FOOTNOTES

1. *Ghana Times*, November 20, 1972, p. 4.
2. *Ibid*.
3. *Ibid*.
4. *Ibid*.
5. *Daily Graphic*, November 21, 1972, p. 10.
6. *Ibid*.
7. Adu Boahen, *Legon Observer*, February 25, 1972, p. 73.
8. *Ibid*.
9. *Ibid*.
10. *Legon Observer*, February 25, 1972, pp. 93-94.
11. *Daily Graphic*, June 3, 1972, p. 5.
12. *Legon Observer*, July 14, 1972, p. 318.
13. *Legon Observer*, July 14, 1972, p. 322.
14. *Legon Observer*, February 24, 1972, p. 60.
15. *Legon Observer*, February 24, 1972, p. 60.
16. *Legon Observer*, February 11, 1972, pp. 65-66.
17. *Daily Graphic*, November 25, 1972, p. 9.
18. *Spectator*, June 17, 1972, p. 12.
19. *Ibid*.
20. *Daily Graphic*, July 15, 1972, p. 16.
21. *Legon Observer*, September 21, 1973, p. 463.
22. *Daily Graphic*, November 20, 1972, p. 1.
23. *Ibid*., p. 48.

CHAPTER IX

THE PRESS AND THE MILITARY REGIMES

"Armies are not democracies. Therefore, where military organizations become the state, order is maintained but training in democratic civility is the less probable outcome."

A. NIGERIA

What is the self-image of the Nigerian press with regard to its role and accomplishments? Observe the self-perception:

> . . . The press had to constantly remind the new masters of their pledges to the electorate . . . The press (after independence, civil war) promptly reflected the opinion of the masses and castigated the profligate ministers for despoiling the treasury. The politicians reacted swiftly. There were attempts to muzzle the press and to make ministerial appointments sacrosanct . . . The new masters were growing intolerant of criticisms but this attitude merely incensed the Press to intensify their fight against corruption, nepotism and tribal jingoism which were the bane of the era.[1]

> . . . The press gave all the support the governments needed to make the new military regime succeed. And it is to the credit of the press that in the course of helping the FMG to accomplish its onerous task, the Press has not shirked its responsibilities of lambasting the government for some of its ineptitudes, excesses and planlessness . . . The Press has been stymied by the federal government and some editors detained for daring to speak the truth or reflect the yearnings of the governed.[2]

Prior to the outbreak of the civil war, the press generally concerned itself with the publicity of local feelings and criticisms about the regime. Newspapers based in Western and Eastern states as well as some of those based in Lagos State tended to be skeptical about the new regime. For example, The Nigerian Outlook in response to the Gowon broadcast of November 30, 1966, where he announced the adjournment of the inter-regional constitutional conference, made it clear that it did not care for the government's action. It seemed that many Nigerian newspapers did not quite appreciate the implication of Gowon's appeal in this broadcast. He had asked that:

> . . . The Press, the radio and other mass communication media must exercise a greater sense of responsibility in what they publish in difficult times.[3]

The *Nigerian Opinion*, published by the Nigerian Current Affairs Society, however, supported General Gowon's action. The paper writes:

> . . . When the delegates to the resumed meeting of the Ad Hoc conference on the constitutional future met in October and went back on what they had previously agreed to, they by that act led people to question the usefulness of their proceedings and by dissolving the conference, Lt. Col. Gowon was doing no more than what anyone would have expected a reasonable man to do in the circumstances. But those who criticize his dissolution of the committee seem to have forgotten that the delegates were not expected to <u>determine</u> the political future of the country. Theirs, after all, was only to advise and to suggest. In this respect, the Supreme Commander was acting within his powers and as such the dissolution cannot be said to have been arbitrary. Pari passu, we must also admit that in putting forward his suggestions, Lt. Col. Gowon cannot be said to have been acting dictatorily.[4]

Understandably, the military regime became apprehensive about its relationship with the press during the war. In the name of security and national interest, attempts were made to control the press. The Federal Commissioner of Information warned some editors that their newspapers were diverting attention from the prosecution of the war and giving false impressions of the government abroad. In November of 1968, the Inspector General of Police and Commissioner for Internal Affairs appealed to editors to refrain from publishing matters likely to embarrass the FMG. From then an array of hostile governmental actions against the press follows. Here are a number of government actions against the press:

1. Soon after publishing a front page story alleging that French arms destined for Biafra had been found aboard a ship in Lagos . . . the editor of the Lagos *Daily Times* was arrested for "security reasons."[5]

2. The editor of the *Nigerian Tribune* was jailed in March 1969 after the paper urged the return to civilian rule:

> It is in the interest of the country . . . and of the Nigerian Army that we return to civilian rule. Some critics have accused some of the military leaders of behaving as if they did not want the war to end. Others have said that the corrective regime has, in fact,

corrected nothing. The most immediate answer to these critics is an immediate return to civilian government . . . .[6]

Again the government said that the arrest was for "security reasons."

3. Even editors of government-owned newspapers such as the Western state-owned Daily Sketch from Ibadan were not immune to reproachments from the military government. The editor of the Daily Sketch, Ayo Adedun, was arrested after an editorial which the FMG considered inimical to its interests.[7] The same editor was arrested two years later for another editorial critical of the government. Upon his release the editor appealed to all Nigerians to support freedom of the press. Gowon responded to his appeal by defending the government's action. "We do not just put people in a cell. Journalists should learn how to criticize constructively. They should re-examine themselves."[8]

After the successful termination of the civil war, a rash of editorials criticizing the government resulted in the detention of many editors, much to the dissatisfaction of the Nigerian Union of Journalists. The fact that no reasons were usually given for these arrests and detentions was most vexing to them. The chairman of the Daily Times of Lagos, Alhaji Babatunde Jose, in an address to the Western State Branch of the Nigerian Union of Journalists in December of 1971 discussed many of the problems of the press under the military regime. He declared: "Those who accused Nigerian journalists and newspapers of being 'dull, timid, spineless, toothless and mealy-mouthed' forget that there are 'formidable constraints' on press freedom, apart from the laws of sedition and defamation which are common to all countries."[9] He pointed out some of the reasons:

1. Nigeria has been under a state of emergency since January 1966 "and all constitutional rights and freedoms ceased to exist."

2. the country has been ruled by the military and by decree.

3. Decree 53 made it an offense to display any item in a manner "likely to cause public alarm or industrial unrest."

4. In the absence of a democratically elected Parliament, newspapers found themselves playing the role of a deliberative assembly "reflecting the feelings of the people, their pecadilloes, their likes and dislikes of government policies and actions and the conduct of the people who run the government.[10]

As a result of these pressures Jose concluded, "Almost every editor of any important newspaper, including those owned by governments, has seen the inside of a police cell or army orderly room."[11] Because these constraints could not be ignored, journalists had to impose self-censorship over what they wrote and reported. Although not censorship by law, such constraints had nearly the same effect. Jose said that the extent to which a government could tolerate a newspaper attack which might endager its existence reflected the extent to which that country and its people accepted the concept of liberal democracy, the rule of law and government stability. He noted that journalists everywhere had the responsibility to inform, educate, entertain and mirror opinions--but in Africa and other developing nations-- journalists also had to help in nation-building where economic resources could not match rising expectations and "where, in many cases, their leaders indulge in corruption, graft and nepotism."[12]

In addition The New Nigerian, owned by the governments of the Northern states editorially lashed out against the harassment of reporters by the armed forces. It listed the arrests, detentions and interrogations of correspondents throughout the federation. It cited a case of a news editor who was arrested and forced to disclose the source of a recent story on reactions to a police raid. It concluded that: "The result, if these actions continue, would be that the vital service of collecting and disseminating information to much of this country--where the New Nigerian is the only daily newspaper distributed--will be paralysed. And the public would know who is responsible."[13]

In a lecture delivered on Press Day to the Press Club of Sokoto Federal Government College by Dr. P. E. Jakapa reflected on the Nigerian press-government relations:

> In my view, the so-called "Freedom of the Press" is a loose expression . . . the Press if generally subject to special press laws by which the government is empowered to suppress and confiscate any matter considered objectionable, and to prosecute those in its publication . . . The Press feels that the present establishment has not kept its "Code of Honour" as the custodian of the rules, laws and rights and as well as its security, especially against internal strife . . . The bitter truth, in my view, is that the establishment, especially its functionaries, are very sensitive to criticisms. Herein lies the estrangement between the Press and the establishment.[14]

Finally, the National Union of Journalists issued a communiqué at the end of a convention held in December, 1972, urging the Federal Government to accelerate the setting up of an independent press council. Talk of such an organization had been going on for four years with little action. The Union also called for the immediate release of the reports of two commissions of inquiry set up to look into the future of the press and radio in Nigeria. They also condemned the "incessant arrest, detention and harassment of journalists by law enforcement agencies" and called for the repeal of what was described as the "obnoxious" press law. A convention of the National Guild of Editors ended with an appeal to government officials for cooperation with journalists in seeking information concerning government activities. The convention deplored the present difficulties encountered by journalists from government officials. The convention also passed a resolution opposing government-control of the proposed national news agency.[15] In late 1968 the Information Commissioners from all of the state governments met with Federal Information Commissioner, Chief Enahoro, to discuss measures to improve Nigeria's publicity machinery, both within and outside of Nigeria. There were discussions on the creation of a national news agency. Allegedly, Chief Enahoro's plan to make the agency independent of government was turned down by the regime. Therefore the Commissioner announced the military government's plan in 1971. He said:

> . . . it is now intended to establish the agency under the direct control of the Federal Government, in order to ensure that the agency has the correct orientation. This is considered particularly necessary in the light of our experience during the Civil War. Steps are therefore being taken to submit fresh proposals

> to accord with the wishes of the Federal Executive Council . . .
> if the agency proves a success, it could acquire independence
> progressively and could, in due course, be constituted into a
> public trust entirely independent of Government.[16]

The Nigerian press found this unacceptable. It seemed that criticism of the government-ownership of the national news agency may have kept the government from putting its plan into operation.

The press, even though closely watched by the military regime, served as a public watch dog by alerting the public to corruption in the government. The military government reacted to the reports of alleged corruption by setting up inquiries to investigate the charges. Anti-corruption campaigns such as the one carried out by the Daily Times criticized some Government Commissioners for holding more than one post. Many civil servants who held joint positions resigned soon after the widespread campaign. In November, 1969, armed police in Lagos sealed off all three offices of the <u>Daily Times</u> and locked in over 1,000 workers. Allegedly, they were searching for "incriminating documents." After several days of suspension, the <u>Daily Times</u> returned to press. No incriminating documents had been found. Like labor, the press has found Decree 53 abominable because it has curbed their ability to analyze and report on potentially volatile occurrences.

The FMG has not had an easy time with the Nigerian press. The government finds itself in a dilemma for it cannot completely supress the press and radio without glaringly appearing to violate one of the key goals it established for itself, that of democracy. Moreover, in the absence of a parliament, the press, if it is free, is an invaluable source for the reflection of public opinion and interests of the literate segments of the society, which the regime needs. Furthermore, a free press is a more credible educator of the literate public regarding the good achievements and understandable problems. However, if the press is perceived to labor under government intimidation it loses credibility with its more independent readers. Under such conditions it cannot be of critical use to its readers, itself and the regime. Complete freedom of the press restrains the regime. Its absence deprives the regime of a valuable source of information and a credible advocate.

The strategy of the Nigerian press has tended to be to criticize the bureaucrat while extolling the personal values and "near saintly" characteristics of General Gowon. Government policy is bad because of the bad advice of bureaucrats who misled him or because the leader did not know the complete facts of the situation. It would be unrealistic for the military regime to control the press completely and still hope to maintain legitimacy with key groups in Nigeria. The literate public could differentiate between government proclamations and editorial review. In order to maintain support, the government had to permit a certain degree of criticism--allegedly they took control in order to preserve certain freedoms that the civilians were taking advantage of. How to minimize criticism without jeopardizing praise became a major problem for the military regime.

Let us return to the general proposition stated at the beginning of the chapter; that of democracy and military regimes. As of July, 1973, the only government measure which can be interpreted as leading ultimately to democracy is the formation of the Nigerian Census Board. Otherwise what we have seen is the government's attempts to restrict the freedom of the press, and individual freedom. There have been abuses of power by the military. During the war, restrictive legislations were justified on security grounds. After the war they are justified in the name of development. The argument is not that Nigeria should be a democracy. Since the military has set this as one of its goals, however, it is not unfair to examine how well the government has performed in this regard.

It might be pointed out that after the end of the war the military continued to encroach upon citizens and institutions.

1. Taxi drivers went on strike because the military had beaten up some of them.[17]

2. Bus drivers went on strike because the soldiers refused to pay fares or follow regulations.[18]

3. Soldiers got into fights with customs officers in the pursuit of the latter's normal duties.[19]

4. Judge Adeshihun warned the State Military Governor of Kwara State against the government's efforts to interfere with the judicial process and independence.

5. The Daily Times reported the arrest and detention of a civilian in the military guardroom because the man refused to give his consent to the proposed marriage of his daughter to an officer. In addition we have various harrassments of the press.

The military leadership is attempting to combat some of these abuses by establishing complaint centers. The fact of the matter is that few people trust the system. The secrecy of military trials and judgments has not helped instill the much needed confidences.

Therefore, the proposition:

> Armies are not democracies. Therefore, where military organizations become the state, order is maintained, but training in democratic civility is the less probable outcome.

would seem to be bourne out in Nigeria. The various attempts of government to maintain order have always succeeded, in the long run, but sometimes at heavy social and political cost.

### B. GHANA

The absence of basic freedoms with the increasing days of Nkrumah's regime is well documented.[20] When the NLC deposed the Nkrumah regime, it declared as one of its priority goals the restoration of freedoms. A journalist writing in the Legon Observer, noted that "In fact not only did almost all the members of the National Liberation Council urge press men to be bold and fearless, one of the leading architects of the coup, Lt. General Afrifa, is on record as having congratulated the members of the Ghanaian Times for daring to criticise him openly."[21] Nevertheless, NLC Decree 92, the Prohibition of Rumours Decree, NLC Decree 131 which puts civilians under the jurisdiction of military laws, and the enactment of some retroactive laws indicate that this goal was not achieved completely. A senior lecturer in the Faculty of Law has commented, "Then came the coup of 24th February, 1966. Our hopes were rekindled: our hopes of a free and just society. But except for a brief period, only a flick of the flame of liberty has appeared. We still cannot sing freedom. Freedom and Justice still remains a pious dream."[22] In other words although Nkrumah's Preventive Detention Act was repealed by the NLC, it promulgated a Protective Custody decree.

At first, it appeared the Ghanaian press was willing to accept NLC exhortations at its face value. The journalists seemed prepared to redeem themselves by letting their vigilant and objective performance atone for the malperformances of the past. Then came the rude awakenings. First, the editor of an independent paper, The Pioneer, openly criticized the rapid promotions in the Army. But according to the editor, he was "summoned before the Army and abused, insulted and humiliated for having criticised the too-rapid promotions in the Army. Wise journalists read the signs of the time and began to dance joyously to the tune the liberators chose to call."[23] Second, three editors who dared to criticize the controversial Abbot Agreement signed by the NLC regime were summarily relieved of their duties. Despite the considerable sympathy which the Ghanaian intellectual community had for these editors' position and in spite of the fact that the civilian commissioner of information felt so strongly about the inadvisability of the NLC decision (to relieve the men of their duties) that he resigned, the NLC did not reconsider its decision. Indeed the civilian commissioner was not consulted prior to the decision.[24] It has been suggested that the latter experience served as "an objective lesson to all Ghanaian journalists. Some of them never forgot that lesson, and they are still in employment. Others forgot it, and they are unemployed."[25] The point apparently is that the Ghanaian press has come to believe that despite all pretensions, the Ghanaian military and political leaders are not serious about the freedom of the press.

It is no wonder, then, that during the Progress Party rule, the press did not critically assert itself. Consider the issue of devaluation. Immediately following the NRC coup, the government papers changed overnight. The Spokesman and the Legon Observer were exceptions. The Spokesman was very vehement and almost psychopathological in its criticism. The Legon Observer, although less effective during the Busia regime, stated its opposition to government policies whenever it deemed it necessary.

Under the Progress Party government, members of the opposition were not imprisoned. However, Busia's "No court, No court" tirade against the Ghana Supreme Court and his dissolution of the Trade Union Congress because he opposed its policy depreciated somewhat from the posture of his regime as a non-repressive one.

In his capacity as the NRC Commissioner for Information, Major Selormey admonished the press to be bold, objective, and courageous. Upon occasion, the government seemed embarrassed by the inaccuracy of its own press. For example, writing about the government's development plan, one of the government's newspapers reported that the NRC had decided to invite West German experts to re-evaluate the viability of the Soviety projects abandoned by the NLC. The government had to issue a denial claiming that the reports were "entirely without foundation."[26] Obviously, the government paper in its eagerness to serve the NRC made no attempt to check the veracity of its story.

On December 4, 1972, the chairman of the NRC addressed thirty-nine district and regional information officers. He "called on them to feed the government with correct information about what the people truly think about the government."[27] He felt the officers "would be doing great disservice to the state if they only filed news items that were favourable to the government . . . . information-officers would be taken seriously only if they are objective and fearless in their presentation of information."[28]

Despite these public declarations, the government is somewhat satisfied with the instrumental use of the press. The government press carried a series of lead articles about the alleged corruption of the Progress Party (PP) and its leadership. Given the affluent style of the PP leadership, the tradition of abuse of office, Ghanaians have tended to have a skeptical attitude toward the integrity of public officials. It was therefore not difficult for them to believe the newspapers' stories.

In any case, it would seem that the NRC government has made a move aimed at protecting the government against prosecution. NRC Decree 67, entitled the "Defamation by Newspaper Decree of 1972," granted indemnity to the editors of Daily Graphic, The Mirror, Ghanaian Times, and The Weekly Spectator regarding publications made in these newspapers on or after January 13, 1972. This move has been interpreted as evidence of the lack of sincereity of the NRC when it professes belief in the freedom of the press. In addition, under the NRC The Pioneer was forced to cease publication in July, 1973, and the editor of The Echo was reprimanded by the NRC for his editorial of June 4, 1972. The editor of Voice of the People has also experienced a similar fate.[29] Moreover, under the NRC, Ghana has witnessed the promulgation of the Newspaper Licensing Decree, a "Prohibition of Rumours Decree" and a retroactive Subversion Decree. Furthermore, the NRC government, like its Nigerian counterpart, has not been favorably disposed toward setting up of the machinery which would guarantee the freedom and independence of the press. The NLC, the Progress Party government, and the .RC have not created a Press Trust despite the clamor for the establishment of such a trust in Ghana.

The Ghanaian press and the academicians appeared to be at each other's throat. The Legon Observer was very scathing in its criticism of the Ghana press. Consider the passage below:

> Within the last six weeks and more, the reading public has been treated to a nauseating spate of unchecked allegations and speculations dished out as well-seasoned and verified facts, accompanied by illogical conclusions and inconsequential editorial commentaries, and followed by abject withdrawals, corrections and refutations. Doubts are cast as to who owns what company, how certain contracts were entered into, how

much was spent on painting buildings and planting trees which were never planted anyhow, how some aircraft or identification equipment were purchased, who received how much loan or severance pay plus gratuity, how people acquired land to put houses on, and a host of other allegations. Most of these allegations have been vigorously refuted, and the journalists challenged to provide evidence in support of their contention. These challenges have not been taken up and the newspapers involved have not had the courage to dispute any of the refutations, presumably because they have only tried to make scoops out of scandalous rumours without taking the elementary precaution of checking on their veracity. The journalistic rumour-mongering, followed by challenges and refutations, has become so typical of recent-day newspaper reports that it is fact becoming normal to expect almost every sensational news item to be refuted in a subsequent issue of the same paper without the slightest editorial comment, however unconvincing or an appropriate apology to the aggrieved person.

The pattern that was clearly emerging indicated a zealous effort to discredit the members of the fallen government on the flimsiest shred of dubious evidence, and this was bad enough, because even a discredited person must be served only his just desserts. But when a newspaper reports that the government has invited a West German firm to re-evaluate projects initiated here by the Soviet Union and proceeds to comment editorially on it in all seriousness, only to publish three days later a statement by the government to the effect that the reports "are entirely without foundation," then we realize that the state of journalism is more dismal than we might have earlier suspected. For, journalism born of malice, carelessness or stark irresponsibility, none of which does much credit to the quality of journalism in this country, is what we have been getting these days and we are clearly fed up with all this rigmarole.[30]

On another occasion, an academician commented: "It is very sickening and mentally unenduring to read newspaper editorials that show blind support and obedience to the government in power. And in this characteristic role of servile obedience and sychophancy our newspapers have become a 'great killer' of the Ghanaian intellect."[31]

In a sense, the Ghana press may well be its own enemy. In their overriding desire to please the new master, Ghanaian journalists have put aside the golden rule. On June 4, 1972, The Echo in an editorial asked that some of the detainees should be considered for release. Under the caption "The Echo's Insolence," The Weekly Spectator declared: "If The Echo thinks that some of the detainees might be security risks who should receive special treatment then the editor of The Echo must be made by the intelligence apparatus of the state to disclose names since he must be in league with them. If The Echo editor refuses to cooperate, then the NRC must ban the paper. Failure to do so would only be a sign of the NRC's own weakness and its implicit agreement with the charge, alleged to have been made by The Echo, that the NRC is (truly) confused!"[32]

Comparatively, the Nigerian press is more concerned about press freedom than the Ghanaian press. At least, it seems clear that they have been more vocal about it and that they have been penalized more for their exercise of press freedom. In my judgment, the Nigerian journalists feel more constrained under the military regime than their Ghanaian counterparts.

FOOTNOTES

1. New Nigeria, October 1, 1971.

2. Ibid.

3. "Towards a New Nigeria." Broadcast by Col. Yakubu Gowon, November 30, 1966.

4. Nigerian Opinion, December, 1966, p. 136.

5. West Africa, November 30, 1968, pp. 14-20.

6. West Africa, March 29, 1969, pp. 370 and 426.

7. West Africa, October 4, 1969, pp. 1197.

8. West Africa, July 9, 1971, p. 793. The journalist had said, "The press must not compromise its freedom and neither must it allow itself to be sacrifice on the altar of power.

9. West Africa, December 17, 1971, p. 1471.

10. Ibid.

11. Ibid.

12. Ibid.

13. Reported in West Africa, March 17, 1972, p. 337.

14. Ibid.

15. West Africa, December 4, 1972, p. 1637.

16. West Africa, November 5, 1971, p. 1309.

17. West Africa, June 30, 1971.

18. West Africa, November 29, 1970

19. West Africa, June 11, 1973.

20. Preventive Detention Act of 1958; Treason Act of 1959; Sedition Act of 1959; Offences Against the State Act of 1959; Criminal Code Act 29 of 1960; Criminal Procedure Amendment Act (Act 91) of 1961.

21. Legon Observer, June 30, 1972, p. 296.

22. Legon Observer, August 24, 1973, p. 403.

23. Legon Observer, June 30, 1972, p. 296.

24. See Jon Kraus, The Politics of the Coup d'etat, p. 120.

25. Legon Observer, June 30, 1972, p. 296.

26. <u>Legon Observer</u>, March 10, 1972, p. 115.

27. <u>Legon Observer</u>, December 15, 1972, p. 607.

28. <u>Ibid</u>.

29.. <u>Legon Observer</u>, June 30, 1972, p. 296.

30. <u>Legon Observer</u>, "Notebook," March 10, 1972, pp. 115-16.

31. Oppong Afrae, <u>Legon Observer</u>, May 5, 1972.

32. <u>Legon Observer</u>, June 30, 1972, p. 306.

CHAPTER X

THE RELATIONSHIP BETWEEN LABOR AND MILITARY REGIMES

A. NIGERIAN LABOR

The editor of The New Nigerian pinpointed the essential problems confronting labor in Nigeria. In an editorial the paper commented:

> No organised group in the country have potentially more power and yet remain more or less powerless than the trade unions . . . The reasons for their weaknesses are not far to see: fractiousness, disunity, poor quality leadership, proneness to foreign cash and influences." It regards the most serious drawback as the inability to "come together and fulfill the basic function of unions: to win maximum pay and the best working conditions for their members.
>
> Many of the more articulate and intelligent unionists have for some years advocated unions through mergers . . . Only when a serious and unified leadership is formed can unionism attract government support and funds . . . Meanshile the real losers are the vast and growing rank and file.[1]

There is no doubt that the efficacy of the Nigerian labor has been hampered by the factors delineated by the editor. The labor movement suffered from the same malaise which afflicted other organizations in the Nigerian society. In addition, Nigerian labor is plagued by the law which makes it possible for any five workers to form a trade union. The consequent proliferation of unions coupled with the absence of meaningful cooperation among them and the alignments with international labor organizations whose ideological predispositions are wo  thless within the framework of Nigeria were added liabilities. There are five central labor organizations in Nigeria: ULC, NTUC, LUF, NWC, NFL.[2]

Although many trade union leaders ran into hot waters with the government, no Nigerian civilian regime banned trade unions. Generally, the major trade union federations were not officially aligned with the political parties. Some of the member unions did have such affiliations, however. For example, in 1964 the Socialist Workers and Farmers Party was established under the leadership of Dr. Utegbeye. In addition, some important labor leaders, as individuals, were active in political parties. After the military take-over and the decree against political parties, formal political activities ceased.

The only notable joint performance of the Nigerian labor organizations during the civilian regime came in 1964.[3] After the government ignored the workers' demand for a revision of the wage standards and working conditions, the Nigerian workers organized and carried out a very effective strike. This is notable because it represents the only time in the history of the Nigerian civilian regime that the entire labor force of the country united together to work as a unit. The government was forced to address itself to the workers' demands and it honored most of them. Parenthetically, I should mention that the relationship between labor and the Ironsi regime was not an entirely peaceful one.

## Labor Under the Gowon Military Regime

Although the FMG appealed for peaceful industrial relations, it felt constrained to introduce Decree 21 in May of 1968. This decree introduced a timetable for intervention in trade disputes if compulsory arbitration did not work. In addition, the decree outlawed strikes. Despite this decree, however, there were 264 trade disputes between 1968 and 1969. Sixty-seven of these disputes led to strikes and lockouts. To complete the statistics, thirty-two were referred for conciliation, four for arbitration, one to a board of inquiry and the rest were directly negotiated by labor and management with assistance from the Ministry of Labour.[4] The FMG therefore felt that Decree 21 was ineffective. Consequently, it opted to introduce a new labor legislation, Decree 53. Under this new Trade Dispute Emergency Provisions Amend Decree, No. 53, of 1969,'

1. an employee cannot initiate a lock-out and a worker cannot take part in a strike;

2. no one can organize or make any preparation for a lock-out or a strike;

3. no worker or employer or any person acting or purporting to act on behalf of a worker or workers can threaten to take part in or organize a strike:

4. no one can publish in the newspaper, television or by any other communication media any material which by dramatization or other defects in the matter of its presentation is likely to cause public alarm or industrial unrest.

Anyone guilty of violating the decree would be sentenced to five years imprisonment. In sum, the decree put a complete ban on strikes and lock-outs for a period of twelve months. This decree has been extended many times. The latest was a six month extension beginning in February of 1973. The implications of the decree are profound because not only do they affect the right to organize or talk about a srrike, but they also affect the freedom of the press.

The government and the union leaders have divergent readings of the union member's reaction to this far-reaching decree. In his 1970 New Year message, General Gowon claimed that most union members welcomed the decree and that only the irresponsible trade union leaders were ready to oppose it. In order to correct what they considered to be wrong impressions of General Gowon, the ULC, NTUC, NWC and LUF attempted another united effort. They prepared and sent a memo to the general. Presumably, this memo incorporated the true feeling which the Nigerian workers and trade unions have about the decree.

In any case, a more convincing evidence of Nigerian workers' negative feelings on the decree is demonstrated by the fact that labor unrests continued; "Go-slows," "work to rules," and strikes mushroomed.

In order to meet war demands taxes were raised, inflation skyrocketed and wages did not keep pace with increased costs. Let me cite a few random samples of labor discontent.

In October, 1968, a pay raise was obtained after 1500 employees of the West Nigerian Marketing Board struck.[6] Four thousand members of the Western State Water Workers Union went on strike and left Ibadan without water for four days until their grievances were met.[7] Over 2000 employees of the Post and Telegraph Division of the Ministry of Communications struck when the government failed to recognize their union.** Employees of the Central Bank of Nigeria struck two times within one month in protest against the refusal of management to continue negotiations on their demands for improved conditions of service. The Government appointed a conciliator, but this turned out to be ineffective, so Chief Awolowo broke his vacation to intervene. The workers returned to work "in view of the assurances and guarantees . . . received both from the Federal Government and bank management."[8] One hundred thousand employees of state-owned corporations struck demanding that the new scale of salaries by the Ani Commission of Inquiry be implemented; the corporations included The Nigerian Railway Corporations; the National Shipping Line; The Nigerian Airways, and the Nigerian Broadcasting Corporation. Most of the strikers were concerned with disparities in salaries between expatriates and local Nigerians. After the rash of strikes, the government called a meeting with trade union representatives to discuss the strikes. Moreover, despite the decree, the doctors at the Lagos University Teaching Hospital went on a "Go-slow." In one month alone, (September, 1970), six government corporations experienced "Go-slow" strikes in support of the demand for higher wages.

There was an intensification of labor dissatisfaction in 1969 despite the civil war. Toward the end of the year strike actions included Central Bank employees, Western State Civil Servants and the National Shipping staff. Economists were becoming alarmed at the dangerous inflationary spiral and warned that wage increases would aggravate the problem. The price control legislation, and Decree 51, aimed at increasing the employment of more Nigerian workers in foreign companies, represented the attempts made by the FMG to accomodate the dissatisfaction of the labor. However, the price control provisions were largely ineffective as an

---

**There was a close relationship between the trade union movement and the civil service. The trade union movement began as trade organizations predominately for government employees. It was often difficult to separate the two as can be seen in the results of the Ayoola and Adebo Commissions of Inquiry.

economic tool. Moreover, they exacerbateed the resentment of some Nigerians against the military regime since they allowed price control inspectors to search, without warrant, the premises of those suspected of contravening the decree.

In response to mounting pressure from the labor, the Adebo Commission recommended the granting of an interim award to labor. It asked that the cost of living allowances be given so as to relieve "the intolerable suffering at or near the bottom of the wages and salary." It should be recalled that the last wage adjustment for labor came during the civilian regime after a general strike (1964). Since then, there had not been a general labor wage adjustment despite the fact that the cost of living had risen by thirty-four percent and the cost of food was up by fifty percent.

Undoubtedly, labor was elated by this interim report. However, the FMG dragged its feet with regard to the implementation of this award. The situation was further complicated by the fact that private workers wanted to be considered for the award. There was another rash of "Go-slows." Major General Adebayo, a member of the Supreme Military Council, called on trade unionists to address themselves to the social welfare of the people and to think less of politics. They were told to be patient and to cooperate fully with the FMG implementation of the four-year development plan. He further urged labor leaders not to allow former politicians to use them against the nation because members of the old regime were "still lurking about ready to pounce on any flimsy situation and use it to return the country to the pre-military era."[9]

The delay in the payment of interim awards caused the government considerable problems. The lack of government desire to encourage private employers to consider an interim award did greater havoc to the economy.
FMG declared that all workers in the private sector would be paid the Adebo interim award. The Adebo final report was somewhat controversial. The FMG accepted only portions of the report.

Government's handling of the Post and Telegraph's (P & T) communications strike of November 1972 is more instructive. The Gill Report had recommended a new scale of salary for P & T workers. The union insisted that the Federal Government and its employees implement this new recommended scale. Under Decree No. 53 the government set up an Industrial Arbitration Tribunal. The union submitted the dispute to the tribunal which ruled in the union's favor, but the government refused to follow the ruling of the tribunal. Instead, the Commissioner of Labor referred the case back to the tribunal for reconsideration. The union then decided to use the ultimate labor weapon, strike, despite the fact that it was illegal. The government not only arrested the labor leaders but threatened to dismiss the strikers. Given the skill of many of these workers, the government was unable to replace the strikers. In the circumstance, the government announced what amounted to a compromise decision. It announced that the P & T would soon be transformed into a corporation and that the staff would be given salary increases which such transformations usually imply. Furthermore, the workers would continue to receive all the fringe benefits of civil servants. Moreover the government instructed the new management to remove existing causes of discontent and to promote those people deserving promotions.

It is significant that the imprisoned leaders were briefed regarding the Federal government's position. More significant is the fact that these leaders were immediately released following the refusal of the rank and file union members to return fully to their jobs. A final point worthy of note in this case is that within a month P & T announced a 33 1/3 percent salary increase for its workers.

The success of the P & T in its confrontation with the military regime can be explained by several factors. The success of the P & T union was dependent on their numbers--they constituted about one-fifth of the Nigerian Federal bureaucracy. In addition, they occupied a strategic position in the Nigerian economy because they held the key to the national communication network, given the sorry state of the transportation system. Moreover, the fact that they had skills which could not be replaced easily, literally held the Federal government to ransom. Finally, it seems that the federal Commissioner of Labor was not very happy about the apparent fact that the government was not respecting the institutional arrangements and procedure which it set up in Decree 53.

Generally, in dealing with labor, the military leadership attempted to use the war as an instrument to bring about industrial peace; (appealing to patriotic emotions in the period of "national crisis"). However, its approach became increasingly punitive and negativistic. As the years went by, restrictive decrees became broken reeds and the use of force in a preemptive fashion became the dominant tool of government. Military leaders and their bureaucratic advisers were distrustful of labor and the lack of mutual trust preempted a more positive instrumental use of labor. Insofar as labor was concerned, therefore, the military government cannot be said to have realistically sought to mobilize all their national resources. Labor was seldom consulted regarding impending policies. Neither was its efforts actively enlisted with regard to modernization. Moreover, there was no attempt to positively involve labor in the integrative attempts. Government strategy with regard to labor has been to maintain low profile. Government seems to be saying, "As much as possible, let us try to stop them from upsetting the apple cart."

On the whole, the military government depended on patriotism and inexpensive symbolic output as an instrument with which to deal with labor. As the civil war dragged on and inflation soared, labor became persistent in its wage demands. In turn, government passed punitive measures and increasingly resorted to the use of force. One of the main results of the use of force by the military government was the engendering of some degree of unity in the labor movement. The strikes and stoppages were somewhat disruptive to the economy. In addition, they were embarrassing to the military regime which was anxious to demonstrate its stability and developmental success to Africa and the rest of the world. The strikes and "go-slows" could be interpreted as an index of widespread dissatisfaction with the

FMG. In addition, the fact that the FMG increasingly failed to settle the labor problems by persuasion could be interpreted as evidence of its poor political performance. A greater indictment on the FMG is the fact that the use of strikes as an instrument for the settlement of disputes has now spread to the professional class; teachers, university lecturers and medical doctors are now rssorting to it.

The Federal Commissioner of Labor would like to see Decrees 21 and 53 nullified. In fact, he had announced that they would be terminated by the end of the year 1972. It is generally believed that General Gowon wants the decrees continued. Consequently, the life of the decrees continues to be extended. In the opinion of the trade union leaders of the ULC,[10] the Commissioner of Labor is friendly with labor. However, he has not received the necessary FMG cooperation because his motives are suspect to the military leadership.

The labor leaders informally interviewed believed that the military government has not really made up its mind on the type of relationship that should exist between labor and the regime. They felt that the government still views labor as a "bunch of agitators always causing troubles." Therefore, government has not adequately responded with positive functions "which the labor could perform in bringing about socio-economic and political changes in our society." Labor leaders complained that they were not consulted before or during the planning of the "now celebrated" Four Year Development Plan. Consequently, "the whole plan has nothing for labor." Some of them claimed that even after the "promulgation of the plan" labor's demand to be consulted on its implementation "was not seriously viewed." Furthermore, they contended that even when a theoretical concession is made to labor, it is often not carried through. For example, they claimed that although the federal government recommended that two representatives of labor should be included on each Price Control Board, some regions have not followed through.

Interestingly, even in the opinion of some ULC leaders who are usually sympathetic to the government, the governmental bureaucracies are to blame for this poor relationship. They claimed that permanent secretaries and heads of service shelter the military governors and particularly the Head of State. Therefore, it has been extremely difficult to have direct access to them. "These people deliberately create barriers which prevent any close ties between labour and government."[11] When pressed as to why the bureaucrats would be interested in these tactics, one labor leader replied, "They advised the civilian governments. It is difficult to teach old dogs new tricks." Another reason given is as follows:

> The FMG speaks of its democratic rule with all the mistakes and double standards of the regime and restrictions on individual freedoms as well as the view that the military is above the law. The fear is therefore there that any close relationship can cause trouble for them. Organized labor can expose all the weaknesses, double standards and point out unfulfilled aspirations of the government. This also explains the fear of the civil servants who are now part of the ruling class.[12]

The perception of labor is that while the military regime might have performed well in the area of Nigerian unity, they did not perform well with regard to the goal of democracy. Insofar as labor was concerned, the FMG's performance has not outclassed that of the civilians.

Finally the following statements which were submitted to the Adebo Committee by the spokesman for the entire workers of the Western State corraborates some of the points made with respect to the perception of the Nigerian workers about the performance of the military regime.

13. Many strikes, lockouts work-to-rule, go-slow actions in the past and presently, if reasons are objectively compiled, nine cases out of ten were caused by intransigence displayed by agents of the employers--both in the public and private sectors. There are examples to quote in support. For instance, let us recall certain events in the Industrial Relations world of Nigeria.
    (a) EVENT No. 1  The workers of the Post and Telecommunications, a Federal Government department went on a "recognition strike" in 1969 because of the intransigence of a Federal Permanent Secretary. The workers struck not because they want to strike for pay increase but because XYZ Permanent Secretary saw no 'immediate reason' to recognise the Postal Workers' Union as the sole bargaining agent for its members. And after the assault had been committed against the Nation's economy, the said Permanent Secretary gave recognition. Isn't that medicine after death? Please note this; the workers and their union were to our mind not the causes.

(b) EVENT No. 2   The workers of all the Western State Statutory Corporations last year September declared a "work-to-rule" action against the State Government.
REASON: A Permanent Secretary altered Cabinet decision without Cabinet approval. News about a successfully concluded negotiation turned the big "YES" to "NO." Again, the Nigerian Worker is to suffer for an act of a dogmatic adviser.

(c) EVENT No. 3   It was in this country that the University authorities allowed several man-days to go unproductive because of just demands made by workers which were firstly unattended but later the authorities conceded same, a thing which could have been met initially without necessarily resulting into industrial action by the workers.

(d) EVENT No. 4   A very Important Spokesman of the Federal Military Government in the Federal Ministry of Labour and Information told the Nation, that Adebo Wages and Salaries Review Commission Cost of Living Allowance Award will not cover certain groups of workers in the private sector. The "official message" came as a "relief" to private firms and even some state-owned companies whose managerial leadership are big exploiters.

(e) EVENT No. 5   The Workers in the Western State Civil Service had cause to "go-slow" in 1969 after exhausting all the channels for redress of their grievances in respect of hours of work and the anomalies in the government's white papers on Elwood Report.
REASON: The High-ups, that is, the bureaucrats Civil Servants were concerned with matters affecting themselves alone and treating with levity, matters affecting the junior civil servants.

(f) The total costs of the go-slow and work-to-rule actions, staged because of the "slip of tongue" from the BIG BOSS in charge of Labour should be assessed. But the Nigerian Worker was worst for it before the situation, though belated, was corrected by the Federal Military Government.

(g) These five big events cannot be assessed in isolation of the industrial relations system of this country.

14. In any case, the Nigerian Worker does not pretend to have no blame for going-slow or working-to-rule as of now or in the past for striking against unruly employers. It is when all efforts to obtain result fail; the "HE", the Nigerian Worker, calls on his fellow workers to mobilise their bargaining strength to obtain justice and fair play through industrial action.

15. The Nigerian Worker of today and his union are aware of their roles to the people of Nigeria and the government. Among other things, "HE", the Nigerian Worker, is to encourage speedy economic progress through efficient production, higher productivity and political stability. His awareness to jointly create an atmosphere for industrial peace by exploring all avenues for settling trade disputes cannot be over-emphasised.

16. How can these lofty ideals be achieved with less (not without) frictions between the Nigerian employers of labour (including the State) the Nigerian Workers and their trade Unions?

17. It is definitely not by sweeping the combined forces of the organised labour unions and the suffering workers under the carpet.

18. It is also not through unprogressive legislations or denial of right to react against an unjust system.

19. The only panacea, to our mind, is the right of Nigerian Worker to participate in Management.

20. Let us not think by this suggestion that only Trade Union leaders should be made State Commissioners, Chairmen of the Boards or Corporations or directors of State Owned Companies. The first thing is, the workers involvement in the Factory level Management, be it State or Foreign Owned Factories. This system has brought great dividends in Japan, Israel, Sweden and United Arab Republic among other Nations.

21. Workers participation in Management will ensure better understanding among all concerned parties such as the State, The Worker and The Capital - Public or Private.
   (a) Such a system will minimise interplay of Industrial-power politics.
   (b) If the suggested system is introduced, the much needed sense of belonging by a worker to his job will be immense and thereby ensure efficiency and higher productivity.

22. In fact, it is absolutely necessary that a Joint Efficiency and Productivity Committee comprising both labour and management be set-up as an essential forum for dialogues in all establishments if the four-year National Development Plan is to fulfill its objectives.

23. It is our joint assignment to build a nation free from imperialistic economic domination and unnecessary political influence by foreign powers - small or big.

24. In our bid to build an egalitarian Society, the Nigerian Worker, his Union should be treated as essential arms of economic power to greatness and their support at all times for social, political and economic schemes MUST be sought. It is through their involvement in the scheme of things that any wage increase now or in future could have any value to the Nigeria peasants, cooperators, petty-traders and the workers.

25. For instance, the consumers in this State would like the unused space of Cocoa House, Ibadan now converted into occasional exhibition centre to be allocated to the Co-operative Supply Association Limited to enable it compete effectively with foreign-owned super markets in Ibadan.

26. In conclusion, Mr. Chairman, your Commission should examine the following suggestions in the light of our experiences:
   (a) - the evolution of a new policy to ensure workers participation in Management at all levels including top policy making bodies;
   (b) - the abrogation of Trade Disputes Emergency Provisions Decree No. 53 of 1969;
   (c) - the creation of an Industrial Court to replace the present Arbitration Tribunal - with Labour, Private employers and the Government representatives on the panel. The court should be answerable through the Head of the Federal Military Government to the Supreme Military Council;
   (d) - to remove all forms of control of State Owned Companies and Statutory Corporations by top Government Beaurocrats who possess no knowledge of modern business methods;
   (e) - the retraining of our Civil Servants especially the "old horses" promised in the country's four-year economic - Blue Print should commence immediately;
   (f) - the urgent task of ensuring better understanding between the Federal Military Government and the Nigerian Labour Movement through closer contacts, representation on Committees; Commissions, Local, State and National Government;
   (g) - the creation of State mechanised farms throughout the country to be manned by those hands now at rest since the end of hostilities. This will help the production of more foodstuffs and finished food products;
   (h) - the rent and price control schemes being pursued by various governments in the Federation are commendable but it is the production of more foodstuffs and building of more low cost houses that can help the situation;

(i) - the Federal Military Government should halt the present exploitation of our resources by foreigners especially in the Oil, Industrial and Agricultural sectore. It should either be in partnership with well organised Nigerian business-man or Government. No foreigner should be allowed to go it alone any more.
(j) - to evolve a sound Industrial Relations Policy, the Federal Military Government should encourage the development and growth of Free and democratic Trade Unions;
(k) - the need for Adebo Commission to ensure a national minimum wage which MUST be made legal throughout the country;
(l) - the existing 1964 Morgan Rates yet to be paid to General Workers by many employers of labour such as School proprietors even those on Government subsidies, General Contractors, as well as other indigenous employers of labour. The Federal Military Government should ensure that the Morgan 1964 rates of pay are attained by all employees;
(m) - the Commission should ensure all the anomalies contained in the Government White Papers on Elwood Report be rectified by all Governments and as well ensure that all employees in the State Statutory Corporations and State-owned Companies are paid the Federal Corporations salary structures as approved under the Federal Military Government Decree No. 59 of 1969;
(n) - to encourage intensive workers education, the present Industrial Relations unit, under the Department of Adult Education at the University of Ibadan should be uplifted to a full-fledged Institute of Industrial Relations.

The course must cater for high level man-power development for both Labour and Management;
(o) - the Commission should evolve a national salary brackets separately for the undermentioned groups and harmonize the structures:
   (i) the Civil Service and the Local Government Service;
   (ii) the Statutory Corporations/Boards and State Owned Companies;
   (iii) the private sector;
   (iv) the Universities/Teaching Hospitals;
and (v) most especially a national minimum wage (without zonalization) for the most cheated group in the society, that is, the tradesmen, Semi-skilled and the unskilled workers.
(p) - the Commission should examine the need to adopt hourly rate system and abolish the present "daily rate" system.

The Workers of this country fully endorsed the case as presented by UCCLO for this cadre of workers and in fact an informal visit to Dugbe Market will further strengthen the workers' case;
(q) - It is no exaggeration if we say that prices of basic and essential commodities had risen as much as over 300 percent;
(r) - The Commission should ensure that its recent Cost of Living Allowance (C.O.L.A.) and the final awards are extended to the pensioners throughout the country;

B. GHANAIAN LABOR

The Trade Union Congress (TUC), which included seventeen national unions in its membership was a strong ally of the CPP. When Nkrumah called for "positive action" in mid-December of 1949 the TUC responded by calling for a general strike. As a result of this two-week strike the British arrested and imprisoned the important leaders of the TUC and the CPP. That was the high point of cooperation between the two organizations. Many workers were disappointed at the seeming failure of the strike and the positive action campaign to accomplish meaningful results. There was also some disagreement within the TUC leadership about the type of relationship that should have been maintained with the CPP.[14] Working with the CPP seemed to be the only viable alternative, however, since the opposition party remained elitist in orientation and labor was unhappy with the colonial regime. Labor's discontent with the colonial government was a result of several factors. To mention two: (1) labor was not mentioned in the Ten-Year Plan set forth by the colonial government in 1951;[15] (2) the cost of food and the cost of living in urban centers continued to rise while workers' wages remained at their 1938 level.

When Nkrumah came to power he directed the union to work for national construction and in 1958, his regime passed the Industrial Relations Act. This act politicized the trade union movement and consolidated the trade unions with the CPP. The unions were asked to concentrate on political tasks that the state gave them. The Secretary General of the TUC, John Tettegah, however, insisted on independence for the TUC and was removed from office. The TUC was then "packed" with CPP men and the Workers Brigade was formed to keep the TUC in line with the party. The next Secretary General, Kwaw Ampah, was allegedly supplied with a slush fund to bribe his subordinates and keep them in line with the political machine.[16]

The ultimate aim of all these was socialism; the trade unions were to serve as a means of educating the labor force to the responsibilities of a socialist working class. Labor leaders were asked to change their orientations; they were not to be concerned with the same issues as labor leaders in capitalist countries. The TUC was to work toward severing traditional relationships of the individual and linking him to the socialist state.[17]

Unfortunately for the Nkrumah regime, labor was plagued by bad working conditions, low wages, and high unemployment rates. Moreover, a fifty to one-hundred percent increase in indirect taxes on coffee, tea, tobacco, vegetables, and fish, and a five percent savings tax on incomes above £150 per year had to be imposed at a time when real wages were falling. Justifiable demands by labor were usually not met. In 1961 when strikes broke out, the demands of the workers were not met and the leaders were jailed.[18] These factors antagonized labor and they explain, in part, why the CPP's political program for labor failed. On the positive side, Nkrumah attempted to help the workers by keeping a number of uneconomical mines open and by providing work on state projects for several thousand workers.

## Labor and NLC

When the NLC came to power, the TUC had over 400,000 members, a large staff, and a modern headquarters in Accra. The TUC was active in two areas. The first was better wages and working conditions and the other was trying to influence the government on broad issues like the cost of living.[19]

The NLC policy toward labor was somewhat contradictory at times: they accepted the freedom of workers to strike but did not want inflationary wage increases or delays in production. They were prepared to listen to the opinion of labor but would base policy on expert advice. The NLC also wanted to close down uneconomical mines and work projects so that the nation could pay her debts, yet she wanted to meet demands in the villages for improved facilities and full employment.[20]

In view of this type of policy it must be said that relations between labor and the NLC were not good. More than 200 strikes and lock-outs occurred during the three and a half years of NLC military rule and many involved violence.[21] Let me cite a few examples. In December, 1967, a series of strikes broke out protesting the dismissals of four workers. Over 2500 workers out of about 5000 stayed off their jobs at the Ashanti Goldfield Corporation. At that time Army Commander E. Kotoka said that the government would not hesitate to deal firmly with anyone who incited or took part in a strike that was against the Industrial Relations Act.[22] In December, 1967, Brigadier General A. A. Afrifa told striking workers at two Ghanaian banks that the government believed that the CPP agents were responsible for industrial unrests and strikes. The most serious of these industrial unrests was a four-day transit strike involving taxi-cabs, buses, and truck fleets which all but stopped traffic in Accra and other large cities.[23]

Again in late 1967 a railway strike began when 200 workers stayed off the job as a protest for better working conditions. Sabotage and subversion were reported to have occurred. The strikes were termed illegal by the government and the workers were told to return to work or face arrest.[24] These strikes and the NLC reactions to them indicate a lack of warmth between labor and the NLC. Indeed, in December, 1968, TUC Secretary-General Bentum charged the NLC with backing illegal lock-outs by management and of overall anti-labor stance in labor-management disputes. He noted that the government had made no plans for the welfare of some 65,000 workers it had declared redundant. In other words, the NLC redeployment declarations were empty words. The NLC insisted that although unemployment was a major concern, the solution to the problem must be a long term one relating to the general rehabilitation and expansion of the economy.[25]

There were many incidents that involved the layoff of over a thousand workers at a time:

1. in June, 1967, 1200 workers were laid off when work at the Tamabe Airport was termed redundant and discontinued;

2. over a thousand workers lost their jobs because the NLC, unlike Nkrumah, closed down several depleted gold mines in an economy move; and

3. in September, 1967, 2000 workers were laid off when Bibiaim mine was closed down.[26]

If the government had been successful in redeploying the retrenched workers, it would have received higher marks from labor. This failure, in addition to the preoccupation of the military regime with orderliness which made them feel that labor conflicts "should be handled through the proper channels" and not by resort to the "illegal instrument" of strikes, made them somewhat unpopular with labor. Although they attempted to restore the independence of labor, trade unions' demands for the amendment of the 1958 Industrial Relations Act and the restoration of the workers' right to strike were rejected.

Despite the illegality of strikes, however, there were fifty-six strikes in 1966 and 1967, thirty-eight in 1968 and fifty-one in 1969.

The NLC performance in labor relations is similar to that of the FMG of Nigeria--the preference for order, the distrust of labor as agents of political parties, the resort to the outlawing of strikes and the apparent inefficacy of strike proscribing legislations. Although the NLC set up commissions to review the salaries and dismissals of workers, in the opinion of labor, these were inconsequential in the face of mass unemployment and rising prices. For example, it was estimated that about one-fourth of the wage labor force was unemployed and that over 300,000 people were actively seeking jobs by the end of the NLC rule.[27]

Under Ghana's second civilian regime, labor fared less satisfactorily despite a brief period of honeymoon. Busia expelled an estimated 2.5 million alien migrant workers. Among other things, Busia expected this to provide greater employment opportunities for Ghanaians. This did not seem to have been the case significantly. There was a ten percent fall in recorded unemployment, however.[28]

When labor put pressure on the government to increase wages by thirty percent in 1971, Busia balked at the idea, because he felt it would be inflationary in the ultimate. In any case, prices rose throughout the PP period,[29] and they really rocketed following the drastic devaluation of the cedi.

There were a number of major incidents which aggravated labor:

1. In the first half of 1971 police opened fire on striking workers at an African Plywood Company factory, killing three.

2. The Railway Engineers Union went on strike for ten days. After the strike was over a special ceremony was held and 120 workers received a cash bonus and letters of commendations for resisting the strike.[30]

3. In August, 1971, the PP started to take drastic action against the TUC. Ministerial Secretary O. K. Richardson recommended the abolition of the check-off system of the TUC whereby deductions were made from union members' salaries before they received them.[31]

The PP government then decided to freeze the assets of the TUC and introduced legislation to abolish the check-off system. Also, a committee was appointed to decide how the TUC's assets should be divided among its seventeen member unions. This action came soon after several ministers of the PP had charged TUC leaders with inciting illegal strikes. Police also raided the offices of the TUC and the home of Secretary General Bentum.[32]

These actions did nothing to ease labor unrest which intensified because the minimum wage remained the same and a ten percent National Development Levy was placed on all workers earning thirty-four new cedis or more a month.[33] In addition to this, some 200,000 workers were unemployed at the end of 1971,[34] and the government's newly introduced surcharges forced food prices up.[35]

The difference between labor and Busia may well be a difference in the perception of the purpose of trade unions. For Busia the trade union was an educational organization for workers, but for the trade union leadership it was an institution responsible for supporting the interests of the workers. To the extent that Nkrumah saw the trade union as an educational instrument for socialism, there is an absence of qualitative and substantive difference between him and Busia.

Under the NRC, TUC has been allowed to reorganize.[36] It has repealed the Industrial Relations Act of 1971 and part of the Industrial Relations Act of 1963.[37] The NRC set up a special committee to review the cases of workers dismissed under the Busia regime. Several hundreds have already been reinstated.[38] It has set up a

Social Security Fund for taking care of the workers. Under it, workers receiving ninety-nine pesewas a day received forty pesewas a day in sick pay. In accordance with this plan, those earning under one cedi twenty-nine pesewas a day received fifty pesewas a day and those earning over one cedi thirty pesewas a day received sixty pesewas a day.[39]

Other steps taken by the NRC to help workers included urging that landlords lower rent for workers,[40] and eventually establishing a rent control act,[41] and forbidding employers to dismiss workers without written permission from the Commissioner of Labour.[42] Steps are being taken to enable workers to have shares in government enterprises in which they are employed.[43]

On the other hand, Colonel Acheampong and Major Asante, Commissioner of Labour, have declared that all strikes are illegal.[44] In fact, he has declared that all strikers will be tried by military tribunal.[45] In his judgment there should be a twenty year industrial truce during which no strikes will be permitted.[46] The commissioner has warned TUC leaders not to incite the workers against the government although they have the right to criticize government programs.[47] There seems to be a very fine line as to how far a person can go in criticizing the government and it appears that the government is the judge of when this line has been crossed. Commenting on the labor walk-out of the Ghana Prices and Income Board, K. Afreh wrote "Unions can only carry out the responsibilities expected of them if they are taken into confidence in the planning of developments, if their views are treated with respect and if they are not suspected of sabotage and obstruction. This has not often been done in this country. Unions often complain of scant information about the economic position of undertakings they have to deal with, about government plans, and the economic policies (if any) of governments."[48] These comments apply equally to the case of the relationship between the Nigerian labor and the military regime.

All in all it appears that more than any previous government of Ghana, the NRC has been receptive to the interest of labor. After the walk-out of labor, the NRC agreed to increase TUC's representation to the Salary Review Committee because the Acting Secretary of the TUC had said that labor would not cooperate unless government increased labor representation. In general, however, labor has not had to flex its muscles before receiving sympathetic consideration.

## FOOTNOTES

1. <u>New Nigeria</u>, April 9, 1973.

2. <u>ULC</u>--United Labour Congress, under the leadership of Alhaji Adebola. Usually moderate with a good percentage of the unions in the private sector such as nurses, transportation, dock workers, ECN.

   <u>NTUC</u>--Nigerian Trade Union Congress, under the leadership of Wahab Goodluck and Samuel Bassey. Usually critical of the ULC and its lack of militancy, linked to the Soviet Union.

   <u>LUF</u>--Labour Unity Front, whose secretary is Gogo Nzeribe. Originally set up as a committee to promote labor unity but eventually became a union. Largely made up of public service workers--railway employees, teachers, etc.; aligned with the NTUC when the Joint-Action Committee split in 1965.

   <u>NWC</u>--Nigerian Workers' Council, led by Nnemeka Chukwure. Linked to the Christian Trade Union Federation in Brussells and aligned with the ULC.

   <u>NFL</u>--Northern Federation of Labour, led by Malam Ibrahim Nock. Regional splinter of the NTUC but was absorbed recently into the LUF; proponent of Northernization policy. <u>West Africa</u>, March 16, 1968, pp. 308-309. Also see March 23, 1968, p. 339, <u>West Africa</u>.

3. <u>Ibid</u>.

4. Olav Stokke, <u>An Introduction to the Politics, Economy and Social Setting of Modern Nigeria</u>, Scandanavia Institute of African Studies, 1970, pp. 97-98.

5. The outgoing President of the Federation of Building and Civil Engineering Contractors said that the war and high taxes had affected contractors tremendously. It held them back from improving service conditions. He appealed to the government to reduce the severe level of taxation for companies. The government also instituted a Compulsory Reconstruction and Development Savings Programme whereby workers each had to pay 10s. This was to last only from January through December, 1968, though. <u>West Africa</u>, July 13, 1968, p. 814.

6. <u>West Africa</u>, July 20, 1968, 2680, p. 1214.

7. <u>West Africa</u>, May 10, 1969, p. 542.

8. <u>West Africa</u>, November 1, 1969, p. 1321.

9. <u>West Africa</u>, January 15, 1971, pp. 29-31.

10. Personal interview with trade union leaders at Ibadan, November 17 and 18, 1972.

11. <u>Ibid</u>.

12. <u>Ibid</u>.

13. "The Nation, The Economy and The Worker, Being the Full Text of the Welcome Address Delivered by Mr. G. Kola Galogun on Behalf of the Entire Workers in the Western State to the Adebo Wages and Salaries Review Commission," pp. 3-9.

14. Bob Fitch and Mary Oppenheimer, *Ghana: End of an Illusion* (New York: Monthly Review Press, 1966), pp. 29-34.

15. *Ibid.*, p. 33.

16. Henry Bretton, *The Rise and Fall of Kwame Nkrumah* (New York: Frederick D. Praeger, Publisher, 1966), pp. 76-78.

17. Barbara Callaway in Michael Lofchie, *The State of the Nations*, p. 76.

18. Bretton, *op. cit.*, p. 78.

19. Robert Pinkney, *op. cit.*, p. 12.

20. *Ibid.*, p. 86.

21. *Ibid.*

22. *Africa Report*, February, 1967, p. 33.

23. *Africa Report*, February, 1968, p. 38.

24. *Africa Report*, March-April, 1969, p. 44.

25. *Ibid.*

26. Pinkney, *op. cit.*, pp. 32-33.

27. *Africa Report*, June, 1966, p. 22. Jon Kraus confirmed that there was seventeen percent unemployment in two years. See *The Politics of Coup D'etat*, p. 120.

28. *Africa Report*, March, 1970, p. 15.

29. *Africa Confidential*, May 28, 1970.

30. *Africa Confidential*, August 20, 1971.

31. *Ibid.*

32. *Ibid.*

33. *West Africa*, February 4, 1972, p. 127.

34. *Ibid.*

35. *Africa Confidential*, May 20, 1971.

36. *West Africa*, May 19, 1972, p. 639.

37. *West Africa*, February 25, 1972, p. 235.

38. *West Africa*, March 3, 1972, p. 263.

39. *West Africa*, July 11, 1973, p. 789.

40. *West Africa*, March 17, 1972, p. 333.

41. _West Africa_, April 2, 1972, p. 449.
42. _West Africa_, May 12, 1972, p. 602.
43. _Daily Graphic_, November 20, 1972, p. 3.
44. _West Africa_, April 14, 1972, p. 462.
45. _West Africa_, April 14, 1973, p. 513.
46. _West Africa_, March 24, 1972, p. 370.
47. _West Africa_, April 2, 1973, p. 449.
48. _Legon Observer_, June 2, 1972, p. 260.

CHAPTER XI

PERCEPTIONS OF PERFORMANCE AS EXPRESSED IN THE INTERVIEWS

A. GHANA

The overall purpose here was to ascertain, as much as possible, the perception of the performance of the Ghana military regimes. To make the project more meaningful, the respondents were also asked to compare the performance of the two military regimes with the performance of the civilian regimes. The various groups interviewed included university lecturers, university students, farmers, craftsmen, traders, workers, traditional rulers and higher civil servants.

### Ghana Traditional Peoples

The entire nine regions of Ghana were included in the sampling of the perception of traditional peoples (farmers, fishermen, chiefs, traders and unskilled workers), relative to the performance of the Ghanaian regimes. Due to limitations of resources the total region could not be sampled. Consequently, in each region, a district was randomly selected. Given the very high homogeneous characteristics of each region with the possible exception of Greater Accra, this pragmatic compromise should not significantly threaten the validity of the findings. The districts randomly selected were as follows:

| District | Region |
|---|---|
| Juaben-Ashanti-Akim | Ashanti |
| Nkoranza | Brong Ahafo |
| Gomoa-Awutu-Effutu | Central |
| Kwahu | Eastern |
| Salanga | Northern |
| Bolgatanga/Tongo | Upper Region |
| Keta | Volta |
| Wassaw/Fiase/Mpohor | Western |
| Accra | Greater Accra |

Unfortunately only the provisional results of the 1970 census were ready at the time of the research. This meant that although we had the regional breakdowns of the 1970 census and we could compute an average growth rate for each region, the regional occupational figures were not available. Therefore, regional quotas were established on the basis of adult population figures of the 1960 census which had the regional occupational breakdowns. Within the randomly selected districts, regional quotas were allocated to the various occupational groups to reflect the regional population characteristics, i.e., if seventy percent of the people in Ashanti were farmers, twenty percent traders and ten percent were craftsmen, then the district ratio of farmers, traders and craftsmen would be seven to two to one respectively. Finally, a strenuous effort was made to avoid an urban bias in a country where over sixty percent of the citizens are non-urban dwellers. As much as possible, about sixty percent of the traditional people respondents came from villages and small towns.

I must warn that in all cases the findings by themselves are not sufficient. However, to the extent that they complement and support the data and arguments previously presented in this book they become more salient and more potent.

## FARMERS

The majority in this sample, 53.1 percent, professed to be farmers. The other professions in order of high representation in the sample, were traders, unskilled workers, traditional rulers and fishermen. When asked to identify the promises made by the National Liberation Council, 43.3 percent listed agricultural and rural development and the stabilization of the Ghanaian economy. About 16 percent identified the promises as economic development, the restoration of democracy and the elimination of corruption from Ghana. An interesting sidelight is the fact that 42.9 percent of the farmers identified the NLC promises to be agricultural development, rural development and the stabilization of the economy. Only 2.4 percent of the total sample agreed that the NLC redeemed all the major promises it made. Most respondents, 47.4 percent, said that the NLC had achieved none of the three major objectives it set for itself. It was said by 38.4 percent that the NLC had achieved only one of its three objectives.

Specifically, the respondents were asked to compare the NLC, Nkrumah and Busia regimes with regard to the achievement of economic prosperity, the basic freedoms available during the period of governance, and the attainment of national pride. Here are some of the general summations of the responses to the questions:

Approximately 52.4 percent of the total sample thought that the country had economic prosperity under Nkrumah regime, while 37.2 percent answered in the negative and the rest (10.4 percent) said they did not know.

About 50 percent of the farmers agreed that there was economic prosperity under Nkrumah while 40.6 percent thought that there was none and 9.4 percent claimed they didn't know.

Nearly 52 percent (51.9) of the sample thought that economic prosperity existed under the NLC while 36.7 percent answered in the negative and 11.4 percent did not know.

Regarding the appraisal of economic prosperity under the Busia government, 27.2% of the sample thought that there was economic prosperity while 63% answered in the negative and 9.8% said they did not know.

Of the total sample 77.1% thought that basic freedoms did not exist under Nkrumah while 15% answered in the positive and 7.9% refused to answer.

There were 80.6% of the sample who were convinced of the existence of basic freedom under the NLC regime while 10.8% answered negatively and 8.7% did not know.

In response to the question about the existence of basic freedom under Busia government, 78.2% of the total sample answered positively, while 12.5% said "no" and 9.3% said that they did not know.

On the question of national pride, 75.5% of the total sample agreed that there was high national pride under Nkrumah while 13% answered in the negative and 11.5% said that they did not know.

Of the total sample, 53% agreed that high national pride existed under the NLC regime while 28.8% answered in the negative and 18.2% refused to answer the question.

There were 36.3% of the sample respondents who thought that under the Busia regime Ghanaians had high national pride while 47.7% answered negatively and 16% said they did not know.

It was conceivable that many of the respondents might not find the three categories of economic prosperity, freedom, national pride, as the comprehensive or even significant measurement of the performance of a regime. Consequently, respondents were also asked to indicate, by whatever measure they chose, the degree of their satisfaction with previous Ghanaian regimes. The result was as follows:

(General Satisfaction with NLC.) Of the sample, 43.4% were satisfied with NLC rule while 39.6% were not and 16.9% said that they did not know. Among the farmers,

43% were not satisfied while 38.5% were satisfied and 18.5% said that they did not know. Fifty-four percent of the traders were satisfied while 30% were not satisfied. If we use this positive expression as the measurement or the index of satisfaction regarding the overall performance of the regimes involved, we can make the following assertions: Ghanaian farmers, traditional rulers and traditional peoples were most satisfied with the NRC, (53.3%). Next comes the NLC with 43.5%, then the CPP with 33.2% and the Busia government with 28%. On the other hand, if we use the degree of negative feeling expressed, we can make the following statements: Ghanaians were almost as dissatisfied with the Busia regime as they were with the CPP regime. In the case of the former, 57% were dissatisfied and in the case of the latter, 57.5% were dissatisfied. The NLC came third in this case with 43% saying they were dissatisfied with the NLC performance. The fact that only 12.7% expressed dissatisfaction with NRC rule may be due to the timidity of the respondent; because the NRC was still in power. Alternatively the low dissatisfaction with the NLC could be attributed to the fact that at that point in time, Ghanaians were willing to give the NRC ample opportunity to demonstrate its competence or incompetence. In any case, if one adds the 34.1% who said they did not know with the 12.7% who said they were dissatisfied with the NRC performance, the respondents' negative view of the military regime's performance still remains significantly lower than the respondents' negative view of the civilian regime's performance. This point is further buttressed by the respondent's answer to the question regarding which Ghanaian regime they found least satisfying. In that case, 38.9% thought the Busia regime was least satisfying, 27.8% thought that Nkrumah regime was the least satisfying, 10.8% chose the NLC as the least satisfying government and 6.3% thought the NRC was the least satisfying. Even if we allow for memory lag and timidity, the difference does not appear insignificant.

The respondents were asked to indicate the chances of the NRC succeeding where the Busia government failed: 63.3% said that the chances of NRC success were high,

13.5% said the chances were poor. Some of the reasons advanced for the optimism included the NRC's "good policies" and "good execution" to date. About 47% of the respondents said that they were optimistic about the immediate future of Ghana, but about 25% said they were not.

There were notable patterns in the answer of respondents with regard to the performance of the various regimes. In the regions such as Ashanti, Eastern, Brong Ahafo, where there was a predominance of Akans, the respondents tended to be positive about the performance of the Busia regime and negative about the performance of the Nkrumah regime. To cite an example, contrary to the answer of the respondents from other regimes, 53.3% of Eastern region respondents, 67.9% of Ashanti respondents, thought that Busia's economic performance was high, while 1.5% of Ewe respondents from Volta region thought so.

Regarding the ill-advised measures of the NLC, 59% felt that the NLC should have made itself less dependent on the old anti-CPP opposition party members. In addition, 34.6% felt that the NLC erred by depending upon higher civil servants for its policy formulation and advice. The respondents were almost equally divided with regard to the question: Should NLC have stayed longer in power? Answering positively were 47.9% and answering negatively were 45.1%. As for the mistakes of the Busia regime, poor economic policies were often cited as his Waterloo. It seemed that the respondents faulted Nkrumah regime not so much for poor economic policies as for the Preventive Detention Acts and a general absence of basic freedoms during his rule. Furthermore, it might be that having seen the economic performances of the two regimes which followed the CPP overthrow, the respondents were less critical of Nkrumah's economic policies. Of course it is possible that with the passage of time the intense economic hardships they suffered during the Nkrumah regime escaped their memory. If this were true, one would expect them to feel less bitter about the denial of personal liberties during Nkrumah's reign. Because this was not the case, the first explanation seems more plausible.

## GHANA STUDENTS AND LECTURERS

### Sampling

At the University of Ghana, Legon, the lecturers and students were randomly selected and were interviewed. The goal was to find out how the more literate and articulate members of Ghanaian society assessed the performance of the military regimes in contrast with those of the civilian regimes. The findings must be compared with the discussions advanced in my chapter on the Ghanaian academicians (Chapter VIII). Non-Ghanaian lecturers and university students were of course eliminated from this sample. In the case of the Ghanaian lecturer the names of prospective respondents were taken out of the 1970-72 University of Ghana Calendar, Legon. A random selection method was used. Some of the people included on the list were on study leave or leave of absence from the university. In some cases, those selected did not cooperate. Some of the reasons given included lack of time, fear of repercussions, and dissatisfaction with the political future of Ghana, past and present. As one non-respondent put it, "In Ghana, politics is all consuming and destructive." In any case, we had the cooperation of about 75% of those included in the sample.

An overwhelming number of the students in the University of Ghana live in the residence halls. All the residence halls were included in the sample and the interviewers came from the same residence halls as the potential respondents. On the basis of the total university population, quotas were assigned to the residence halls. Within the residence halls, however, the quota was filled through random sampling. Even though we used a random method, there was an amazing closeness between the regional distribution of the student respondents in our sample and what a quota sampling technique would have produced. The interviewers reported that about 95% of the students contacted cooperated willingly.

## Students

Nearly 30% of the student respondents believed that the NLC was not successful. However, a total of 68.7% felt that the NLC was moderately successful. None felt it was very successful. Over 81% felt that the NLC would have been more successful if it had depended less on the leaders of the old opposition party. Unlike the farmers and other traditional Ghanaians, only 20% of the students felt that NLC rule would have been improved if NLC had stayed in power longer, and only 20% felt that lesser dependence on higher civil servants would have had a more solitary effect on NLC rule. Nevertheless, in the student's perception, government officials and traditional rulers were the most contented with the NLC policies and performance although academicians and businessmen were also seen as beneficiaries of the NLC rule.

In general, the students expressed low satisfaction with the Busia government; 48.3% ranked their level of satisfaction as low and 15% ranked it as very low. Only 18% ranked it as high. When students were asked if they felt the negative terms applied to the Busia regime were appropriate, 26% said "very appropriate," 29% felt that they were appropriate and 32% said they were somewhat appropriate. Significantly only 6% felt that they were inappropriate. Part of the student's negative assessment of Busia government performance was based on his introduction of the Student Loan Scheme which I discussed earlier in Chapter VIII. Another reason derived from the public humiliation which the student leaders were subjected to following their demand that the political leaders of the Progress Party should, in accordance with Ghana law, disclose their assets. To the question: Do you believe that Ghana under Busia was a free, just, developed, egalitarian, dynamic society?, we had the following answers:

|  | True | Somewhat True | False | Somewhat False |
|---|---|---|---|---|
| A free society | 23.0% | 50.3% | 24.0% | 2.7% |
| A just society | 7.3% | 32.0% | 57.0% | 3.7% |
| A developed society | 3.3% | 27.7% | 63.7% | 2.3% |
| An egalitarian society | 5.0% | 23.0% | 59.7% | 12.3% |
| A dynamic society | 5.0% | 17.0% | 72.3% | 5.7% |

The NRC leader publicly advanced many reasons for the overthrow of the Busia government. In my effort to see how many of these were acceptable by the students, I asked the question: Why, in your opinion, did the Army step in on January 13, 1972? The responses were as follows:

|  | True | False | Somewhat False |
|---|---|---|---|
| Poor economic conditions | 86.0% | 9.3% | 4.7% |
| Corruption of Busia regime | 66.3% | 11.3% | 22.4% |
| Lack of justice | 51.7% | 29.3% | 19.0% |
| Persecution of workers | 44.0% | 31.3% | 24.7% |
| Maltreatment of Army by Busia | 41.0% | 20.0% | 39.0% |
| Desire for power | 27.0% | 39.0% | 34.0% |
| Absence of freedom | 14.3% | 73.7% | 12.0% |

These responses clearly indicate that the reasons advanced by the Acheampong regime seem credible to the student. Only 27% of the students believed that the take-over was motivated by the military's desire for political power. One notable exception was the refusal of students to believe that there was a significant absence of freedom during the reign of Dr. Busia.

The fact that a total of 51.3% of the students believed that the chances of the military regime succeeding were either high or very high is notable; only 35.4% believed otherwise. The reasons cited for the optimism included the fact that the military regimes "are efficient" and that the NRC "is receptive to the ideas of the people." About 77.3% of the respondents believed that the NRC regime would remain in power for a long time.

## Ghana Lecturers

Nearly 60% of those in the sample of lecturers identified agricultural development, rural development, the restoration of democracy and the elimination of corruption as the major tasks to which the NLC addressed itself. About 74% of those interviewed regarded the NLC rule as generally successfully. More specifically, about 20% described it as successful and the remainder preferred to use the words, "somewhat successful" or "fairly successful." Approximately 12% of the respondents regarded NLC rule as unsuccessful. Surprisingly, 66% of the respondents felt that the NLC would have achieved more if it had depended less on the leaders of the old opposition party. Other measures advocated included less dependence on civil servants, dealing more ruthlessly with Nkrumah's former associates and increasing the influence of civilian commissioners. Another somewhat surprising finding was the respondents' ranking of groups perceived as satisfied with NLC political performance. In order of high priority, the lecturers listed traders and businessmen, intellectuals, traditional rulers, government officials, farmers, and workers. Notice the contrast with the student respondents who listed government officials and traditional leaders as the Ghanaians most contented with the NLC performance and rule.

The only specific policy of the NLC which a relatively significant number of the academicians (about 25%) disagreed with, is the policy of rescheduling of the national debt. They preferred outright repudiation of debts incurred under Nkrumah. On the other hand, about half of the respondents praised the NLC for the restoration of freedom in Ghana. Only one-eighth of the respondents agreed with the general economic policies pursued by the NLC, however. The Abbott agreement was often cited as a case of poor economic policy. It is also interesting that about 10% felt that the NLC regime was corrupt and about 6% said that the NLC introduced "tribalism" into Ghanaian politics.

The lecturers were asked whether or not the negative terms used for old Progress Party politicians were appropriate and justifiable. Only 37% of them felt the terms were appropriate. This can be interpreted as an index of a relatively strong sympathy for the Busia government. In addition, it may be a reflection of a lack of faith in the objectivity of Ghanaian newspapers. A majority of the respondents felt that Ghanaian newspapers reported events inaccurately. In any case, it may suggest a lack of credibility in the utterances of the new military leaders who initiated and/or encouraged anti-Progress Party campaigns. Other signs of support for the Busia government included the fact that nearly 80% regarded Ghana under Busia to be a free society. A majority also regarded Ghana under Busia to be an egalitarian society. However, only about a quarter of the sample found Ghana under Busia to be a developed or dynamic society. In the opinion of about 45% of the respondents, Ghana at the time of the coup d'etat had a weaker sense of national identity than was the case prior to the Busia rule. By far the most predominant reason given for the disappearance of national identity was tribalism.

The reasons advanced by the lecturers for the coup d'etat of January 13, 1972, included the following: poor economic conditions, maltreatment of the military by the Busia regime, desire for personal power and political corruption of Busia regime. When asked to assess the chances of the NRC succeeding where the Busia regime failed, about 42% felt the chances were either high or very high. Those who answered optimistically based their answers on the fact that the NRC revalued the cedi and repudiated certain categories of the national debt. About one-third of the respondents thought the chances of NRC's success were poor. Most of those not responding to the question indicated a high degree of skepticism about NRC capabilities in general. This is further supported by the fact that nearly one-half saw "gloom" in the immediate future of Ghana. Another one-third predicted poor prospects for Ghana in the immediate future. The immediate future was interpreted to respondents as one to three years. Only about one-sixth of the respondents saw a bright immediate future for Ghana. About three-fourths of the lecturers interviewed believed that Ghana was in for a long period of military rule. All interviewers reported that what seemed to bother the academicians about the coup d'etat was not so much that the government whose policy they supported was overthrown, but rather it was the fear that the military intervention in politics would become a permanent feature of Ghanaian politics, more specifically, the fact that military rule would tend to ride roughshod over basic freedoms. There also was expressed skepticism with regard to the competence of the NRC to tackle the gigantic tasks and problems confronting Ghana.

## GHANA BUREAUCRATS

Using the legal definition of the "Administrative Class" as synonymous with higher civil servants, we randomly selected some higher civil servants. In many instances, there was reluctance on the part of the civil servants to answer questions. In fact, only about 60% of those contacted cooperated with us. It must be pointed out that at the time of the research most of the civil servants were under tremendous pressure and constraints. Given the discontinuities which followed the dramatic change in the political leadership, style and philosophy, the entire Ghanaian bureaucracy and the higher civil servants, in particular, had to work harder and longer. In many cases, they had to work literarily under the barrell of the gun; soldiers were posted to the ministries in order to ensure that civil servants did not "loiter." Permanent secretaries were subjected to military drills, publicly, if they came to work late. Given the extraordinary circumstances, we were indeed fortunate to have any cooperation.

About 80% of the higher civil servants interviewed felt that under the NLC the political leadership considered the advisory role of the civil servants to be very important. For their part, the civil servants said they were very enthusiastic because they felt that their advice would be given very serious considerations. Furthermore, over 55% of those interviewed indicated that the political leadership of the NLC allowed the civil service to take initiative.

When similar inquiries were made with regard to the NRC, about 70% of those interviewed felt that the NRC considered the advice of the civil servants very important. Although about 60% of the respondents felt it was too early to assess the achievement of the NRC, about 30% pointed out the improvement in the civil servants' conditions of service as one of the achievements of the NRC.

By contrast, over 64% of those interviewed felt that under the Busia government, the civil servants' advice was not seriously considered and that this depreciated from the work, morale and energies of the civil servant. Indeed some, 40%, of those interviewed, went as far as to say that nothing was achieved under the Busia government while another 25% indicated that the effect of Busia rule was negative as far as they were concerned. Only 10% of the civil servants were prepared to attest to high civil service morale under the Progress Party leadership. Some specific accusations made against the Busia regime included the introduction of CI17 and the Industrial Relations Act of 1971, both of which had the effect of reducing civil service morale. As for the CPP regime, over 72% felt that the civil service advice was ever a significant factor in the decision making process.

All in all about 64% of the civil servants bluntly indicated that they felt more comfortable under military rule. Approximately 64% said they felt a higher degree of satisfaction under them than under civilian regimes. In addition, they said that under military rule, the processes of policy formulation and execution were more efficient. Strangely enough, the civil servants credited the military regimes with strict adherence to the policy of non-interference as well as assiduous cultivation of the proper atmosphere conducive to maximum performance of the bureaucracy. Unfortunately, about half of the respondents said whatever the impact of military rules might be on the bureaucracy, it could only be temporary since civilian governments have a tendency to negate the attainment of military rules either directly or indirectly. When respondents were asked to rank regimes in order of high receptivity to civil service advice, NLC came first, NRC second, Busia third and CPP fourth. In the case of the NLC, 60% found them receptive to advice and 30% found them most receptive. Thirty-two percent found the NRC most receptive to advice and 16% found them receptive. By contrast, the two civilian governments did poorly. Finding the Busia government to be less than receptive were 64%, and about 70% found the CPP to be less than receptive to civil service professional advice.

Regarding civil service morale, 88% felt that under the Progress Party, civil service morale was lowest. Of the respondents, 76% felt that the civil service morale was low or very low under CPP rule. On the other hand, about 70% felt that under NLC rule, civil service morale was high or very high, and 76% found civil service morale to be high or very high under the NRC. Although about 6% said that they were only prepared to give the NRC little support, 90% said that they were prepared to give the NRC adequate and enthusiastic support.

Quite apart from these formal interviews, we had scores of informal interviews with the people who preferred this approach. In addition, we carried out informal discussions with some military officers. Generally, the Ghanaian military rulers were quite open about their goals, aspirations and intentions. Furthermore, they had no qualms about their own perceptions regarding their performance. On the basis of the informal discussions, we felt it would be redundant to carry out formal interviews with the military officers because the informal discussions yielded little information that was not evident in the public utterances of the military officers.

## NIGERIA

Given the limitations of time and money, we were not able to interview in all Nigerian universities. In any case, the availability of alternative ways of assessing Nigerian students' perception of the military's developmental performance made this exercise less essential (see Chapter VII). The students at the University of Ibadan were interviewed using random sampling.

On the same random selection basis, Nigerian lecturers listed on the University of Ibadan staff list were selected for interview. Again, the discussion in Chapter VII suggests that altnerative sources for the measurement of the lecturers' perception of military performance were available and used. In other words, this discussion is supplementary to Chapter VII.

### Nigerian Students

In the effort to find the barometer of the students' identity with various governments, they were asked to rank stipulated periods in order of the student feelings of high identification with the government. The students indicated the following high-low rank order: Civil War period; 1960, the year of formal independence from Britain; 1971 following the end of the Civil War; 1965, the year before the first coup d'etat. The students interviewed in 1972 ranked 1972 with 1965 as representing the nadir of their identification with the government.

Specifically, the students were asked to indicate their reactions to specific government policies and positions. Below is a tabulation of the results:

| Policy or Position | No response | Support policy % | Disagree with policy % |
|---|---|---|---|
| Public executions | 2 | 64 | 34 |
| Commissions of Enquiry into alleged corruption | 2 | 54 | 44 |
| Bringing old politicians into Executive Council | 8 | 48 | 44 |
| Government response to striking doctors and other labor unrest | 28 | 30 | 42 |
| Wage and Price Control | 6 | 46 | 48 |
| Present high military budget | 4 | 26 | 70 |
| Scholarships and loans | 2 | 16 | 82 |

About 54% of the student respondents felt that the creation of the 12 state structure represented a successful attempt to solve Nigeria's basic political problem. Indeed about 76% believed that the creation of more Nigerian states would be a political step in the right direction. The students were largely of the opinion that the celebrated military government's goal to make Nigeria a just and an egalitarian society has not yet been put into operation. They nevertheless felt that some meaningful implementation of this goal might soon be forthcoming. About 70% of the students gave the military government high marks for helping to bring about a relatively high degree of national unity in Nigeria. Similarly nearly 60% of the students believed that on the aggregate, the military government had been successful in creating a dynamic economy and bringing about economic growth in Nigeria.

In the perception of the students interviewed, the armed forces as a unit was not involved in the process of political decision making. Rather, only the individual military officers of the armed forces who were either military governors, or members of the Federal Executive Council, or the Supreme Military Council were involved. The very few military officers who were appointed to governmental boards and bodies were also involved in the process of political decision making. It was the students' opinion that the military regime very seldom seriously consulted with workers, farmers, and students before taking actions or making policies which affected these groups. The students saw the higher civil servants and the Nigerian businessmen as comprising the political powerhouse. Surprisingly, the students had very little faith in the capacity of the Nigerian government-bureaucrats. Only 14% expressed positive view on this score.

Although 72% of the students thought that the deposed Nigerian politicians earned their bad reputations, about 46% expressed the view that they should not be banned from future participation in Nigerian political leadership. About 44% disagreed with this position. Approximately 20% of the students believed that by 1976 Nigeria would have disposed of all of its most nagging political problems.

About 60% of the students expressed a keen desire in seeing greater mass participation in post-military Nigerian political life. Surprisingly, 82% of the students did not believe that constitutional provisions should be made in future for military participation in politics. An overwhelming 84% believed that structurally Nigeria should remain a federation. This may explain the popularity of the creation of more states in Nigeria.

### Nigerian Lecturers

Just as the students, the lecturers indicated that they felt closest to Nigerian government during the Civil War; about 63% agreed with this position. However, only about 9% indicated that they remained close to the military government by late 1972. Only 30% expressed confidence that the primary problems confronting Nigeria would be solved by 1976. The lecturers were very apprehensive about the prospect for the return to civilian government because they believed that the military leadership had a lust for power. Over 42% felt that the military government's leadership needed to show good example. They believed a credibility gap existed between what the military leaders preached and what they practiced. Furthermore, they expressed both hope and desire that the military would improve its communication with the people and would expedite its policy in an efficient way.

Approximately a quarter of the lecturers interviewed claimed to have served as consultants to either a state government of the Federal government. Many of them expressed some disappointment that the number of lecturer-consultants was decreasing "these days." About 60% of those who have acted in consulting capacities to the military governments said they found the experience rewarding. A majority (approximately 60%) saw significant differences between acting as advisor to the military regime and advising the civilian government. They felt that an advisor to the military regime had status, and they suggested that the military regime tended to respond more favorably to their advice.

By a margin of two to one, the lecturers felt that the military leaders' attitude to the lecturers had changed significantly following the end of the Civil War. They felt as a result of this, lecturers were being slowly excluded from the political class. The lecturers expressed a feeling of status loss. Of the lecturers questioned, 60% of the lecturers said that between August 1966 and January 1970, Nigerian lecturers played an important or very important political role in the country. Agreeing that this role had changed were 66%. Among the reasons for the change in the political role of Nigerian lecturers were (1) the increasing arrogant attitude of the military in general; (2) a change in the political situation of the country which led to a feeling that the lecturers were dispensable; and (3) a change in the attitude of the Nigerian lecturers themselves. The lecturers conceded the fact that as a result of the academic community's support for the military regime during the Civil War, the Nigerian universities retained considerable degree of independence. Furthermore, some political plums were handed to some lecturers. When the war was successfully terminated, however, and the military announced its intention to remain in power until 1976, the university students and activist lecturers became increasingly vocal and open about their criticisms of the military regime. This has drawn the ire of the military leadership and the bureaucratic leadership as well. Since the interview was successfully terminated in December of 1972, the disaffection of the students and lecturers cannot be completely represented here. Unquestionably, however, the level of satisfaction has decreased significantly following the Nigerian University Teachers Strike and the National Youth Service Corps controversy.

## NIGERIAN FARMERS

With regard to the sampling of Nigerian farmers, only those in the Western state were interviewed. Five districts of the Western states were randomly selected. Parenthetically, I must note that historically the Nigerian farmers living in the Western states have exhibited strong political consciousness. Although their feelings cannot be said to be representative of all Nigerian farmers, these farmers are significant in assessing the political effectiveness and otherwise of the military regime. In other words, given the importance of Western state farmers in terms of their contribution to Nigeria agricultural output, the political perceptions of these farmers is very important.

Generally, most of the farmers interviewed (about two-thirds) felt that the military regime had embarked upon most of the tasks it promised. On the overall, about 60% felt that these tasks would be or had been successfully completed. About a third were skeptical on this score, however. In order to increase the chances of success, a majority felt that the military rulers needed to be more responsive. They felt that effective communication linkages must be built and used. The farmers were somewhat distrustful of the executors of public policy. Despite the farmers' revolt, the farmers claimed that they felt close to Nigerian government. When asked to order the years according to high degree of closeness to the government, a majority answered 1971, 1960, 1965. In terms of their perception of the participation of groups in policy decision, the farmers saw women, workers, students and themselves as very low participants in political decision making. The farmers were asked to indicate whether or not they agreed with the following specific government actions or policies. The result is tabulated below:

| Specific Government Policies and Actions | Support % (app.) | Does not support % (app.) |
|---|---|---|
| Public executions | 90 | 4 |
| Government harsh response to doctors strikes and other labor problems | 76 | 4 |
| Wage and price control | 82 | 10 |
| Military budget | 22 | 66 |
| Bringing back old politicians into cabinet | 16 | 76 |
| Agricultural credit corporation | 76 | 20 |
| Commissions of Inquiry into allegations of corruption | 88 | 4 |

The farmers were also asked to assess the performance of the military regime in goals which the military regimes promised to accomplish. The responses were as follows:

| Type of Performance | Yes | No | Don't Know |
|---|---|---|---|
| United Country | 52 | 8 | 40 |
| Strong economy | 62 | 12 | 26 |
| Just society | 62 | 18 | 20 |
| Free society | 28 | 65 | 3 |

With regard to the future, notice the farmers' responses tabulated below:

| Question | Yes | No |
|---|---|---|
| In future, the mass should be given more power | 70 | 22 |
| In future, the military should not be involved in politics | 22 | 70 |
| In future, Nigeria should be a centralized government | 36 | 60 |
| In future, Nigeria should be a federation | 54 | 36 |
| Do you think the military should create more than 12 states in Nigeria | 42 | 44 |
| Will the Nigerian military relinquish political power in 1976 | 42 | 44 |

## NIGERIAN TRADERS

The sampling of Nigerian traders was done by randomly choosing two markets, each in Ibadan and Lagos. Many traders from the interior and many parts of Nigeria come to Lagos and Ibadan markets to buy commodities which are later sold in the interior. We found no significant distinction among the views of the traders from different Nigerian states.

The petty traders interviewed listed 1960 as the period when they were most satisfied with their government. It should be recalled that 1960 was the year that Nigeria received its independence from Britain. The air of optimism was reflected in the hustle and bustle of economic life which percolated to the level of the petty traders. Next came the period after the Civil War. This represents a notable departure from the responses of the other groups who usually ranked the Civil War period higher than the post-Civil War era. A closer examination suggests that there is nothing surprising about the choice of post-Civil War period over the Civil War. During the Civil War there were economic hardships and restrictions. Import restrictions made it difficult for petty traders to get adequate supplies. Such supplies as were available were not easily accessible to the petty traders low in the hierarchy of power. The "military boys," so they were called, during periods of excesses, created an environment unconducive to the free flow of trade. For example, there were excessive military check points with long delays. In any case, the Civil War period was put third, just ahead of 1965, when by all accounts, the Nigerian government performance was at its nadir. The petty traders, it should be added, saw themselves, farmers and women, as hardly involved in the process of decision making. Decisions involving them, in their perceptions, were made without consultations with them. Surprisingly, only 56% of the traders were opposed to the future involvement of the Nigerian military in politics. Indeed, about one-third of the respondents welcomed such involvement.

In terms of specific actions and policies of the military regime and the reactions of the traders to them, the table below is enlightening:

| Specific Actions | Support or agree % | Do not support/disagree % |
|---|---|---|
| Public execution | 72 | 24 |
| Doctors strikes, labor problems and government actions on them | 48 | 18 |
| Commissions of Enquiry into alleged political corruption | 76 | 22 |
| Returning the assets of politicians seized by government | 76 | 22 |
| Wage and Price Control | 32 | 66 |

With regard to price control, about 75% felt it was ineffective because the government was corrupt. In addition, it was felt that the price ceilings were unrealistic given the cost of the goods to the retailers. The execution of the policy was also faulted. On the matter of whether the military had accomplished some specific goals it set for itself, we had the following itemized responses:

| Specific Performance Category | Yes | No |
|---|---|---|
| Has the military brought political stability | 66 | 28 |
| Has the military ended inflation | 14 | 86 |
| Has the military brought national loyalty | 28 | 60 |
| Has the military brought economic growth | 68 | 24 |
| Has the military brought equality | 8 | 86 |
| Will the military listen to the common men if the commoners would organize | 52 | 44 |

Among the expectations of the petty traders were (1) liberalization of import restrictions, (2) more realistic ceilings on prices, (3) a desire for closer communication between the military regime and petty traders, (4) more vigorous Nigerianization of the retail market--(this was before the policy came into effect), (5) desire for availability of loans to traders, (6) the feeling that government should produce goods which may not be available at "good" price, from foreign countries. However this demand was usually coupled with the exhortations that government should get out of the retail business. Over 80% of the respondents took this position. All in all, about 58% felt that the regime had not done much for the petty traders. Others felt that despite everything, traders had not done badly under this regime.

CHAPTER XII

POLITICAL STYLE

A. Nigeria

Southern military governors and those of Kwara state fondly and consistently have mentioned that one of the benefits of the creation of the twelve state structure is that no one state can be in a position to hold the Federal government to ransom as under the civilian regime. The implication is obvious; the twelve state structure has led to a natural diminuation of state power vis a vis the Federal government. One can therefore anticipate that, given the gigantic nature of the task it set for itself, the FMG would use its opportunity to transform Nigeria from its essentially ineffective reconciliatory pattern to a more dynamically reconcilliatory or even mobilization system. For example, in an essentially mobilization oriented military regime one should expect to see either complete and direct organizational involvement of the military in basic political and economic life or, pervasive involvement of the military at all decision levels of society. More importantly, the military representatives would perceive themselves as central government representatives, not as local representatives.

The Nigerian military governors are appointed by General Gowon. Technically, therefore, he has the authority to transfer or dismiss them. Furthermore, given the military chain of command, one would expect them to view themselves not as local representatives but as central government representatives. However, as it will be obvious, definitely in the cases of the Western State Governor and the Rivers State Governor (and there are many more cases and governors), the attitudes of the military governors are distinctively ambivalent on this score. At a time when Nigeria was striving toward unity, a military governor appointed by General Gowon, Col. Abba Kyari, Governor of the North Central State, publicly contended that the division of the North into six states would not threaten the power of the North because, "People in the old geographical North always think . . . alike. The old elephant will rise from slumber and work with determination and vigour knowing its position in the country."[1] This is an obvious open disapproval of this fundamental policy of General Gowon.

It has been argued that since the FMG is composed of units governed by representatives who are organically part of the "power structure of a politically monolithic regime" it is "obliged to seek relatively static balance among its units." This means that since military governors in the states are an organic part of a constitutionally monolithic power structure, it is, in fact, difficult for the federal center to impose its will on them. In operational terms, therefore, on many issues, government becomes government by consensus.

"Hence, the stubborn unwillingness of a particular state may hold up a decision that involves the entire federation."[2] Thus, a state can exercise a *de facto* veto.

The protection of the freedom of movement of any Nigerian in any part of the Federation falls directly within the purview of the Federal government. The Federal Military Government and General Gowon have strongly expressed their desire and determination to see that this right of Nigerians is not undermined. Yet, the Rivers State for over two years after the end of the war has refused to have Ibos of East-Central State return to the state. The Federal government, although disgusted with the Rivers State, has not forced the state to comply with the law. It is this that has led Professor O'Connell to observe that a Federal Military Government "is less well-placed to curb the state than a Federal government in which stronger politicians sought positions at the center because they reckoned that power lay there."[3] But the failure of the FMG to compel the Rivers State to abide by the law testifies, in my judgment, to the political skill of the Federal government.

It may be logical to think that no state can hold the Federal government to ransom as was the case in Nigeria's First Republic. But is it impossible for a coalition of states to do so? In a situation of "Animal Farm" in which all states

are equal but some are more equal than others, some states are politically strong
while others are well organized. In terms of Revenue Allocation, the Dina Report
has been shelved because it is considered politically explosive. One can only guess
that if and when the present military regime leaves, it may well be the last major
task to which it will address itself. All in all, it would seem that:

> Only occasionally and for acute political reasons has the present
> FMG government followed the unitary logic of the military.
> Generally in its administration it has respected the federal logic
> of the country's constitutional order.[4]

It is important to note that in the cases where the FMG has taken a direct and
politically forceful leadership style over the states, it has done so either
hesitantly or apologetically. In dealing with the military governors, General Gowon
has been concilliatory, persuasive and compromising. Even in the two known cases
where military governors have failed to be masters of their house or failed to keep
peace in their states, he resisted for a long time direct and indirect pressures to
replace them. In one case, after repeated failures, a military governor was kicked
upstairs. The Federal bureaucracy has been more outspoken and active in their
attempts to impose the federal will on the states. State governments have
complained about the Federal bureaucracy. In short, the normal Gowon style is not
mobilizational. He tends to allow the military governors and their states maximum
freedom.

Typically, General Gowon has concentrated on the image of the "Head of State,"
projecting Nigerian personality and leadership on the world scene and particularly
in Africa. Except on state occasions such as independence day or "state" visits to
other states, occasions replete with protocol, or during periods of near emergencies
such as the illegal strikes, General Gowon has not been an activist. He prefers a
low profile devoid of ideological content. As I have argued in Chapter VII, however,
the National Youth Service Corp represents, perhaps, the only cogent example of
General Gowon's serious and uncompromising attempt at a high profile approach to
political integration in post civil war Nigeria.

Financially the FMG is growing stronger. It has the largest reservoir of technical experts. It is obvious from the Four Year Development Plan, that the FMG envisaged a situation in which the center can bring along the state or, in fact, control it because of its dominant and healthy financial posture as well as its superior manpower resources vis a vis the states. Generally, the FMG has looked upon this as its greatest leverage and weapon in dealing with the state governments. The logic of military authority will suggest the chain of command as the greatest instrument of the central government. To the extent that this is not the case, the FMG cannot be seen as a mobilization regime or even as pursuing a high political profile (see Chapter VII).

In contrast, most of the military governors have been activists and have used high profile style. In theory they have the power of colonial governors. Let me cite Col. Ogbemedia of the Midwest State and Major General Adebayo of the Western State in this connection.

1. The Midwest government passed an edict against passengers loading and unloading outside of designated motor parks. The military governor personally carried out surprise checks and ordered the close-downs of petrol stations where he found the loading and unloading of passengers.[5]

2. The Midwest government set the rate for taxi fare. When the taxi drivers went on strike, he gave them an ultimatum, "If you go on strike we will operate taxis." The only choice was for the taxi drivers to sell their services at stipulated prices or comply with the rate schedule.[6] The threat was obvious; the government would commandeer the taxicabs.

3. The Midwest Governor paid a surprise visit in a medium sized bus to government road projects. The workers found "idling" were suspended on the spot and their supervisors were demoted on the spot without going through the public service commission or the civil service procedure.[7]

4. To aid in reconstruction, the government established shops for building materials in war-affected areas.[8]

5. The Midwest government established a state transport corporation (The Midwest Line). The governor's surprise checks have been credited with the efficiency and productivity of the "Midwest Line." The government's success has led other state governments to examine the possibility of such systems. Here I should point out that the Chamber of Commerce has been critical of government incursions into the road transport business.[9]

6. The Midwest government also went into the bulk purchasing business. For example, the Bulk Purchasing Unit established in the Ministry of Trade, ordered scarce commodities and sold them at more reasonable prices. These efforts have been credited with reducing the retail prices on canned tomatoes, milk and cement, (cement from twenty-six shillings to nineteen shillings). Again, some states have followed the Midwest example.[10]

7. Immediately after his tour of European countries, the governor unilaterally declared that his government's overseas scholarship would be terminated because he believed the scholarship recipients were not making proper use of the opportunities. It took concentrated efforts of newspaper editorials to get the Midwest governor to change his mind.[11]

8. When the university students at the University of Benin boycotted lecturers in protest against what they regarded as intervention of the governor in academic affairs, the governor used his dramatic personalistic approach. The military governor appeared on the university grounds carrying placards which read, "Grant the Visitor Freedom of Speech," "Remember your Poor Tax Payers," "Listening is an Excellent Investment." In response, the students called off the strike.[12]

Talking about an aspect of his direct personalistic style, a correspondent, commenting on the governor's visit to the scenes of disaster, observed, "In his characteristic manner he visited the scenes of damages and not only did he supervise reconstruction work, but personally participated in it. He showed the people that soldiers could do anything."[13]

The military governor feels this must be done because "when the history of this country is written many of the pages will be devoted to the 'success or failures of the military administration.' Therefore, there should be concrete evidence of what we have done for our people for posterity to see."[14] Explaining the philosophy of active government intervention in economy, he said the "Midwest government established projects because it was one important way by which the government could fill the gap in economic development created by shortage of private capital." He feels that as soon as the projects become paying concerns members of the public will be invited to hold interests in such projects, e.g., bus services are being handed over to local councils."[15]

Major General Adebayo's style of performance as military governor must be put in a frame of reference involving the man, the state and the circumstances of the country when General Gowon took over.

Governor Adebayo took over from a popular military governor who had been assassinated as a result of the second coup. Consequently, the new military rulers needed to pacify the West for his death. Secondly, the West had been weary of the power of the Northern establishment and most Yorubas were very suspicious that as a group the Northern Region, in the face of Eastern Region secession, would dominate the military. Consequently, there was talk of the establishment of the Republic of Oduduwa if the Republic of Biafra was allowed to exist unchallenged.[16] This distrust of Northern soldiers also led to the demand that Northern soldiers leave the Western Region lock, stock and barrel and be replaced with Yoruba soldiers through a vigorous recruitment of Yorubas for the military. On November 19, 1967, twenty-five Western State leaders led by Awolowo presented General Gowon with a memo to this effect.[17] If one traces the military career of Major General Adebayo one notices that he is one of the enlisted men who were promoted into the officer class following a short officer course. Therefore, the impact of the social grace which is usually presumed to be a consequence of Sandhurst training is not likely to be maximum. Moreover he is the oldest of the most senior Nigerian army officers.

His administration was personalistic to the extreme. He had tremendous difficulties with the higher civil servants who saw him as usurping their functions. In an editorial headed "Civil Servants or Personal Servants" the *Daily Times*[18] claimed that the Solicitor General of the Western State and the Permanent Secretary of the state's Ministry of Justice was sent home on compulsory indefinite vacation because he was reported to have advised the governor against making a certain appointment in the Ministry of Justice. The editorial castigated the Governor for not following the proper disciplinary procedure, and it questioned the value of senior civil servant's advice if all the Governor wanted was "pallative thinkers." Moreover, he single-handedly changed the process by which contracts are awarded. He was accused of being blatantly sectional in the distribution of public amenities and rebuked for living a highly privileged social life without a commensurate sense of public responsibility. His relationship with the farmers, the university students and the traditional leaders were turbulent. The following scathing remarks about his administration were shared by quite a number of Western Nigerians that we interviewed.

> Brigadier Robert Adebayo leaves the Western State today after serving as Military Governor for nearly five years. He spent the last one month in a marathon tour of the state during which he laid the foundation-stones of several projects, some of whose plans are yet to be completed. The purpose of this exercise is to have the Governor's name inscribed on each of the foundation-stones so that he may be remembered long after he is gone. This desire is perfectly legitimate and understandable. The ambition of any public man is to immortalise his name and to be remembered forever. But neither nature nor history can be cheated. It is not the number of foundation-stones laid that will immortalise Brigadier Adebayo in the annals of this country. He will be judged entirely on the services which he rendered or failed to render during his term of office.
>
> For example, Brigadier Adebayo's predecessor in office, Colonel Adekunle Fajuyi, hardly laid any foundation-stone or performed

any flamboyant ceremonies. But in six months of firm, responsible, honest, disciplined and uncorrupt government, Colonel Fajuyi carved for himself a place of honour in the history of not only the Western State but Nigeria as a whole.

There were many who expected Brigadier Adebayo to follow in the footsteps of Colonel Fajuyi and carry forward the task he had so well begun. But such expectations were misplaced; for nothing is more evident now than that the two governors belonged to two different worlds.

The most important thing for which Brigadier Adebayo will be remembered is his advocacy for Yoruba unity. He advocated Yoruba unity with missionary zeal and made several appeals in and out of season for the Yoruba to unify in their own interest as well as that of the Federation. But it was never known whether the Governor himself had a clear idea of what he meant by Yoruba unity. In any case, actions speak louder than preachments. And the actions of the outgoing Military Governor never matched his words in this respect. In fact, the net effect of all his actions was divisive rather than unifying.

Brigadier Adebayo has some achievements to his credit. He awarded bursaries to all university students of Western State origin, thus virtually providing free university education for the state. But he also burdened the state with many ill-considered schemes such as self-help projects and the ill-fated cottage hospitals. Beside, some of his administrative decisions in chieftaincy and other matters have only created problems for his successor.

The outgoing Governor's style of administration and his social activities were subjects of open criticism by well-meaning citizens. But these criticisms must be tempered by the realisation that the man is, after all, a soldier and that the governorship of a state was not part of his military training. What cannot be excused is the apparent relish with which he took decisions clearly at variance with the declared policies of the Federal Military Government. For example, his decision to return to the public men found guilty of abuse of office the properties seized from them was made on the eve of a crucial broadcast by the Head of State promising tougher measures against corruption. If, as a soldier, the Governor did not learn the art of government, one expected him, at least, to know a thing or two about discipline.

The transfer of Brigadier Adebayo to the Military Academy in Kaduna establishes the principle that any Military Governor can be re-assigned to any post. Brigadier Adebayo has said that it is in order to demonstrate the inadvisability of staying too long in office that he is returning to the barracks after nearly five years. However incredible this may sound, one must welcome the explanation and hope that the other Governors of the Federation will take notice of it. As for the Brigadier himself, his departure comes as a great relief to the majority of the people of the state and came rather too late. Nevertheless we wholeheartedly wish him success in his new assignments, and look forward to seeing him in his new role of

Adebayo, Brigadier sans despatch riders sans the paraphenalia of gubernatorial office.[19]

The administration of Brigadier Esuene, Lt. Commander Diet Spiff and Col. Bamgboye were also perceived as personalistic (see Chapter V on Col. Bamgboye).

## B. Ghana

Unlike the Nigerian military regime, the NRC regime of Ghana is directly and completely involved in governance almost at every important level and segment of Ghanaian life. They are in the diplomatic corps; they are members of boards; they are commissioners. Some are attached to universities and public corporations. They are directly involved in some agricultural activities, and they are partially involved in administering law enforcement. In short, the military personnel involved itself directly in the administration of state enterprises and governmental agencies.

The dangers of direct, active military rule are multivarious. Among these dangers are over-enthusiasm, hasty decision-making because of desires for excessive speed, and the danger of alienating civilians because of the tendency of the military to administer instant justice. Let me cite some policies of the NRC which it had to reverse because of its hasty decisions. First, is the NRC order for a twenty percent rent reduction by all landlords. This order had to be made inoperative because "certain important details" such as property valuation and rent assessment were not properly examined prior to the declaration of the policy. Second, the use of passbooks was cancelled by the regime because passbook holders were middlemen who "were impeding the free flow of goods at reasonable prices." But the government soon realized that these middlemen in Ghana were crucial to the system of distribution. So the regime restored the passbooks.[20] Another example is the removal of essential commodities subsidy.

In a speech on the eve of the first anniversary of the NRC, Col. Acheampong declared that the government subsidy to essential commodities would continue despite the fact that the government purpose had been frustrated in many ways.[21] Three weeks later, the announcement of Major Felli clearly showed that the government had reversed its categorical position. The Commissioner of Trade and Tourism contended that the decision to withdraw the thirty million cedis annual subsidy on certain foreign foods and commodities was "another corrective measure" introduced "in the interest of the economy and the well-being of the people of this country." In addition, the commissioner maintained that the subsidy was no longer necessary because as a result of the NRC's increase in the producer price of cocoa, the restoration of certain allowances of public servants, the increase of up to thirty-three percent in the salaries and wages of workers, vigorous price controls, etc., the people were now in a position to do without the subsidies.[22]

Although these could be taken as examples of poor political performance because of the absence of prior careful planning and reflection, the fact that the government is not afraid to review or change its policies once it has decided that they are inappropriate may be perceived as a political asset by the citizenry. However, when the reversal of policies becomes commonplace, the government may become a "big joke."

As an active and pervasive military regime, the Ghana NRC has succumbed to few temptations of instant justice. Consider the following:

Government workers who came late to work were not treated in accordance with civil service procedure and regulations. Rather they were publicly drilled. The Legon Observer reported the case of a former ambassador who had returned to Ghana to become a Principal Secretary in the Ministry of Foreign Affairs. The paper claimed that the Principal Secretary was publicly drilled for coming late. After the incident, the Principal Secretary was reappointed ambassador to another country![23] Suspected thieves were arrested and drilled. The Daily Graphic reported that in one case suspected thieves were drilled for three and a half hours, forced into some sort of gladiatorial contest, and then put into jail.[24] All of these incidents occurred prior to trial or conviction. There also was the case of the regional commissioner who forced striking workers to go back to work after the commissioner had drilled them.[25] While these activities may bring about the immediate effects desired, the danger is abuse of power and the alienation of the citizenry. Although cases of these are not as frequent as in other military regimes, it is becoming a problem for the NRC. An example of the abuse of power is the case of a military officer who arrested police officers in a police station because the police officer refused to grant bail to the officer's friend.[26] Reacting to the incident, the Public Relations Directorate of the Ministry of Defense announced that fifteen service personnel had been dismissed in recent times from the Ghana Armed Forces "for behavior contrary to military rules and regulations." It also revealed that "preliminary disciplinary action had been instituted against the Air Force lieutenant involved in the incident with the police.[27]

In addition to these problems, active and total involvement of the armed forces may spread the limited officers too thin and create a problem of overload for political leadership. Consequently, the rank and file of the military may be left unsupervised leading ultimately to misbehavior on the part of the NCO and rank and file membership. Of course, maximum participation minimizes the chances of internal military disgruntlement which the involvement of a few officers could engender. Finally, the total and pervasive presence of the military in the political, administrative, and enforcement processes has damaging implications for the credibility and viability of the military if the regime should fail.

While the NRC policy is that of introducing military personnel into every civilian public institution, under the NLC, governmental and administrative processes were controlled by predominantly civilian personnel "with token but powerful military and police presence.[28]

Soon after Col. Acheampong seized power, he declared: "I believe that no matter how power is taken, those who wield it have a primary duty to be at one with the people and with their hopes and aspirations. Being at one with them means understanding them, and listening to them and taking account of their views. One way of doing this is by a system of popular consultations with the people, not only with their representatives but with people of all walks of life and of all manner of persuasions who can be brought together to hear and exchange ideas. I can hear the cynics cry: 'Anarchy the rule of the mob!' I answer them and say: We shall prove you wrong."[29]

He has met with market women, Kwahu traders, businessmen, manufacturers, students, traditional rulers, and other groups. How representative are these groups? How seriously are their views taken to heart? There are some who doubt the representativeness of these groups. A more significant question is the seriousness or lack of seriousness with which the military regime takes these views into account in the formulation and amendment of policies. There is no question about the fact that the regime has attempted to be receptive to pressures. I have cited the case of the abolition of the loan scheme, and the restoration of the T.U.C. The nationalization of the mines can be added. In fact, the NRC suggests that the disbandment of the National Advisory Council which it appointed was in response to popular demand.

Col. Acheampong and his fellow commissioners are attempting to practice what they preach. For example, the Northern Regional Commissioner, Lt. Col. Iddisa led about 600 members of the Northern Youth Association in harvesting a 250 acre rice farm at Nabogy.[30] Moreover, Col. Acheampong has attempted to set the example of modesty by driving a very small car and by leading a modest life. In a speech marking the first anniversary of the coup, he urged the armed forces to be "modest, honest, approachable, understanding, courteous and sympathetic to the civilian population."[31] The hope is that his officers and men would follow his example.

Although the NRC would prefer to use persuasion rather than compulsion, its leadership has experienced some frustration in the use of persuasion. The frustration is betrayed by the following outburst of Col. Acheampong: ". . . humane methods have not succeeded much."[32] ". . . no appeals for the exercise of the prerogative of mercy shall be entertained for such economic crimes as smuggling, hoarding, profiteering and wickedly-contrived rackets to rob state institutions."[33] ". . . our traders are guilty, our market women are guilty. Equally guilty are the consumers, you the people, who should benefit from these concerns. You have been guilty of condoning crimes against your very selves . . ."[34]

The failure of persuasion seems well illustrated by the fact that only two landlords responded to the NRC appeal to reduce house rents. Ultimately, the NRC had to issue a rent control edict.

Possibly the use of compulsion which is condemned by some intellectuals is a manifestation of this frustration. The passage below is illustrative of another type of political style as well as the response of some segments of society to this style.

> In these days of unreliable and unedifying journalism when press reports are being refuted with disturbing frequency, one is naturally wary about commenting on matters reported in the press. However, since Colonel F. G. Bernasko appears to have a very good and obliging press, and since the incident I am going to comment on has not yet been refuted, I presume that it is true, until the contrary is affirmed.
>
> The said colonel was reported in the recent past to have threatened some villagers with conscription. These villagers were alleged to have refused to harvest sugar-cane at Komenda because remuneration was small. The threat of conscription however had some beneficial repercussions, because it highlighted the shortage of manpower in the harvesting of sugar-cane, and this whipped up the nationalist enthusiasm of students to make their contribution to salvaging our tottering economy by harvesting sugar-cane. Perhaps this positive result compensates for the tortuous way in which this crusading spirit was inadvertently aroused.
>
> Spurred no doubt by this initial success, the same Colonel Bernasko is reported in the Graphic and Times of the 29th of February to have foiled a strike threat by workers at Komenda. He achieved this feat in a very original way. The Colonel is reported to have subjected the aggrieved workers to a 45-minute drill after which he examined his first results by asking the recalcitrant workers who had not been sobered by the drill to step forward. A further dispensation of the drill dose did the trick, and after 30-minutes the strike threat had been averted.
>
> People may want to condemn the "irresponsible" workers and congratulate the Colonel on his singular achievement, irrespective of the unorthodox methods he used. What I would want to impress on Colonel Bernasko is that he has obtained respite at the expense of

considerable good will. Why did Colonel Bernasko not take the trouble to find out whether the workers had a case or not? Could he not have achieved the same result through reasoned argument? Admittedly our economy is in such a perilous state that we cannot afford strikes, but this is no excuse for subjecting workers to bullying and humiliation, especially not at a time when some other categories of workers have had their allowances and other privileges restored. Putting the economy on a war footing as far as I am concerned is not tantamount to turning the whole country into an army camp. This country cannot be built through threats and exhibitions of force.

It is true that as a people we are lazy and that we should be made to change our attitude to work in a radical way. But is it not possible to achieve this goal without resorting to such disciplinary histrionics? People need to be disciplined, but there are well-established methods like suspension, etc., for doing this. Drilling latecomers and those who threaten to go on strike is a crude form of disciplining people outside military camps and academies.

Even in the critical situation of the country's economy, it is important that basic human dignity and rights should not be trampled under foot through bullying and other unnecessary forms of coercion. And Colonel Bernasko, it must be conceded, does not have a monopoly over this unorthodox form of enforcing civilian discipline!

By the way, in case the incident referred to did not transpire in the manner reported, I apologise unreservedly to the said Colonel, but if the reports are correct, then I appeal to the higher authorities to check the exuberance and zeal of that obstreperous military administrator. It is still true, I believe, that one can catch more flies with a teaspoonful of honey than with a barrelful of vinegar.[35]

By and large the FMG and the NRC represent divergent political style, at least on the national scope.

## FOOTNOTES

1. Africa Report, XII, No. 1, January, 1967, p. 39.
2. James O'Connell. The Quarterly of Administration, April, 1971, pp. 315-316.
3. Ibid., p. 316.
4. Ibid.
5. Nigerian Observer, August 31, 1970, p. 15.
6. Nigerian Observer, July 17, 1969, p. 10.
7. Midwest West (Midwest Information Service Publication), No. 677, July 27, 1971.
8. Nigerian Observer, April 15, 1970, p. 12.
9. Midwest, op. cit.
10. Ibid.
11. Ibid.
12. West Africa, February 5, 1973.
13. Nigerian Observer, op. cit., April 15, 1970.
14. Daily Times, May 1, 1971, p. 5.
15. Ibid.
16. West Africa, April 5, 1969, p. 397.
17. Africa Report, January, 1967, p. 34.
18. Daily Times, February 15, 1971, p. 3.
19. Nigerian Tribune, April 3, 1971, p. 4.
20. Legon Observer, October 5, 1972, pp. 448-52.
21. Col. Acheampong, Broadcast on the first anniversary of the NRC, January 12, 1973.
22. Major Felli's news conference reported in Legon Observer, February 23, 1973.
23. Legon Observer, February 23, 1973, p. 76.
24. The Daily Graphic, January 29, 1973.
25. Legon Observer, February 23, 1973, p. 78.

26. The Weekly Spectator, February 3, 1973.
27. Legon Observer, February 10, 1973.
28. Legon Observer, January 26, 1973, p. 29.
29. Legon Observer, January 26, 1973, pp. 38-40.
30. Daily Graphic, November 20, 1972, p. 4.
31. West Africa, January 22, 1973, p. 95.
32. West Africa, January 22, 1973, pp. 95-97.
33. Ibid.
34. Ibid.
35. Legon Observer, March 10, 1972, p. 128.

CHAPTER XIII

CONCLUSION

Generalizations and comparisons, while difficult, are at the same time necessary. Consequently although one should not shy away from them, one should exercise great care in undertaking them. Mindful of the inherent limitations of my task, let me address myself to the economic performance propositions.

The Ironsi regime lasted for a period of six months. During this period it was bedeviled by the crisis of legitimacy. Because the solution to the problem eluded it, it was incapacitated and ultimately doomed. In the face of this necessary preoccupation, not much was done by way of delineation and pursuance of economic goals. Therefore, as far as the economic development propositions are concerned, the Ironsi regime did not provide us with meaningful data which can serve a comparative effort.

The NLC of Ghana presents us with a different case. Although it was haunted by poor economic conditions, it seems to have had little trouble in establishing itself. In the pursuit of its economic goals, the regime did appear to be pro-Western and anti-Eastern. It sought and received financial assistance from the Western powers, while it terminated financial and economic linkages which had existed between Ghana and the Eastern as well as Socialist states. In terms of its economic philosophy, it seemed to have pursued a <u>laissez faire</u> economy with high capitalistic overtones while it drastically reduced the role of the state in the economy. Many state enterprises were sold to private concerns; some of these concerns were foreign owned. The NLC regime offered to sell seven state industries out of about fifty state industries undertaken by the Nkrumah regime. Moreover, it invited private participation in eleven others and promised to sell others provided buyers could be found.[1] The NLC refrained from taking the drastic economic step of repudiating Ghana's foreign debts. Instead, it opted for the rescheduling of these debts and it did not advocate any radical (socialistic) changes in the economy. However, there were indications to show the regime's concern for economic nationalism. For example, the regime reserved retail trade, taxis, small businesses and wholesale trade representatives of overseas manufacturers for Ghanaians. The performance here, however, was non-fundamental and indeed minimal. Thus on the face of it, Price's reference group theory would appear to hold in the case of the NLC. Upon a closer look, however, the picture becomes less clear. The question, in my judgment, should not only be were the policies pro-West? We must also ask why were they pro-West? I would argue that given the fact that the Nigerian military regime under Gowon, and the NRC regime under Acheampong--both of which are led and ruled by officers trained in the West--do not seem particularly pro-West, there is an intervening variable which needs to be considered. It seems to me that having replaced an allegedly pro-Eastern regime, which preached socialism, it would have been unwise for the NLC to seek the active support of the East. Indeed in the interests of NLC survival, the strategy should call for the destruction of Eastern influence, and within the framework of a modified cold war, the solicitation of the friendship of the West. Finally, if the reason for Ghana's woes were derived from "Nkrumah and his socialist boys and friends," then the issue was joined and the policy alternative unambiguous. It is in this context that one must regard the NLC policies. That this was a strategic and pragmatic posture on the part of the NLC, given the circumstances of the take-over, is at least as credible as Price's argument.

Chapter III demonstrates that on the overall, the economic performance of the Nigerian military regime under Gowon does not support Price's economic performance propositions. Both the first and second economic performance propositions were negated despite the fact that the Nigerian military is an ex-colonial army whose military leadership were trained in the West. There is no absence of economic nationalism. Despite their Western training, they differ from the civilian government of Sir Tafawa Balewa because they do not deal with the Eastern bloc in an irrational manner when and where the Nigerian economic interests are involved. The bulk of the evidence does not support the proposition that the Nigerian military leaders are unconcerned with economic change. In fact, the Nigerian military leaders have initiated certain structural changes in the economy; witness the reform of the cooperative system. To say all these, of course, is not to say that the Gowon regime has been overwhelmingly successful in bringing about economic growth and development. Despite the inflationary spirals, on the overall, the Nigerian economy is in a better and more dynamic posture than it has been at any time in its history. More people are sharing in the wealth. Significantly, however, the peasant farmers are still out of the main stream. Hopefully the government's agricultural development project will be successful since the government has in fact recognized its poor performance in this area.

The data presented in Chapter IV shows that the NRC economic performance also negates the economic performance propositions a la Price. In short, we find that:

1. The military regime of Acheampong is favorably disposed toward the realization of economic change and reform and that there is no evidence to suggest that the NRC members are opposed to civilian groups advocating such reforms.

2. In spite of their Western military training, the military leaders of the NRC are not irrational with regard to the West or the East insofar as their general economic policies are concerned.

3. Despite the fact that the Ghanaian military was an ex-colonial army, the NLC does not behave in non-nationalistic fashion--they practiced economic nationalism which they like to refer to as the policy of "Ghanaian's capturing the commanding heights of their own economy."

In the overall, they have attained notable success in their agricultural efforts. The continuing problem of smuggling, which reduces the amount of agricultural products available in Ghanaian markets, tends to obfuscate the relatively high degree of government success. Unfortunately the alleviation of the smuggling problem is hard to effect because of the difficulty of tight border control and the reluctance of the government to put realistic price limits on Ghanaian agricultural products.

Moreover, the distribution system can stand some improvement. Unfortunately this requires improved transportation and storage systems--these call for heavy capital outlay.

The Legon Observer, not known for its timidity, in its January 25, 1974, edition, gracefully admitted that "in the main, the government's concern with the financial lot of Ghanaians has been admirable."[2] The NRC members must have been intensely gratified to receive such high accolades from their erstwhile critic and vociferous skeptics of their ability and potential. The editor of the Legon Observer wrote: "Finally, we believe that the NRC has over the past two years shown evidence of its good intentions--even if it has made some mistakes. In the youth in particular it has aroused a keen sense of purposeful patriotism which it would do well to encourage, if it can. It has also been responsive to the needs of the workers and also, to some extent, of the farmers. More has to be done in the way of controlling prices, constructing feeder roads to bring the fruits of Operation Feed Yourself to the markets, and to ensure that the low-cost accommodation is abundant and really of low cost."[3]

Next let me turn to the modernization strategy. The propositions are as follows: In states with a recent colonial past, a strategy characterized by heavy foreign participation of a financial and technical nature and limited mobilization of indigenous humor and material resources would be followed. There would be a low profile approach to nation-building, and in the sphere of political integration the government would make only minimal efforts to penetrate society. Political integration would occur with trickle-down effect because of the application of political laissez faire strategy.

Under the NLC, Ghana depended highly on help from the Western nations both in the financial and agricultural areas. For example, Canada supplied Ghana with agricultural commodities. In addition, the technical advisers from the socialist states were replaced with Western advisers. Indeed some state industries were sold to

Western private concerns. The Busia government continued to retain the Harvard and Oxford advisory groups; allegedly these groups became more important under the Busia regime. With the overthrow of the Busia regime, substantial changes have become visible. First is the de-emphasis of Foreign Aid as a revenue source and the reliance on domestic sources to raise capital. Second is the constant declaration about putting Ghanaians at the commanding height of the economy. These declarations have been concretized by the nationalization of certain industries, the increase of Ghanaian shares and control in other industries, and the operationalization of fundamental restructuring in the financing of Ghanaian development. Chapter IV documents these points. Furthermore, Operation Feed Yourself represents more than a limited mobilization of the available resources in Ghana. The increased participation of all Ghanaians in agriculture as well as the psychological feat of raising farming to the status of a respectable if not crucial profession, testifies to this point. The pervasive involvement of the military in the administration of the country, the posting of military men to bureaucratic and pseudo-governmental corporations, as well as the newly established practice of assigning many regional commissioners to regions outside of their native region--positively underscore a desire to establish fundamental changes in Ghana. Such modernization strategy and style resembles Apter's mobilization model more than his reconcilliatory typology. The total involvement of the military in the government and administration of Ghana has been defended on the grounds that it will hasten the attainment of total mobilization of Ghana. In the opinion of the NRC, this is a _sine_ _qua_ _non_ for lifting Ghana out of the apparent doldrums. To say all this is not to argue that political brokers in Ghana are not unimportant. However it suggests that the military is not hesitant to project a high political profile.

Undoubtedly the NRC is concerned about the importance of primordial variables in Ghanaian politics. Even the friends of Busia agree that primordial variables soared to alarming proportions during the Busia reign. However several Ghanaians concur that primordial variables were also important during the closing days of the NLC. In any case, the NRC is trying to diminish their importance by fostering national orientation in the young and by posting regional commissioners outside of their areas of origin. Although the Nigerian FMG has expressed greater anxiety about primordial variables, I doubt that they have been as successful as the NRC. Quite frankly, even NRC success is not overwhelming in this respect.

In assessing Nigeria's modernization strategy, it is useful to note that in its development plan, the Nigerian Federal Military Government has declared that it will hold at least fifty-five percent of the shares in the iron and steel bar complex, petro-chemical industry, fertilizer production, and petroleum products. It also wants to minimize foreign control over the Nigerian economy. The FMG has espoused an uncompromising attitude toward the economic independence of Nigeria and the defeat of neo-colonial forces in Africa. If the government takes this declaration seriously, there cannot be any doubt that it will be vigorously opposed to heavy foreign financial and technical participation in its economy. Chapter III documents the extent of government success with economic nationalism. I need to add that the increased share of Nigerian interest in banking establishments as well as the Nigerianization decree are added tangible evidence. The argument is not that these things are operating flawlessly. Rather, the fact that such changes are perceived as desirable and are allowed to go into operation at all lends credibility to government declarations. At this point in time the FMG modernization approach cannot be viewed as mobilizational. It seems more reconciliatory than mobilizational. With the possible exception of the federal government's reluctant decision on the Farmers Cooperatives in Nigeria and the issue of the National Youth Service Corps, the FMG has been careful not to take radical steps which might alter the federal-state authority relationships. Unlike Ghana, the Nigerian military is not completely immersed in the administration of the country. Despite the possible weakening of the power of regionalism by the creation of new states, the states have very seldom been compelled by the FMG to do things against which they hold strong views, or objections. Even the effective nationalization of the university, in the end, was made voluntary. For the discussion of this and the Nigerian National Youth Service Corps, see Chapter VII. In addition, Chapter XI argues that the political style of General Gowon both in his dealing with the states and other military governors is not that of compulsion but persuasion, not that of revolution but reform, not that of total mobilization but reconciliation. However, when it comes to the administration of the states by the governors, it can be argued that the styles of a few like Governor Ogbemudia is decidedly mobilizational.

Now let us turn to the first political proposition. Chapter V shows that in the initial phase of Gowon's regime the military attempted to use the traditional and religious institutions to bolster and underscore its power, authority, and policies. In a sense the farmers' uprisings in the West, particularly the killing of some traditional rulers by the protestors, seemed to be a recognition of the successful instrumental use of the traditional institutions and rulers by the military regime. Obviously, the protestors resented this fact. Moreover, in Chapter V, I discussed the adroit instrumental use of religion by the military. However, in dealing with modern organizational groups such as labor and the students, the Nigerian military has tended to rely on martial rituals and symbols, i.e. the show of force. Of course it may well be that these groups are transitional in the normative sense. Consequently, peacefully dealing with them is perceived as difficult, if not impossible, by the military. As long as the military regime can deliver on its developmental promises, these groups can be diffused. If the military should fail in this regard, however, such groupings together with the <u>lumpen proletariat</u> may become the political time bomb.

In Chapter VI, I discussed the instrumental manipulation of the Ghanaian traditional rulers by the NLC. Indeed one of the justifications for the coup was based on traditional grounds. Kwame Nkumah was constantly portrayed as an atheist in an essentially deeply religious society. By definition, then, his overthrow was the liberation of religion and the rescue of religion from the anti-God. As in Nigeria therefore, abundant prayers were offered to God for the success of the NLC regime, and weekly admonitions were made to worshippers to support the regime. Individual members of the NLC cultivated these services both in the Christian as well as the Moslem communities. Moslems were indeed allowed public holidays on appropriate religious occasions. Col. Acheampong also has carefully cultivated the support of the Catholic and Apostolic Churches in Ghana. Even though Nigerian and Ghanaian societies are essentially religious, at least formalistically, interestingly enough, no Nigerian or Ghanaian military leader has attempted to manipulate traditional values to the Zairean and Ugandan extent. None attempted Gan. Amin's theocratic style. The ecumentical effort of Gen. Amin is well discussed by Professor Mazrui in a paper entitled, "Piety and Puritanism in a Military Theocracy, Uganda Soldiers' Apostolic Successes."[4] For a leader to recognize his limitation is not necessarily bad politics. The Nigerian and Ghanaian military leaders have wisely refrained from the extremities in their manipulations of the traditional and religious values of their societies. I will argue on the overall that the military regimes discussed are no less politically shrewd than their civilian predecessors in similar circumstances. In Chapter V and Chapter VI, I examined the legitimacy engineering of the military. In the case of the NLC and the Gowon regimes it was quite clear that both regimes exercised considerable political sagacity in the establishment of their authority. Even in the case of the Ironsi regime, we see that essentially its downfall was not due to the lack of political skill. By and large, these military men do not operate as total political novices. Having registered these general impressions we still must address ourselves to the comparative summations regarding specific political postulates.

<u>Political Performance Propositions</u>. Political leadership potential of military officers is decisively undermined by the fact that the military is unlikely to relate to the political symbols that have meaning in their own society. Since successful

modernization requires both the mobilization of popular sentiment around collective values and goals of development, and the building of solidarity in a fragile political community, the military elite is unsuited for the task. Reliance on martial rituals and symbols of a foreign cultural milieu surely reduces their political capacity. Armies are not democracies. Therefore where military organizations become the state, order is maintained, but a training in democratic civility is an unlikely outcome.

The Federal Military Regime of Nigeria as well as the National Liberation Council of Ghana declared the attainment of democratic society as one of their most important objectives (see Chapters III and IV). In Chapter IX A and B, I discussed the absence of the freedom of the press and the constraint under which journalists labor in the military regimes of Nigeria and Ghana. Similarly in Chapters X A and B I discussed the strong restraint to labor activities and, in the case of Nigeria and the NLC of Ghana, a feeling of impotence on the part of the labor groups. Chapter VII documents the perception of the lack of freedom as far as the students and the academicians are concerned.

Unquestionably, then, despite the declaration of democracy as a major societal goal, the operations of the military regimes concerned have not established them as bastions of democracy. Obviously, some military regimes are less undemocratic than others. Consider for example the NRC which, in response to popular pressures, dismissed the committee it appointed (The National Advisory Committee) even before that committee has had the opportunity to meet. Consider its abolition of the Student Loan Schemes, among other things. Clearly, the NLC performance on the democratic scale is higher and less dismal than that of the FMG. The NLC, despite its democratic proclamation, became somewhat less scrupulous in observing democratic principles in its day-to-day operations as the years of the administration went by. This is particularly true following the unsuccessful counter-coup. In Ghana, under the NRC, there seems to be great responsiveness to the wishes of the people on the part of the military. Again, even a staunch critic of NRC performance--the Legon Observer, had to admit after two years of the NRC that, "More than most governments, this one has been very responsive to the people's needs, no doubt as a means to securing a popular base, but some of these relief gestures have been ill advised."[5]

The more important point here in terms of political development is the government's responsiveness to people's needs and demands. Obviously mistakes are going to be made; no government can perform perfectly.

In fairness to the military regimes under consideration we must remember that they are "corrective regimes." Therefore the test of democratization lies in their actual rule as well as the kind of arrangements made so as to insure a high prospect for democratic government upon the exist of the military regime. In that sense, then, the data for conclusive assertion are absent for the FMG as well as for the NRC. By and large, the military regime's posture regarding public opinion and participation tends to be manipulative. However, even Western democracies are not free from such operational abuses. Certainly the NRC has demonstrated a degree of responsiveness which surpass that of the civilian predecessors. Although meaningful mass participation in the process of decision making of a military regime might be low, the military regime's responsiveness to the needs of the people is not necessarily low. So, it boils down to what one perceives as the most important criterion of a democracy: responsiveness, the rigorous pursuit of such things as procedures, the assertion of the rule of law, or individual liberty and freedom. On the issue of democracy, the NRC's performance is less divergent from its declaration, while the performance of the FMG seems to suggest a wider credibility gap.

In Chapter II, I identified some of the political problems confronting the Nigerian polity. It is proper to return to these in our concluding chapter. The question is whether all or some of these problems have been solved or eliminated. Unfortunately, the answer to the question cannot be truly and fairly answered until after 1976 when the FMG would have handed power over to civilians, presumably after it is satisfied that its Nine-Point Program has been fully operationalized and concretized. Nevertheless, let us make a few observations regarding these problems as they now stand in December, 1973.

It seems to me that although the creation of the twelve state structure aggravated the "Biafrans," it created a framework within which some Nigerian problems could be successfully tackled. Of course, one needs to avoid the mistaken notion that structural rearrangements, of and by themselves, provide the permanent solution. It is true, however, that in Nigeria, this structural rearrangement has eliminated one of the major sources of conflict between the North and the South. The image of a powerful, domineering, monolithic North has disappeared. Somehow the southerners feel less insecure about a potential coalition of Northern states than they did about the old "North." At the same time, the examination of recent budgets of northern states and discussions with various officials amply demonstrate a more vigorous commitment to education and an accelerated pace of modernization. No Northern state better illustrates these goals than Kano state. If Kano state is a good indicator we can assume that success in these endeavors will eradicate northern insecurity in its relationships with the South. While the Ibos are still suspect and perhaps unwelcome in the Rivers state, there is plenty of evidence to suggest that the other states are not actively engaged now in attempts to limit or restrict the freedom of Nigerians to live in any part of the country. Of course the preference of state governments to employ their own people remains.

On the whole, the response to the questionnaire suggests that Nigerians are rather optimistic about the future. The sense of optimism may have been a consequence of the reduction in citizens' expectations following the rude awakenings of the earlier years. On the other hand, it may derive from favorable economic prognostication. Once again there seems to be some air of hopefulness in many quarters. Some caution is in order because this is reminiscent of the climate which reigned in Ghana in

1970 during the transition from the NLC to the Busia regime. Many fundamental political issues have not been dealt with, the census exercise is just underway, the formation of "national political parties" has not yet begun, the institutional and constitutional arrangements for civilian rule has not been agreed upon as yet. Nor are we sure of the place of the military in future Nigeria. To the extent that these variables remain unknown, we cannot realistically predict citizens' reactions to them. However, we do know that on the surface, many Nigerian problems seem to be less active and potent. Perhaps this is a product of a "no politics state." It may also be that politicians are eager not to provide the military regime with an excuse to remain in power longer than the stipulated period. If the latter is correct, Nigeria may be back to square one because a similar situation prevailed during the colonial period. The indigenous political elite labored to maintain a facade of unity in order to ensure the quick exit of the colonial overlords.

The lasting effect of the creation of the twelve state structure may be an unanticipated one; it has made it possible to decentralize development projects. Presumably, such decentralization will increase the citizens' influence on government policy, in the long run. The Federal bureaucracy is developing a professionalism which appears to be national in its orientation and concerns. The division of Nigeria into smaller states has decreased the power of a state(s) *vis* *a* *vis* the Federal government. The defeat of Biafra has discouraged the utility of secession or threat of secession as a viable political option in the Nigerian context.

The Nigerian military is trying to portray the image of national orientation. However the state governors tend to betray strong sectionalism whenever, in their perception, the interests of their state is threatened. While the military officers may appear to be totally modern, a closer examination of them and their behavior patterns will show this image to be somewhat misleading. At the most, they are culturally ecclectic. As an objective observer, it seemed to me that a Yoruba officer, for example, is most comfortable in traditional social situations such as traditional weddings, naming, and burial ceremonies. He feels more comfortable with high life than the waltz. His Beethoven recordings, if he has any, will not wear out from use, but his highlife records may show signs of overuse. In the North, with the exception of duty hours, the sight of a northern officer in military uniform is unusual indeed. I would argue that there is really little or no concrete evidence to suggest that the Nigerian military officer is more dedicated to his profession than any other educated groups in Nigeria. Similarly not much in the behavior of the officer suggests that he is markedly less likely to be influenced by traditional values, norms and primordial sentiments.

We have found that the Federal Military Government can relate to many political symbols of meaning to the society. The selective use of civilian commissioners, traditional rulers, academicians and bureaucrats during the period of the civil war is a testimony to the considerable political capability of the military government. Since the end of the civil war, however, there has been a decrease in the consultation with most of these people. The decrease may be interpreted as an indication of the confidence the FMG has in its own political capability, or it could be seen as a sign of their basic distrust of the civilian commissioners, former politicians and traditional leadership who may have ambitions of their own or may have become disenchanted with the FMG. The extreme reluctance of the FMG to put the military in a police role has been criticized by some. Seemingly, the problem is not that the military government on the federal level is unable to mobilize popular sentiment around collective values and goals. It did so during the civil war. Rather, the problem is that in the federal sphere it has been somewhat reluctant to mobilize all popular sentiment (labor, management, farmers and military) as a means of increasing input of human and material resources. It has elected this route in deference to the political style of General Gowon. What is in doubt is whether the sense of a strengthened political community which the military has developed can be sustained by it or by anybody else. Quite frankly FMG's economic performance has been more successful than its political performance. We must never forget that these are not mutually exclusive categories. Seemingly, the economic performance has helped sustain the FMG politically. Finally, let us remember that political performance requires a longer gestation period.

The NLC defined Ghana's political problem as essentially the problem of a dictator and a sick economy. It assumed that the elimination of the dictator as well as the creation of a democratic structure the organization would ensure democracy in Ghana. It also presumed that wise economic decision-making would thrive under a democratic set up. The ensuing elaborate democratic machinery which they bequeathed to Ghana proved to be inadequate insurance of stability and development. What the NRC will leave to succeeding Ghanaian regime remains to be seen.

I have argued and demonstrated that in the cases presented, the reference group theory à la Price does not seem validated. I do not see any evidence of a powerful significant foreign referent in the FMG and NRC regimes. I also argue that in the case of the NLC, the evidence is definitely mixed and remains unconvincing. However, this does not mean that the reference group theory is inoperative. I am confident that, by and large, the domestic forces and considerations are paramount. I contend that in all cases, the regimes are most concerned about their "self preservation." Whether or not a military regime gives priority to a domestic group and how long it will do so, depends on a complex set of variables which I have only illustrated in this book. Variables such as the circumstances of the take-over, the nature of the military, the degree of unity within the military, the power distribution among various groups in the society, the native and tradition of conflict in the society, the composition of the military junta, the junta's perception of its mission and its resolve to pursue its goals. More cases need to be considered before we can delineate the relative strength of these variables in a definitive way. In the meantime we must recognize that some military regimes can bring about economic growth and development while others may not. It is wishful thinking to argue that a military regime in a developing country, no matter how puritanic or idealistic, will drastically reduce the economic resources of the military with impunity. However, the NRC is attempting to demonstrate that even under grave economic constraints, a military regime can attempt to manage its economy without suffering disastrous consequences. Certainly, the FMG and the NRC are making substantial headway in this connection.

We need to admit that military regimes do not conform to the classic democratic model. Nevertheless, to say this is not to ignore the most important variable of political development, responsiveness. This book shows that a military regime can be more responsive to the needs of its people than some democratically elected governments.

One parting word, my discussion here is based on the examination of the performance of the military regimes concerned as of December, 1973. There is still a long way to go for the FMG and the NRC. Indeed, the "institutionalization stage"[6] is only being contemplated in Nigeria. The NRC has not even outlined its plan of action in this connection. Necessarily then, no posture of permanence can be asserted in this analysis.

## FOOTNOTES

1. Jon Krause, in *The Politics of Coup d'etat*, op. cit., p. 120.

2. *Legon Observer*, January 25, 1974, p. 26.

3. *Ibid*.

4. Ali Mazrui, "Moral and Economic Puritanism under a Military Theocracy: The Case of Amin's Uganda," paper presented to Inter University Seminar on Armed Forces and Society, October 13, 1973.

5. *Legon Observer*, January 25, 1974, p. 26.

6. See Introduction for a definition of this stage.